CHALLENGES

TO

PARTY GOVERNMENT

EDITED BY
John Kenneth White
AND
Jerome M. Mileur

SOUTHERN ILLINOIS UNIVERSITY PRESS
Carbondale and Edwardsville

Printed in the United States of America
Design and production by Natalia Nadraga
95 94 93 92 4 3 2 1

Library of Congress Cataloging-in-Publication Data

Challenges to party government / edited by John Kenneth White and Jerome M. Mileur.
p. cm.
Includes index.
1. Political parties—United States. I. White, John Kenneth, 1952–
II. Mileur, Jerome M.
JK2261.C43 1992
324.273—dc20 91-41855
ISBN 0-8093-1799-0. — ISBN 0-8093-1834-2 (pbk.) CIP

The paper used in this publication meets the minimum requirements of American National Standard for Information Sciences—Permanence of Paper for Printed Library Materials, ANSI 239.48-1984. ♾

Contents

Acknowledgments

In completing this book, we have incurred more than the usual number of obligations. First and foremost, we would like to thank the contributors, who willingly gave both their time and talent: Everett Carll Ladd of the University of Connecticut and the Roper Center, John S. Jackson III of Southern Illinois University, Wilson Carey McWilliams of Rutgers University, Sidney M. Milkis of Brandeis University, and A. James Reichley of the Brookings Institution. Two members of Congress, who also happen to be political scientists, added their unique perspectives: David E. Price, a Democrat from North Carolina, and William M. Thomas, a Republican from California. We would also like to thank the Committee for Party Renewal for its sponsorship of a workshop that included the participants of this book. Allen Blume, a graduate student at the Catholic University of America, provided invaluable assistance in organizing the workshop.

Our colleagues at our home institutions, the Catholic University of America and the University of Massachusetts at Amherst, gave us their insights and comments on the various incarnations of the outline for this book. In addition, our colleagues from the Committee for Party Renewal, a bipartisan organization consisting of political scientists and party activists, contributed their thoughts to the editors and the contributors, and we gratefully acknowledge their assistance. Richard DeBacher, editorial director at Southern Illinois University Press, was a faithful supporter throughout. John White would also like to thank the Catholic University of America for a research grant to complete the book. Timothy Sifert, a graduate student at the Catholic University of America, faithfully typed many of the chapters submitted by the contributors onto a computer disk and performed several research tasks.

Introduction

Shortly after the Persian Gulf War ended, Samira Hunaidi, a Kuwaiti housewife, told a reporter from the *Washington Post*: "We want to have more democracy because democracy means sharing. We have to share with our rulers the destiny of our country because they cannot do it alone."[1] Hunaidi's grasp of the central problem facing the citizens and rulers of her war-ravaged country reflects a preoccupation of students of government through the ages. In *The Politics*, Aristotle categorized governments based in a sense on the character of sharing between the governors and the governed. These included kingship (rule of the single just man) and tyranny (rule of one man seeking his own advantage); aristocracy (rule by the best citizens) and oligarchy (rule by the self-interested wealthy); and republic (rule by the civic-minded property owners) and democracy (rule by the avaricious masses).[2] The search for a government in which citizens could partake at the same table with their rulers persisted long after Aristotle. James Madison maintained that the U.S. Constitution crafted a sturdy republican table that would "refine and enlarge the public views by passing them through the medium of a chosen body of citizens, whose wisdom may best discern the true interest of their country and whose patriotism and love of justice will be least likely to sacrifice it to temporary or partial considerations."[3]

What Madison did not foresee in his constitutional designs is that the political parties would be the "legs" supporting the new table of government. Parties have become the single most important article in our unwritten constitution, and in the opinion of many political sci-

1. Caryle Murphy, "Kuwaitis Weigh Rebirth of a Nation, 'More Democracy' Urged in Emirate; Right to Vote Becoming Key Issue," *Washington Post*, 10 March 1991, p. A-1.

2. Cited in James MacGregor Burns with L. Marvin Overby, *Cobblestone Leadership: Majority Rule, Minority Power* (Norman, Oklahoma: University of Okla. Press, 1990), p. 64.

3. James Madison, "Federalist Number 10," in Alexander Hamilton, James Madison, and John Jay, *The Federalist Papers*, ed. Clinton Rossiter (New York: New American Library, 1961), p. 82.

tists, they make the written one work. Ergo, if the political parties are not working, government is not working. David Broder created this tautology in 1972, and every present indicator suggests that the party "legs" have grown rickety with age.[4]

The result has been a dwindling of public confidence in government. Numerous public opinion surveys have tracked the growing disillusionment. In 1958, 75 percent agreed with the statement "Government can be trusted to do what is right most of the time"; by 1991, just 36 percent agreed. Those who thought "quite a few politicians were crooked" stood at 25 percent in 1958, rising to nearly half those surveyed by 1991. In 1952 only 36 percent agreed "I don't think that public officials care much what people like me think"; by 1991, those concurring climbed to 59 percent. In 1964, the year of the Johnson landslide, just 31 percent believed that "government is run by a few big interests"; by 1991, 71 percent thought this was true. Not surprisingly, the public thought that in 1991 forty-nine cents of every tax dollar was "wasted." Most disturbing are the growing ranks of voters who think "My vote doesn't really matter in an election." In 1980 only 9 percent agreed; by 1983, 14 percent; and in October 1991 the figure rose to 27 percent.[5]

As we enter the 1990s, the complaints against Washington have reached ear-splitting decibels. A series of "focus-group" interviews sponsored by the Kettering Foundation captured the prevailing anomie that exists between the rulers and the ruled. The views of a Seattle participant were typical:

> People have lost faith in their policymakers because they always tell what they're going to do and they never follow through. Or they stand up there and tell blatant lies—at least it seems in recent years—and they make statements that you know can't be true. [For instance,] you know it's going to cost money to run a government and they tell you "no new taxes."[6]

---

4. David Broder, *The Party's Over: The Failure of Politics in America* (New York: Harper and Row, 1972), p. xxiii.

5. Dan Baltz and Richard Morin, "A Tide of Pessimism and Political Powerlessness Rises," *Washington Post*, 3 November 1991, pp. A-1, A-16. Figures are based on the ABC News–*Washington Post* surveys conducted between 1983 and October 1991. Earlier results are based on the National Election Study (NES), which has been conducted every other year since 1952 by the University of Michigan.

6. *Citizens and Politics: A View from Main Street America* (Dayton, Ohio: Kettering Foundation, 1991), p. 27. Focus groups consisting of twelve persons each were conducted in 1990 and 1991 in ten cities.

The cynicism expressed by that Seattle man does not mean that voters suffer from a bad case of malaise about politics and government. Civic-mindedness is not the problem. Indeed, there has been a noticeable increase in patriotism beginning with the Reagan presidency and following the Gulf War. The problem lies in the fact that many Americans believe they lack the *power* to alter the course of government.

This book is about power—*political power*. In 1942, a seminal book, *Party Government*, was published. Its author, E. E. Schattschneider, sought to redefine democracy and popular control of government by formulating a concept that has since become known as the "doctrine of responsible party government."[7] Political scientists Nelson Polsby and Aaron Wildavsky summarized its essential features:

> [The parties] (1) make policy commitments to the electorate, (2) are willing and able to carry them out when in office, (3) develop alternatives to government policies when out of office, and (4) differ sufficiently between themselves to provide the electorate with a proper range of choice between alternatives of action.[8]

Schattschneider believed that "a more responsible two-party system" was required to meet the unprecedented domestic and foreign challenges facing the nation in the chaotic years following World War II. In 1948 he declared an "emergency" and claimed it could not be met "by tinkering with the apparatus of government." What was required, Schattschneider argued, was "a plan and an effort appropriate to the magnitude of the problem."[9] Schattschneider already had the outlines of a bold plan in mind. In 1946 he accepted the chairmanship of the Committee on Political Parties, a group sanctioned by the American Political Science Association. By 1948, Schattschneider was halfway through a set of prolonged discussions with his colleagues that culminated with the publication of *Toward a More Responsible Two-Party System* in 1950.[10]

---

7. E. E. Schattschneider, *Party Government* (New York: Rinehart, 1942). Austin Ranney gave the concept its name with publication of *The Doctrine of Responsible Party Government* (Urbana: University of Illinois Press, 1954).

8. Nelson Polsby and Aaron Wildavsky, *Presidential Elections* (New York: Free Press, 1971), p. 225.

9. E. E. Schattschneider, *The Struggle for Party Government* (College Park: University of Maryland, 1948), p. 2.

10. *Toward a More Responsible Two-Party System* was first published as a supplement to *The American Political Science Review*, 44 (September 1950). It was subsequently published as a small book by Rinehart. In addition to

The APSA report continued to sound the alarm bells Schattschneider had already rung: "The existing party system is inadequately prepared to meet the demands now being made upon it."[11] The problem, the committee declared, was that the political parties had disintegrated to the point where they could no longer give clarity to the election debate and propose national solutions to what the committee saw as increasingly national problems. The report warned that unless the party system was overhauled, three disastrous consequences were possible. First, a shift of "excessive responsibility to the President,"[12] who would have to build support for his program "through his personal effort without benefit of party."[13] Second, the "disintegration of the two major parties," caused by a growing alienation between a sizable body of the electorate and party leaders, resulting in "a great incentive for voters to dispose of the parties as intermediaries between themselves and the government."[14] Finally, the governmental impasse "might set in motion more extreme tendencies to the political left and the political right."[15]

Schattschneider and his colleagues proved prescient. In some measure, each of the dire consequences they associated with the decline of political parties has come to pass. Presidents blithely campaign for office using a "Rose Garden strategy" that all but ignores the parties. If presidents do not need parties, then why do the voters? A. James Reichley writes that voters tend to view parties "much as they view competing supermarkets or movie theaters. Voters may develop a degree of customer loyalty but are less likely than before to regard a party as their political home." And all the while candidates outside the mainstream, from George Wallace to Jesse Jackson, push those in charge further away from the mainstream, as detailed by John S. Jackson III.

Schattschneider (whose affiliation was Wesleyan University), the members of the Committee of Political Parties were Thomas S. Barclay, Stanford University; Clarence A. Berdahl, University of Illinois; Hugh A. Bone, University of Washington; Franklin L. Burdette, University of Maryland; Paul T. David, Brookings Institution; Merle Fainsod, Harvard University; Bertram M. Gross, Council of Economic Advisers; E. Allen Helms, Ohio State University; E. M. Kirkpatrick, Department of State; John W. Lederle, University of Michigan; Fritz Morstein Marx, American University; Louise Overacker, Wellesley College; Howard Penniman, Department of State; Kirk H. Porter, State University of Iowa; and J. B. Shannon, University of Kentucky.

11. *Toward a More Responsible Two-Party System*, p. 23.
12. Ibid., p. 92.
13. Ibid., p. 94.
14. Ibid., p. 95.
15. Ibid.

But the cause of all the trouble, the decline of political parties, remains undiagnosed by most citizens and many commentators. In the four decades since the Committee on Political Parties completed its work, the problems afflicting the parties have worsened. David Broder writes: "In an era of debilitated political parties, Washington is run by 536 individual political entrepreneurs—one president, 100 senators and 435 members of the House—each of whom got here essentially on his own. Each chooses the office he seeks, raises his own money, hires his own pollster and ad-maker and recruits his own volunteers."[16]

The result has been the advent of the career politician. A listing of Massachusetts legislators compiled by *The Almanac: Massachusetts State Officials, 1979–1980* illustrates the trend.[17] While some legislators checked their occupation as lawyer or teacher, several answered "legislator." Professionalism has replaced partisanship. The result has been a "gutless government."[18] Although the career legislators are serving longer terms than ever before, they have become increasingly timid in proposing bold solutions to national problems. After all, every two, four, or six years their "jobs" are on the line. Lacking the shield of party, these officials do not want to face the voters alone. Thus, political action committees, interest groups, and enlarged personal staffs form the provisions of a new insurance policy designed to protect the elected officials from those they supposedly serve.

The condition of the Democratic and Republican parties does not concern most Americans. Since the two-party system firmly took root in the 1830s, Americans have tolerated parties but continually expressed their distaste for them. The Committee on Political Parties believed that the weaknesses of the two-party system "could be overcome as soon as a substantial part of the electorate wants it overcome."[19] Hence the need for a crash course in civics, with political parties composing much of the syllabus. Since 1950, the need for such a course has grown more acute. Today it is commonly said that if those in power would "rise above partisanship," the nation's problems would be solved. What such senti-

16. David S. Broder, "Gutless Government," *Washington Post National Weekly Edition*, 6 November 1989, p. 4. Quoted in Martin P. Wattenberg, *The Rise of Candidate-Centered Politics* (Cambridge, Mass.: Harvard University Press, 1991), p. 165.

17. State Legislative Leaders Foundation, *The Almanac: Massachusetts State Officials, 1979–1980* (Milwaukee, Wis.: State Legislative Leaders Foundation, 1980).

18. See Broder, "Gutless Government," p. 4.

19. *Toward a More Responsible Two-Party System*, p. v.

ments ignore is that a reinvigorated partisanship is a *precondition* for solving the nation's problems.

The contributors to this volume believe in the utility of political parties and would like to see their resurgence. Yet the unwillingness of the electorate to give their full backing to one party has become a staple of our time. Not since the 1880s have voters so consistently placed one party in charge of the presidency while putting another in charge of Congress. Thus, the doctrine of responsible party government has taken a beating—not from the political science community, which by and large heartily endorses it, but from the voters themselves.

This book comes at an important time: fifty years after publication of *Party Government* and forty-two years after publication of *Toward a More Responsible Two-Party System*. *Challenges to Party Government* contains several criticisms of the 1950 report. That is to be expected. But chiefly it is a celebration of the report. We believe that parties remain the indispensable instruments of communication between voters and elected officials. The downing of these "party lines" does not mean that they cannot be restored. Nor does it mean that responsible party government is obsolete. Quite the contrary. The contributors to this volume are rightly pessimistic in their analyses of the present prospects for party government. But at the same time we side with the sentiments expressed by former British Prime Minister Benjamin Disraeli: "In times of great political change and rapid political transition it will generally be observed that political parties find it convenient to re-baptize themselves."[20] Immersing the parties into the "born again" waters of baptism remains the single most important challenge facing political scientists, elected officials, and the voters in the decade ahead.

20. Quoted in Ronald P. Formisano, *The Transformation of Political Culture: Massachusetts Parties, 1790s–1840s* (New York: Oxford University Press, 1983), p. 18.

Contributors

JOHN S. JACKSON III is dean of the College of Liberal Arts and professor of political science at Southern Illinois University at Carbondale. He is the coauthor of *Presidential Primaries and Nominations* (1985). His work on political parties and presidential elections has appeared in several leading journals, including the *Journal of Politics*, *American Politics Quarterly*, *Polity*, *The Midwestern Journal of Political Science*, and *The Western Journal of Political Science.*

EVERETT CARLL LADD is professor of political science at the University of Connecticut, and executive director and president of the Roper Center for Public Opinion Research. He is the author of more than one hundred journal articles and ten books, including three on the American party system. He writes a bimonthly column on American politics for the *Christian Science Monitor.*

WILSON CAREY MCWILLIAMS is professor of political science at Rutgers University and the author of *The Idea of Fraternity in America* (1973).

JEROME M. MILEUR is professor of political science at the University of Massachusetts at Amherst and editor of *Polity*, the journal of the Northeastern Political Science Association. He is the coauthor of *Campaigning for the Massachusetts Senate* (1974) and editor of *The Liberal Tradition in Crisis: American Politics in the 1960s* (1974).

SIDNEY M. MILKIS teaches politics and is a senior research associate at the Gordon Public Policy Center at Brandeis University. He is the author of numerous articles on the presidency and political parties and has coauthored *The Politics of Regulatory Change: A Tale of Two Agencies* (1989), *Remaking American Politics* (1989), and *The American Presidency: Origins and Development* (1990). He is the author of *The New Deal and the Transformation of the American Party System* (1992).

DAVID E. PRICE was first elected to Congress from the Fourth District of North Carolina in 1986. He currently serves on the House Appropriations Committee. Prior to his election to Congress, Price served as chairman of the North Carolina Democratic Party. He is professor of political science and policy sciences at Duke University and the author of numerous books and articles, including *Bringing Back the Parties* (1984) and *The Congressional Experience* (1992).

A. James Reichley is the author of many books and articles on American politics. His most recent books are *Party Struggle* (1992) and *Religion in American Public Life* (1985). He was a senior fellow at the Brookings Institution from 1977 to 1991. Before that, he served on the White House staff under President Gerald R. Ford and was political editor of *Fortune*.

William M. Thomas was first elected to Congress from the Twentieth District of California in 1978. He currently serves as the ranking Republican on the Committee on House Administration. Prior to his election to Congress, Thomas served as a California state assemblyman and was professor of American government at Bakersfield College.

John Kenneth White is associate professor of politics at the Catholic University of America. He is the author of *The Fractured Electorate* (1983) and *The New Politics of Old Values* (1990) as well as the coeditor of *New York State Today* (1989). He serves as executive director of the Committee for Party Renewal.

CHALLENGES

TO

PARTY GOVERNMENT

Prologue

Intellectual Challenges to Party Government

JOHN KENNETH WHITE

Responsible party government. These three words are often thought an oxymoron by scholars and voters alike. Academics contend that responsible party government is possible and that it is the ornery voter, ignorant of the benefits associated with it, who poses the principal obstacle to its realization. For its part, the electorate wants a responsible government, but *without* the political wrangling that responsible parties entail. The American dislike of political parties stems from the earliest days of the Republic. In his Farewell Address, George Washington warned that parties "distract the public councils and enfeeble the public administration" by their "ill-founded jealousies and false alarms."[1] Thomas Jefferson, one of the founders of American parties, was not especially proud of his achievement. Shortly after he assumed the presidency, he promised "to obliterate the traces of party and consolidate the nation, if it can be done without the abandonment of principle."[2]

Jefferson nearly succeeded in separating parties from politics. But purging partisanship from the councils of government was an impossible task because parties were linked to social, regional, and economic interests as well as status and class. By the 1830s, political parties had become an integral part of government. Americans still did not like them much, but party leaders sought to ameliorate the public's disdain by imbuing themselves with a nobler purpose: Parties were shapers of public opinion organized on the basis of commitments to issues and principles, not class or social standing, but dedicated to promoting the general welfare. Martin Van Buren wrote that because parties were so constituted, they rendered an invaluable public service: "It has always therefore struck me as more honorable and manly and more in harmony with the character of our people and of our institutions to deal with the subject of political parties in a sincerer and wiser spirit—to recognize their necessity, to prove and to elevate the principles and objects to our own [party] and to support it faithfully."[3]

Van Buren's belief in the ability of parties to articulate policies and programs has been accepted as an article of faith in the political science community. Two corollaries follow: When the parties work, issues are clarified, and voters can render intelligent judgments. When parties do not work, the people are unable to speak clearly, and the functioning of government is impaired.

Believing that the party system was not working and in urgent need of repair, the American Political Science Association in 1946 authorized the creation of a Committee on Political Parties. Composed of sixteen distinguished political scientists, the group held several hearings before issuing a report entitled *Toward a More Responsible Two-Party System*.[4] The committee's goals were lofty, even quixotic. But short of having its recommendations adopted, the committee hoped that its ninety-six-page document would achieve some notoriety: "Nothing would be more satisfying to the whole committee membership than to know that its report has served as a starting point for constructive public debate, creative political action, and more intensive scientific studies."[5]

Forty years after its publication, the report remains required reading for political scientists. Austin Ranney heralded its publication as "an event which has evoked a considerable and ever-growing volume of literature on these important and difficult problems."[6] Evron Kirkpatrick, a member of the committee who later became a prominent critic, praised the report as "a landmark in the history of political science as policy science."[7] Clinton Rossiter wrote that he would "recommend it . . . to all who are interested in moving toward stronger party government."[8] Theodore J. Lowi ranked the report as "second only to the 1937 President's Committee on Administrative Management as a contribution by academics to public discourse on the fundamentals of American democracy."[9] William Crotty claimed it "may have been the most significant influence on the debate over the operation of political parties that occurred between the Progressive period and the party reform movement of the 1970s."[10] A survey of several textbooks finds the report mentioned in all of them, with most devoting several pages to it. Frank B. Feigert and M. Margaret Conway used it to introduce students to the concept of responsible party government.[11] David Price wrote that "much of the debate on the role of American parties" began with the report's publication.[12] In a similar vein, Robert Huckshorn maintained that the report "triggered a controversy that simmers to this day in political science circles."[13] Frank J. Sorauf and Paul Allen Beck lavished praise on the report, calling it "the classic American statement on party government."[14]

The uncertain state of political parties over the past three decades only enhanced the report's standing in the political science community. Gerald M. Pomper argues that the failure to heed the committee's plea for a more responsible party government resulted in many of the ills foreseen by it, including the "incoherence in public policies, a dangerous enlargement of presidential power, public cynicism, and the growth of extremist movements."[15]

Pomper's apoplectic tone was anticipated in the report. The committee believed that the American party system was "ill-equipped to organize its members in the legislative and executive branches into a government held together and guided by the party program." In the words of the committee, this was "a very serious matter, for it affects the very heartbeat of American democracy."[16]

E. E. Schattschneider, chairman of the committee, wrote in his masterful book *Party Government* that "modern democracy is unthinkable save in terms of the parties."[17] Thus, if the parties were in trouble, so was democracy. These suppositions guided the committee's deliberations, and in the post–World War II years, it appeared that the parties were in trouble. Democrat Harry Truman was president, but there were doubts about his leadership. In 1946, voters gave the Republicans control of the Congress, producing the first divided-party government since 1930. The New Deal was floundering as the bipartisan conservative coalition in Congress continued to control Congress and strangle liberal initiatives for new civil rights laws. In 1948, the national Democratic coalition seemed to splinter. The Democratic Convention applauded Minneapolis Mayor Hubert Humphrey's call for southern Democrats "to get out of the shadow of states rights and walk forthrightly into the bright sunshine of human rights."[18] It prompted a Dixiecrat revolt, a third party of the South, which kept the Democratic party off the ballot in some states. Yet it did not allay the Left, who broke to support the Progressive candidacy of Henry Wallace. Truman's surprise win did not relieve the anxieties of many Democrats, some of whom hoped that Dwight Eisenhower, whose party affiliation remained a mystery, could be persuaded to accept their party's presidential nomination in 1952. At the same time, Thomas E. Dewey's defeat in 1948 sharpened divisions between moderates and conservatives in the Republican party. Theodore Lowi writes that the committee's diagnosis of the New Deal's anemia was "remarkable . . . when the dust had hardly settled over FDR."[19]

In its charge, the American Political Science Association made it clear that the Committee on Political Parties "should center its attention on the condition and improvement of *national* party organization."[20] The committee made several recommendations to that end, including

1. Biennial convening of national party conventions.
2. Active participation of national conventions in selecting national committee members.
3. Strengthening the national Democratic and Republican parties by reapportioning their national conventions and committees to reflect population and actual party strength in the states, and upgrading their headquarters and operations.
4. Establishing a party council that would draft the platform and interpret it in relation to current problems, review prospective presidential candidates, endorse congressional candidates, and make disciplinary recommendations with respect to conspicuous departures from general party decisions by state or local party organizations.[21]
5. Lengthening the terms for those in the House of Representatives from two to four years, with members chosen in the presidential election year.

The report also contained what might be called a wish list. It hoped that Congress would rely less on the seniority system in choosing committee chairmen. Regarding the presidential selection process, the committee wrote: "In time it may be feasible and desirable to substitute a direct, national presidential primary for the indirect procedure of the convention."[22] Some of these wishes have come true. Congress has strengthened the party caucus, and Democrats in particular have used it to dislodge recalcitrant committee chairs. In 1975, they ousted three from their posts, and in 1984 the caucus chose the seventh person in seniority to chair the House Armed Services Committee.[23] As for presidential selection, the McGovern-Fraser Commission began a revolution that has given greater weight to primaries and caucuses, thus advancing the destruction of those party structures that once housed the infamous "smoke-filled rooms."

The report claimed that its findings represented "a summation of professional knowledge."[24] It is remarkable that so many of its recommendations were realized since they were made in an era when television was a novelty and presidential candidates whistle-stopped from one railroad station to another.[25] The 1974 Democratic Party Charter, for example, established a party conference to be held between quadrennial conventions. These so-called midterm conferences convened in 1974, 1978, and 1982, but were abandoned after that.[26] The charter also reapportioned the Democratic National Convention and Democratic National Committee to reflect party strength in the electorate.[27] Republicans, meanwhile, have been faithful to the report's call for revamping and modernizing party operations. Beginning in 1975, the GOP began turning its party headquarters into a computerized hum of fund-raising activity and began to offer an extensive menu of campaign services to their candidates. Democrats have more recently struggled to match the Republican capacity for technological innovation but continue to lag behind. In addition, both national parties have their own office buildings in Washington and have been working more closely with their party's congressional campaign committees.

Despite its prescience, the Committee on Political Parties was subjected to a barrage of criticism, the most prominent critic, perhaps, one of its members, Evron M. Kirkpatrick.[28] In 1970, he renounced the report as both "relevant and disturbing," explaining that it was

> relevant to our collective past, to current discussion of party reform, and to any serious consideration of political science as policy science: disturbing to any political scientist who believes that the discipline can provide knowledge applicable to the solution of human problems and the achievement of human goals.[29]

Kirkpatrick likened the committee's product to "a political campaign document or program for political action than the report of a committee of scholars." He added that the work of the McGovern-Fraser Commission "is more like reading political science than reading the APSA Committee Report."[30]

Others criticized the report for its disparagement of federalism. The committee itself had noted that the national and state party organizations were "largely independent of one another, without appreciable common approach to problems of party policy and strategy" and urged greater nationalization of power.[31] Clearly, federalism accentuates the contrasting state political cultures that often result in fifty separate political parties. In an article critical of the report, Norton E. Long took note of this fact: "The existence in the United States of a multitudinous army of governmental institutions, each capable of supporting a private political army with its spoils, makes the electoral map resemble the free cities, dukedoms, petty principalities and bishoprics of the Holy Roman Empire, though Democrats and Republicans may look little enough like the Guelphs and Ghibbelines of yore."[32] Two critics of the report, Murray S. Stedman, Jr., and Herbert Sonthoff, took a swipe at the committee: "The advocates of greater party centralization, in neglecting or sidestepping the issues of profound Constitutional revision, have not made an effective case."[33] Failing a rewriting of the Constitution, federalism was not about to be repealed.

In a similar vein, many critics believed the committee was unduly influenced by the British parliamentary system. Clearly, the committee admired the British example of "responsible cabinet government."[34] Evron Kirkpatrick thought that the committee wanted American parties "to become like the British parties were believed to be."[35] Leon D. Epstein speculated that the British system had an unusual hold on the committee. After World War II, Epstein notes, the British Labour government enacted a sweeping program of social welfare legislation coupled with nationalization of key industries. Party-line voting in the House of Commons was at an all-time high, reflecting sharp and meaningful class divisions.[36]

In contrast, Democratic liberals could not muster much support for President Truman's domestic program. A Republican-controlled Congress passed the Taft-Hartley law over Truman's veto in 1947. The 1948 Democratic Convention endorsed new civil rights laws, but none was forthcoming. Truman wanted Congress to enact Medicare, but nothing happened until Lyndon Johnson got it passed in 1965. Thus, the Committee on Political Parties, some of whom had been in the Roosevelt administration, could not help but notice the contrast between the political stalemate in the United States and the enactment of a liberal agenda an ocean away.

The inability of Democratic liberals to prevail in Congress prompted a debate between supporters and critics of the report over the proper balance between majority rule and minority rights. Unlike Great Britain, the United States had deliberately resisted placing total political power in the hands of the majority. To the Federalists, the word *power* had such negative connotations that they substituted the word *energy* for it.[37] Their concerns were justified. A Democratic-Republican party leader spoke out against the Federalist energizers in 1802: "I would as soon give my vote to a wolf to be a shepard, as to a man, who is always contending for the *energy of government*."[38] Thus, the Framers were quite reluctant to mediate the debate over the proper relation of majority rule and minority rights, deferring it to the First Congress, which enacted a Bill of Rights, and successive congressional and Supreme Court decisions. If anything, the Framers tried to make a virtue out of the political stalemate. Writing in *Federalist* 51, James Madison extolled the constitution his peers had written, claiming that the ambitions of one branch would be countered by those of another.[39] A proper arrangement of interests, each with checks upon the others, was in Madison's view the ultimate guarantor of a republic, that is, a free and popular government. That it might also result in political stalemate was not Madison's primary concern.

Responsible-party advocates, however, do not like stalemate. They are drawn to active, purposeful government like moths to light. Their aim is that the majority govern. But in the two centuries since the Constitution was ratified, the debate between advocates of majority rule and defenders of minority rights continues, with minority rights advocates strengthening their position since the committee published its report in 1950.[40] Blacks and Hispanics have protection under the umbrella of "civil rights" to ensure their voting and employment privileges. Women's rights organizations claim they are due comparable pay for work performed by men. Homosexuals assert their right to an alternative lifestyle. All claim their "right" to exercise a veto over the majority.

This proliferation of minority rights only complicates the argument for responsible party government. But as Austin Ranney observes, the Committee on Political Parties believed that they could "sell" their fellow countrymen on the benefits of a more responsible party government without dealing with such "theoretical" subjects as majority rule and minority rights.[41]

Critics also noted a tension in the report between those who advocated intraparty debate and those who preferred interparty conflict. Austin Ranney wondered if it is "possible for twenty-seven million Democrats to 'participate' in the close supervision of their government any more than it is for one-hundred-fifty million Americans to do so?"[42] Clearly, the committee envisioned an enlightened issue-activism, with the rank and file guiding the party's direction and emboldening it with purpose. But the committee also proposed a party council, an elitist national body that suggested party responsibility was something that flowed from the top down. Stedman and Sonthoff thought the party council was another illustration of "the increasingly administrative or even quasi-military approach to the study of political problems."[43] Julius Turner worried that such power in the hands of party elites would result in control by unrepresentative factions. He feared in particular that the party council would disrupt the Republican Party, giving its unpopular conservative wing undue influence.[44]

"A World of Perceptions, Not Reality"

In the midst of the Iran-Contra Affair, Lieutenant Colonel Oliver North reminded his boss, John Poindexter, that the White House lived "in a world of perceptions, not reality."[45] Much the same can be said for advocates of responsible party government. Although publication of *Toward a More Responsible Two-Party System* produced a plethora of critics, two perceptions that guided the committee still shape the literature about responsible party government. Ironically, far from furthering academic inquiry, the report *froze* the subsequent debate, as both supporters and critics accepted the key assumptions contained in it. Foremost among these was that only political parties could produce responsible party government.

The committee began its work on the following premise: "Throughout this report political parties are treated as indispensable instruments of government."[46] This assumption reflected the thinking of committee chairman E. E. Schattschneider. Shortly before his death, Schattschneider said, "I suppose the most important thing I have done in my field is that I have talked longer and harder and more persistently and enthusiastically about political parties than anyone else alive."[47] Schattschneider was not the only party fan in the academic community. For decades, political scientists had accepted the inevitability of parties and assigned many desirable characteristics to them. Herbert Agar called them "unique," adding: "Unforeseen and unwanted by the fathers, they form the heart of the unwritten constitution and help the written one to work."[48] Giovanni Sartori claimed they were "*the* central intermediate structures between society and government."[49] The Committee for Party Renewal, a bipartisan organization consisting of academics and party activists, declared in 1976: "Without parties there can be no organized and coherent politics. When politics lacks coherence, there can be no accountable democracy. Parties are indispensable to the realization of democracy. The stakes are no less than that."[50] Gerald M. Pomper, a cochair of the Committee for Party Renewal, declared: "We must either acknowledge the mutual reliance of our parties and democracy—or lose both."[51] This article of faith has remained sacrosanct, even when it is universally acknowledged that today's parties have lost much of their former influence.

The clinging of political science to parties stems from a notion that the party system, not individual officeholders, should be the object of greatest concern in a democracy. Among the first to follow this prescription was James Bryce. In his masterpiece, *The American Commonwealth*, Bryce devotes nearly two hundred pages to the political parties.[52] His conclusions remain simple but powerful: "Parties are inevitable. No free large country has been without them. No-one has shown how representative government could be worked without them. They bring order out of chaos to a multitude of voters."[53]

The premise that parties are vital to successful governing appears so self-evident that it is often forgotten that it was a contentious subject in the early years of political science. At the turn of the century, some scholars wondered whether the American polity could (or should) be characterized by a commitment to *collective* (meaning party) responsibility or *individual* responsibility. M. I. Ostrogorski criticized the infatuation of some of his colleagues with collective responsibility: "This theory appeared alluring enough to be adopted by some writers of prominence, and expanded in certain cases, with brilliancy of literary style. It has, however, one defect: it is not borne out by the facts."[54]

William Graham Sumner agreed. A believer in individual responsibility, Sumner wrote in 1914 that it was an inevitable consequence of the American constitutional division of power: "I cannot trust a party; I can trust a man. I cannot hold a party responsible; I can hold a man responsible. I cannot get an expression of opinion which is single and simple from a party; I can get that only from a man."[55]

A debate ensued. In 1900, the political scientist Frank A. Goodnow argued the case for collective party responsibility: "The individual candidate must be sunk to a large extent in the party. Individual responsibility must give place to party responsibility."[56] The Progressives disagreed. Herbert Croly argued that party government was undesirable because it "interfered with genuine popular government both by a mischievous, artificial and irresponsible [i.e., parochial and localistic] method of representation, and by an enfeeblement of the administration in the interest of partisan subsistence."[57]

Perhaps no scholar better demonstrated the inexorable movement of political science toward party responsibility (and the inherent conflicts contained therein) than Woodrow Wilson. At first, Wilson maintained that party responsibility was more fiction than fact. Addressing the Virginia Bar Association in 1897, he declared:

> I, for my part, when I vote at a critical election, should like to be able to vote for a definite line of policy with regard to the great questions of the day—not for platforms, which Heaven knows, mean little enough—but for *men* known and tried in public service; with records open to be scrutinized with reference to these very matters; and pledged to do this or that particular thing; to take a definite course of action. As it is, I vote for nobody I can depend upon to do anything—no, not if I were to vote for myself.[58]

Later, Wilson saw collective responsibility as not only desirable but necessary. In a 1908 book, *Constitutional Government in the United States*, Wilson wrote: "There is a sense in which our parties may be said to have been our real body politic. Not the authority of Congress, not the leadership of the President, but the discipline and zest of parties has held us together, has made it possible for us to form and to carry out national programs." He added, "We must think less of checks and balances and more of coordinated power, less of separation of functions and more of the synthesis of action."[59]

There is a tension in Wilson's scholarship. He believes that collective responsibility is essential but couples it with a plea for individual responsibility by emphasizing the president's role as party leader.[60] In an article about Grover Cleveland's cabinet, Wilson observes: "What we need is harmonious, consistent, responsible party government, instead of a wide dispersion of function and responsibility; and we can get it only by connecting the President as closely as may be with his party in Congress."[61] In subsequent editions of *Congressional Government*, Wilson goes further to place the president at the apex of responsible party government:

> If there be one principle clearer than another, it is this: that in any business, whether of government or of mere merchandising, *somebody must be trusted*, in order that when things go wrong it may be quite plain who should be punished. . . . *Power and strict accountability for its use* are the essential constituents of good government. A sense of highest responsibility, a dignifying and elevating sense of being trusted, together with a consciousness of being in an official station so conspicuous that no faithful discharge of duty can go unacknowledged and unrewarded, and no breach of trust undiscovered and unpunished,—these are the influences, the only influences, which foster practical, energetic, and trustworthy statesmanship.[62]

Wilson's predilection for individual (read presidential) responsibility was not universally accepted by subsequent generations of political scientists. Ironically, the idea of collective responsibility may have been enhanced by Franklin D. Roosevelt. To members of the Committee on Political Parties, Roosevelt was a formative and formidable figure. He reinvigorated the Democratic Party and brought into its ranks those like Lyndon Johnson and Hubert Humphrey who shared his programmatic commitment to the New Deal. The lively partisan debate that followed was welcomed by political scientists, most of whom agreed with FDR. The party itself seemed at the center of the political universe.[63] In 1955, former committee member V. O. Key introduced the concept of "critical elections," with political parties acting as catalysts in electoral realignments.[64]

By 1950, collective party responsibility had become political science's First Commandment, and digressions from it were considered heretical. In a now famous warning, the committee predicted that placing individual responsibility in the president rather than the parties would endanger liberty itself.[65] Moreover, political scientists saw collective party responsibility as the way to limit conflict by channeling competition. In *The Semi-Sovereign People*, E. E. Schattschneider wrote: "The best point at which to manage conflict is before it starts."[66] His argument reinforced one made by social scientist Lewis Coser. In Coser's *The Functions of Social Conflict*, Schattschneider heavily underlined this passage: "One unites in order to fight, and one fights under the mutually recognized control of norms and rules."[67] Parties, therefore, became a sort of "thought police" in the establishment and maintenance of order.

In sum, publication of *Toward a More Responsible Two-Party System* placed the argument between collective and individual responsibility on ice. It is time to for political scientists to revisit the old arguments once more and to discard assumptions previously thought sacrosanct.

Thinking Anew: Responsible Party Government in America

A critical reexamination of whether responsible party government is desirable or attainable must take into account the major contours of the American political landscape, a prominent feature of which is the persistence of divided party control of the federal government and most of the states. In the four decades since the publication of *Toward a More Responsible Two-Party System*, Republicans have resided in the White House for twenty-six years, and Democrats have controlled the Senate and House for thirty-two and thirty-six years, respectively. Moreover, the gap between reelected presidents of one party and a House of Representatives dominated by another has widened considerably. The first instance of divided government occurred in 1792 when Federalist President George Washington was reelected and Thomas Jefferson's Democratic-Republican Party won a nine-seat majority in the House. When Republican Ronald Reagan was reelected in 1984, the opposition Democrats had a seventy-one-seat margin in the lower chamber. The pattern persisted in 1988. Republican George Bush easily beat Democrat Michael Dukakis in the presidential election, but the Democrats increased their majority in the House to an impressive eighty-nine-seat plurality.

Voters have seemed to approve of divided party government. An Institute for Social Inquiry survey conducted after the 1988 balloting asked Connecticut voters whether it was "good for the country" that Bush won the presidency and the Democrats controlled Congress. Sixty-seven percent answered yes. Moreover, by a 55 to 36 percent margin, *Bush supporters* welcomed divided government.[68] Recent polls show little change of opinion. One 1990 survey found that 51 percent believed that divided government is "a good thing, because it has kept either political party from having too much power." Only 37 percent deemed it "bad because it has made it impossible to work on solutions to the important problems facing the country."[69]

This extraconstitutional "check and balance" is not new. In a 1944 Elmo Roper poll, only 31 percent agreed it would be a bad thing "if a president from one party is elected next time, and the majority in Congress belongs to the other party."[70]

But this relatively new balancing act by the voters rests on firmer foundations. The electorate has decidedly mixed assessments of the two major parties, something not true in 1950. In a March 1991 ABC News–*Washington Post* survey, respondents said the Republicans were better than the Democrats on a litany of what can be termed "presidential issues," including maintaining a strong national defense, increasing U.S. influence overseas, handling foreign affairs, making American industry competitive, handling the economy, controlling inflation, controlling the spread of illegal drugs, handling crime, holding taxes down, reducing the threat of nuclear war, and shrinking the federal budget deficit.[71] The same poll showed the Democrats winning support on "congressional issues," most of which involve some redistribution of federal monies. For example, respondents thought the Democrats better at protecting the Social Security system, handling the problems of the homeless, and helping the elderly and the poor. Democrats had somewhat more modest advantages on reducing unemployment and helping the middle class.[72]

These mixed assessments reflect the contradictory feelings voters have about government. In 1967, Lloyd Free and Hadley Cantril noted the dissonance between the public's preference for "ideological conservatism" and its penchant for "programmatic liberalism."[73] Voters want government in the abstract to be kept to a minimum, but when asked about specific programs, they continually voice strong support for a more intrusive federal establishment. Today, the contradictions are translated in partisan terms, with the Republicans playing the role of the "ideological conservatives" and the Democrats acting as the "programmatic liberals."

With the passage of time, the allure of divided party government is becoming stronger. Early in 1990, Democratic pollster Peter Hart found that the mixed partisan assessments were being reinforced by the gargantuan federal budget deficits and the growing public concern about them: "While George Bush personally is at an all-time high in both job rating and how he is viewed personally, when we ask the public who they trust more to make the right decisions on the federal budget deficit cuts—28 percent say the president and 55 percent say the Congress."[74]

Divided government results in partisan behavior different from that anticipated in the responsible party literature. The Committee on Political Parties prescribed a code of conduct for the party-in-government and its loyal opposition:

> The party in power has a responsibility, broadly defined, for the general management of the government, for its manner of getting results, for the results achieved, for the consequences of inaction as well as action, for the intended and unintended outcome of its conduct of public affairs, for all that it plans to do, for all that it might have foreseen, for the leadership it provides, for the acts of all its agents, and for what it says as well as for what it does.
>
> Party responsibility includes the responsibility of the opposition party, also broadly defined, for the conduct of its opposition, for the management of public discussion, for the development of alternative policies and programs, for the bipartisan policies which it supports, for its failures and successes in developing the issues of public policy, and for its leadership of public opinion.[75]

Historically, such patterns of party behavior are anomalies. Only four times in this century have the parties acted in the manner prescribed by the report: once in 1913–14 with Democratic passage of Woodrow Wilson's New Freedoms, again in 1933–36 with the enactment of Franklin Roosevelt's New Deal, in 1964–65 when a Democratic Congress passed Lyndon Johnson's Great Society, and in 1981–82 when Congress enacted Ronald Reagan's tax and budget cuts. Each of these illustrations represents a party articulating a *national* program with the public's approbation resulting in unified party control of the government.[76] Today the parties are not conforming to the model envisioned by the responsible party supporters—nor can they. This is because neither the Democrats nor the Republicans can articulate a national program that is compelling enough to win an outright majority.[77] Those who believe the Democrats should cast themselves in opposition to a Republican president have received a sharp retort from House Speaker Thomas Foley:

> I keep having people say to me, "You ought to be the constant daily scourge of George Bush," that I ought to get up in the morning and figure out what I can say or do to embarrass the president or obstruct the president or whatever. That's not my concept of the job. . . . There are issues on which you have to stand even if you fail, but for the most part I would rather have a successful and important achievement in cooperation with the executive branch than just have a political issue.[78]

Cooperation is not a pattern of behavior associated with opposition parties. But because the Democrats share power with the Republicans and are not exclusively limited to seeking it, the resultant coalition government has a different set of characteristics than the responsible party government envisioned by the Committee on Political Parties.[79] Moreover, it has a set of advantages that the committee never associated with divided government. For one thing, this coalition government has *not* been beset by stalemate but has produced more than its fair share of what Speaker Foley terms "successful and important achievements." During the past forty years, landmark legislation has won approval from a Democratic Congress and a Republican president, including a federal highway program, revenue sharing, creation of the Environmental Protection Agency, deregulation of the airline and other industries, the 1981 tax cut, the 1986 overhaul of the federal tax code, a Free Trade Agreement with the Canadians, an Intermediate Nuclear Forces Treaty with the Soviet Union, reform of immigration laws, clean-air legislation, child care, an increase in the minimum wage, a defense budget that outlines Pentagon spending for the 1990s, and a landmark "bill of rights" law for the disabled.

This is far from the "do-nothing" government that the committee thought the norm in periods of divided party control. George Bush, in a 1991 interview, characterized the successes of the Democratic Congress and his Republican administration as "rather impressive on a wide array of issues."[80] In short, Democratic congresses and Republican presidents have done "big things"—or more accurately, about as many "big things" as the public wants. When Congress has failed to support the president, as in its refusal to back the proposed Reagan and Bush reductions in entitlement programs or Reagan's call for military aid to the Nicaraguan Contras, its rejection reflects the majority view.

Thus, it can be argued that the American polity is acting more "responsibly" than many political scientists believe. Moreover, it is responding to pleas for action from a national perspective that the committee would have applauded. James Q. Wilson writes that

> policy making has been rationalized in the sense that partial interests are now suspect and "general" interests are thought paramount. Everywhere the "old-style client politics" is on the defensive: Even the redoubtable tobacco farmers of North Carolina and their champion Jesse Helms have been forced to abandon any hope of large federal subsidies for their crops, and to turn instead to a federally administered plan that is financed by the contribution of the farmers themselves.[81]

Today, Wilson continues, the claims made upon government are not industrial or territorial in nature but "national, ideological or system-wide interests such as those pressing for tax reform, abortion on demand, the right to life, campaign finance reform, an end to the civil war in El Salvador, or the prevention of global warming."[82] Wilson's "system-wide interests" are code words for responsible government.

E. E. Schattschneider wrote in *Party Government*: "The greatest difficulties in the way of the development of party government in the United States have been intellectual, not legal."[83] The contributors to this volume have accepted Schattschneider's invitation to think anew the intellectual underpinnings of responsible party government and its prospects in the United States.

Everett Carll Ladd discusses the attempts by the Progressives and the responsible-parties school to "reform" the American party system, noting that the Progressives have succeeded all too well, whereas the responsible parties advocates have had little institutional impact. Successive chapters explain why it has been so difficult to reform the party system.

A. James Reichley describes the development of party organizations in the United States, noting that in recent years the political parties have become more national in character and scope. John S. Jackson III explores the competing models of party—elite versus participatory—implicit in the report and how these have played out in the politics of presidential nominations. John Kenneth White explores the relationship between voters and parties, specifically the question of mandates.

Sidney M. Milkis describes how Franklin Roosevelt effected a revolution in the executive branch that resulted in the diminishment of political parties and the prospects for responsible party government. Two members of Congress who are political scientists, Democrat David Price and Republican William M. Thomas, reflect on their relationships with their respective parties and how their experiences comport with the extant literature.

Jerome M. Mileur explores the history of party regulation, focusing especially on Supreme Court decisions in recent years that have "deregulated" the parties. Wilson Carey McWilliams compares and contrasts the conceptions of the American parties embraced by Alexis de Tocqueville and the Committee on Political Parties.

Notes

1. From Washington's Farewell Address, quoted in David E. Price, *Bringing Back the Parties* (Washington, D.C.: Congressional Quarterly, 1984), p. 97.
2. Ibid., p. 98.
3. Ibid., p. 100.

4. The Committee on Political Parties had a predecessor, the Committee on Congress, established by the American Political Science Association in 1941. Chaired by George Galloway, the committee was composed of ten members: Joseph P. Chamberlain, Marshall E. Dimock, George B. Galloway, Pendleton Herring, Arthur N. Holcombe, Meyer Jacobstein, Robert D. Leigh, Benjamin B. Wallace, Schuyler C. Wallace, and Roland Young. Like its successor, the Committee on Congress issued a short report (89 pages) advocating several reforms, including abolishing the seniority system and replacing it with a legislative council composed of the Vice President, Speaker of the House, the majority leaders in both chambers, and the chairmen of the newly constituted congressional committees.

The Committee on Political Parties recognized its debt to the Committee on Congress, saying it had "made a large and widely acknowledged contribution toward the strengthening of Congress and the passage in 1946 of the Legislative Reorganization Act." Committee on Political Parties, *Toward a More Responsible Two-Party System*, (New York: Rinehart, 1950), p. viii (hereinafter, CPP). The Committee on Congress did not achieve the notoriety that the Committee on Political Parties did. Nevertheless, the report was used as a justification for the reorganization of the congressional committee system in 1946.

5. CPP, p. ix.

6. Austin Ranney, *The Doctrine of Responsible Party Government: Its Origins and Present State* (Urbana: The University of Illinois Press, 1954), preface. This book is based upon Ranney's dissertation, directed by committee member Howard Penniman, and was revised in the wake of publication of the committee's report into this book.

7. Evron M. Kirkpatrick, "Toward A More Responsible Party System: Political Science, Policy Science, or Pseudo Science?" *The American Political Science Review*, 65 (December 1971): 965–90.

8. Clinton Rossiter, *Parties and Politics in America* (Ithaca, N.Y.: Cornell University Press, 1960), p. 180.

9. Theodore J. Lowi, *The Personal President: Power Invested, Promise Unfulfilled* (Ithaca, N.Y.: Cornell University Press, 1985), p. 68.

10. William J. Crotty, "The Philosophies of Party Reform," in *Party Renewal in America*, ed. Gerald M. Pomper (New York: Praeger, 1980), p. 35.

11. Frank B. Feigert and M. Margaret Conway, *Parties and Politics in America* (Boston: Allyn and Bacon, 1976), pp. 380–84.

12. Price, *Bringing Back the Parties*, p. 104.

13. Robert J. Huckshorn, *Political Parties in America,* 2d ed. (Monterey, Calif.: Brooks/Cole, 1984), p. 17.

14. Frank J. Sorauf and Paul Allen Beck, *Party Politics in America*, 6th ed. (Boston: Scott, Foresman; Little, Brown, 1988), p. 393.

15. Gerald M. Pomper, "The Contribution of Political Parties to American Democracy," in *Party Renewal in America*, p. 15.

16. CPP, p. v.

17. E. E. Schattschneider, *Party Government* (New York: Rinehart, 1942), p. 1.

18. Quoted in Carl Solberg, *Hubert Humphrey: A Biography* (New York: W. W. Norton, 1984), p. 17.

19. Lowi, *Personal President*, p. 68.

20. CPP, pp. viii–ix.

21. CPP, p. 43. The fifty members of the party council would consist of five members from the national committee, ten members of Congress (five from each house), ten members of state party committees (determined by region), five governors, representatives from other recognized groups such as the Young Democrats or Young Republicans, and twenty at-large members to be chosen by the delegates at the presidential nominating convention. The president, vice president, and members of the president's cabinet would be ex-officio members of the council. The idea for a party council was originally proposed by Charles E. Merriam in an article entitled "Nomination of Presidential Candidates" in the February 1921 issue of the *American Bar Association Journal*. Merriam's council included the president, vice president, and cabinet for the majority party (the presidential candidates in the last election would be included on the minority party council), the majority members of Congress (and the minority for its counterpart), state governors (and their runners-up), the chair of the national committee, state party chairs, and party leaders chosen by the national or state party committees. The Republican Party established a party council in 1919. It consisted of twenty-four members: twelve from the Republican National Committee, twelve prominent noncommittee Republicans. But it was short-lived, given the persistent GOP control of the executive and legislative branches.

The Committee on Political Parties also suggested that a smaller subgroup of the party council could form a "party cabinet" consisting of the Chair of the national convention, the chair of the national committee, the chair of the party council, the chairs of the Joint Congressional Caucus, congressional floor leaders, the vice president, and the Speaker of the House.

22. CPP, p. 10.

23. That was Les Aspin. The three ousted from their posts in 1975 were Wright Patman, chairman of the House Banking Committee; F. Edward Hebert, chairman of the House Armed Services Committee; and W. R. (Bob) Poage, chairman of the House Agriculture Committee. Both national parties have also acted to denounce congressional candidates not to their liking. In 1980, Democratic Party leaders condemned a California congressional candidate who had once been a member of the Ku Klux Klan. Ten years later, Ronald Reagan, George Bush, and the Republican National Committee denounced David Duke, a former Klan member from Louisiana who was seeking election to the U.S. Senate. Several Republican senators also condemned Duke and backed Democrat J. Bennett Johnston.

24. CPP, p. v.

25. Even the report's call for a party council was briefly adopted. In 1956, Democratic national chairman Paul Butler created the Democratic Advisory Council, whose purpose was to "provide a collective voice for the Democratic Party, representing on a year-round basis the millions of Democrats who may or

may not be represented in either House of the Congress." Congressional Democrats led by Sam Rayburn and Lyndon B. Johnson ignored the council, and after John F. Kennedy won the presidency, it was disbanded. Quoted in Stephen K. Bailey, *The Condition of Our National Parties* (New York: Fund for the Republic, 1959), p. 10.

26. The 1974 conference saw an unknown Georgia governor named Jimmy Carter occupy a hospitality suite to court prospective presidential delegates. The 1978 gathering proved to be an embarrassment to the Carter administration, and the 1982 meeting saw Walter Mondale and Edward Kennedy face off in anticipation of a prospective presidential nomination battle.

27. The Democrats also gave seats to the lesbian-gay caucus, an Asian-Pacific caucus, the Black caucus, the women's caucus, the liberal-progressive caucus, the business-professional caucus, and the Hispanic caucus. These caucuses became objects of derision, and in 1985 national chairman Paul Kirk withdrew their recognition.

28. One reason the report may have been subjected to so much criticism is that its recommendations appeared to have the imprimatur of the American Political Science Association. But the APSA took no position as to the recommendations made in the report, and in fact the *American Political Science Review* provided a forum for critics, including Julius Turner's "Responsible Parties: A Dissent from the Floor," *American Political Science Review*, (March 1951): 143–52.

29. Kirkpatrick, "Toward a More Responsible Party System," p. 1.

30. Ibid., p. 47. Asked why he signed the report, Kirkpatrick blamed it on "group-think": "Social norms—'not rocking the boat,' being a good fellow—come into play; so may careerism, unwillingness to alienate influential and respected colleagues, and even the desire to end an interminable committee meeting!" (p. 53).

31. CPP, p. 3.

32. Norton E. Long, "Party Government and the United States," *Journal of Politics*, 13 (1951): 211.

33. Murray S. Stedman, Jr. and Herbert Sonthoff, "Party Responsibility—A Critical Inquiry," *Western Political Quarterly*, 4 (September 1951): 468.

34. CPP, p. 35.

35. Kirkpatrick, "Toward a More Responsible Party System," p. 42.

36. Leon D. Epstein, *Political Parties in the American Mold* (Madison: University of Wisconsin Press, 1986), p. 36.

37. In *The Federalist Papers*, Hamilton stoutly defended the presidency, maintaining: "Energy in the executive is the leading character in the definition of good government." See Alexander Hamilton, "*Federalist* Number 70," in Alexander Hamilton, James Madison, and John Jay, *The Federalist Papers*, ed. Clinton Rossiter (New York: New American Library, 1961), p. 423.

38. Quoted in Ronald P. Formisano, *The Transformation of Political Culture: Massachusetts Parties, 1790s–1840s* (New York: Oxford University Press, 1983), p. 8. The spokesman was John Leland, and the emphasis is his.

39. James Madison, "*Federalist* Number 51," in *The Federalist Papers*, p. 322.

40. James MacGregor Burns writes that there have been seven "bills of rights" in the United States: the first ten amendments to the Constitution; the presence of an opposition party (first tolerated by the ruling Federalists in the 1790s); the 1803 Supreme Court ruling in *Marbury v. Madison* which established the principle of judicial review; the emancipation of the slaves and their subsequent reception of legal and political rights by the Civil War amendments; the extension of the franchise to women; Franklin Roosevelt's "economic bill of rights," including the freedom from fear and want; and the "social bill of rights" contained in Lyndon Johnson's much maligned Great Society. See James MacGregor Burns (with L. Marvin Overby), *Cobblestone Leadership: Majority Rule, Minority Power* (Norman: University of Oklahoma Press, 1990).

41. Austin Ranney, "Toward a More Responsible Two-Party System: A Commentary," *American Political Science Review*, 45 (1951): 498.

42. Ibid., p. 491.

43. Stedman and Sonthoff, "Party Responsibility—A Critical Inquiry," p. 460.

44. Turner, "Responsible Parties," p. 151. Turner's forecast proved accurate. After the hostility that surrounded Barry Goldwater's presidential nomination in 1964, Aaron Wildavsky branded the Goldwater delegates "purists" and wondered whether it is possible that the United States was "producing large numbers of half-educated people with college degrees who have learned that participation (passion and commitment) is good but who do not understand (or cannot stand) the normal practices of democratic politics." See Aaron Wildavsky, "The Goldwater Phenomenon: Purists, Politicians, and the Two-Party System," *Review of Politics*, 27 (January 1965): 413. Party activists, though excoriated by most students of political parties, began to seize power in both parties. James Q. Wilson attached the pejorative word *amateur* to the Democratic variety. James Q. Wilson, *The Amateur Democrat* (Chicago: University of Chicago Press, 1962).

45. "In Their Own Words: How the Iran-Contra Affair Took Shape," *New York Times*, 28 February 1987, p. 8.

46. CPP, p. 15.

47. Quoted in Epstein, *Political Parties*, p. 32.

48. Quoted in Richard L. Strout, "Restoring America's Parties," *Christian Science Monitor*, 23 September 1977, p. 31.

49. Giovanni Sartori, *Parties and Party System: A Framework for Analysis* (Cambridge, Mass.: Harvard University Press, 1976), p. ix.

50. "Strengthening the Political Parties," a position paper adopted by the Committee for Party Renewal in 1980 and presented to both national party committees.

51. Pomper, "Contribution of Political Parties," p. 5.

52. Although Bryce believed political parties were in need of reform, he thought they mattered more in the United States than in Europe. Bryce wanted to curb the excesses of party patronage. The discipline's early entanglement with

reform led to what Leon D. Epstein calls "an uncertain start." See Epstein, *Political Parties*, p. 12.

53. Quoted in Epstein, *Political Parties*, p. 18.

54. M. I. Ostrogorski, *Democracy and the Party System in the United States* (New York: Macmillan, 1910), p. 380. Quoted in Ranney, *Doctrine of Responsible Party Government*, p. 116.

55. From *The Challenge of Facts and Other Essays*, ed. A. G. Keller (New Haven: Yale University Press, 1914), p. 367. Quoted in Ranney, *Doctrine of Responsible Party Government*, p. 14.

56. Quoted in Ranney, *Doctrine of Responsible Party Government*, p. 96.

57. Quoted in Price, *Bringing Back the Parties*, p. 102.

58. Woodrow Wilson, "Leaderless Government," an address before the Virginia Bar Association, 4 August 1897, in *Public Papers*, vol. 1, pp. 336–59. Quoted in Ranney, *Doctrine of Responsible Party Government*, p. 33. The emphasis is Wilson's.

59. Quoted in Price, *Bringing Back the Parties*, p. 103.

60. Wilson may have been influenced by Theodore Roosevelt's presidency. Roosevelt's vigor and passions dominated American politics for more than a decade.

61. Woodrow Wilson, "Mr. Cleveland's Cabinet," in *Public Papers*, I, pp. 221–22. Quoted in Ranney, *The Doctrine of Responsible Party Government*, p. 30.

62. Quoted in Ranney, *Doctrine of Responsible Party Government*, p. 29. The emphasis is Wilson's.

63. Sidney Milkis disagrees herein, noting that Roosevelt sought to transcend the Democratic party in his reorganization of the executive branch.

64. V. O. Key, "A Theory of Critical Elections," *Journal of Politics*, 17 (February 1955): 3–18.

65. CPP, p. 93.

66. E. E. Schattschneider, *The Semi-Sovereign People: A Realist's View of Democracy in America* (Hinsdale, Ill.: Dryden Press, 1975, reprint), p. 15.

67. Lewis Coser, *The Functions of Social Conflict* (Glencoe, Ill.: Free Press, 1956), p. 121. I am grateful to Professor Morton Tenzer of the University of Connecticut for giving me Schattschneider's marked copy of Coser's book.

68. Cited in Everett Carll Ladd, "Public Opinion and the 'Congress Problem,'" *Public Interest*, 100 (Summer 1990): 66.

69. *Market Opinion Reports*, May 1990, p. 4.

70. Ladd, "Public Opinion," p. 67.

71. ABC News–*Washington Post* poll, 4–6 March 1991. Strong Republican leads were found on such issues as maintaining a strong national defense (68 percent to 17 percent); increasing U.S. influence overseas (60 percent to 26 percent); handling foreign affairs (59 percent to 23 percent); making U.S. industry competitive overseas (55 percent to 26 percent). The Republicans had modest advantages on handling the nation's economy (49 percent to 32 percent); controlling inflation (49 percent to 34 percent); reducing the problem of illegal

drugs (48 percent to 26 percent); handling crime (46 percent to 28 percent); holding taxes down (44 percent to 35 percent); reducing the threat of nuclear war (43 percent to 34 percent); and reducing the federal budget deficit (43 percent to 35 percent).

72. Ibid. On keeping unemployment down, Democrats led 45 percent to 38 percent; helping the middle class, Democrats had a 48 percent to 34 percent advantage. Stronger Democratic leads were found on issues such as helping the poor (64 percent to 22 percent); helping the elderly (60 percent to 24 percent); handling the homeless problem (54 percent to 27 percent); and protecting the Social Security system (52 percent to 29 percent).

73. Lloyd Free and Hadley Cantril, *The Political Beliefs of Americans* (New Brunswick, N.J.: Rutgers University Press, 1967).

74. "An Interview with Peter Hart," *Public Perspective*, (March–April 1990): 7.

75. CPP, p. 22.

76. Ronald Reagan's tax and budget cuts were not deterred by Democratic control of the House of Representatives.

77. See E. J. Dionne, *Why Americans Hate Politics* (New York: Simon and Schuster, 1991).

78. Tom Kenworthy, "Democratic Critics Want for Foley to Push Back," *Washington Post*, 7 June 1990, p. A-1.

79. New York investment banker Felix Rohaytn declares: "[T]he Democrats are not an opposition party; they share power, they do not seek it. Seeking power requires putting forward alternatives to the voters and competing for their allegiance; sharing power is an entirely different matter. The Democratic leaders in the Congress are excellent men, but they are part of the existing political power structure, and have formed something close to a coalition government with a Republican administration." Felix Rohaytn, "Becoming What They Think We Are," *New York Review of Books*, 12 April 1990.

80. "Determined to Do What Is Right" (Interview with George Bush), *Time*, 7 November 1991, p. 32.

81. James Q. Wilson, "The Newer Deal," *New Republic*, 2 July 1990, p. 35.

82. Ibid.

83. Schattschneider, *Party Government*, p. 209.

1

Political Parties, "Reform," and American Democracy

Everett Carll Ladd

Clinton Rossiter began his splendid little volume on the U.S. party system with an elegant summation of the parties' essential role: "No America without democracy, no democracy without politics, no politics without political parties."[1] Surely he was right in insisting that democracy without parties is inconceivable. He was also right, I believe, to lament that "for a people that invented the modern political party, we have been strangely reluctant to take pride in our handiwork."[2] It has been all too easy in this stable democracy of ours to become preoccupied with the evident shortcomings of politicians and their partisan institutions and to lose sight of the many vital links between political parties and the fabric of democratic life.

Why is it that one cannot envision democracy without parties? Primarily for the reason given by James Madison in his famous exposition in *Federalist* 10: "Liberty is to faction what air is to fire, an aliment without which it instantly expires. But it could not be a less folly to abolish liberty, which is essential to political life, because it nourishes faction than it would be to wish the annihilation of air, which is essential to animal life, because it imparts to fire its destructive agency." Madison was, of course, primarily intent on arguing that "factions" or interest groups, for all of the problems they caused, had to be permitted to operate freely. But the core of the argument is more general: If people are permitted to participate freely in the great enterprise of self-governance, they will surely organize themselves into many contending groups. And some of these groups will seek to organize the electorate in leadership selection—presenting candidates for elective office and providing voters with programs, traditions, and identities to help orient them in their political choices. If the liberty without which democracy is impossible is provided, people will in fact form political parties. The absence of a flourishing party system can mean only the absence of political freedom.

No America without democracy, no democracy without politics, no politics without parties.

Calls for Party Reform: The Progressives

At times, we know, observers have concluded that the American party system, while evincing the essential attributes of popular choice, was nonetheless performing inadequately with regard to other democratic requirements. There have been two major intellectual efforts aimed at party reform: (1) the Progressive Movement and its descendants and (2) the various calls of the last half century for strengthening parties. The two are wildly different in many regards. The Progressives were a highly successful political movement, operating within both the Republican and Democratic parties and at times as a third party. They took their case for party reform to the voters and often triumphed. Their institutional legacies are very much with us today: most notably, direct primaries as the principal means of candidate selection, an innovation that still sets the United States apart from most of the world's democracies, and direct public enactment of statutes through the initiative and the referendum. Those calling for stronger parties, in contrast, have never constituted more than an intellectual movement, indeed one finding support in academic political science along with a small coterie of sympathetic journalists and occasional politicians like those who have lent their energies to the Committee for Party Renewal.[3] This effort has no substantial institutional legacy. Nonetheless, its proponents have kept alive an alternative to the Progressive idea of a minimal place for parties in American democracy. The responsible-parties school, which produced the 1950 report *Toward a More Responsible Two-Party System*, is a distinct example of the intellectual effort to strengthen American parties.[4]

The Progressives saw the problem as parties being too strong.[5] Democracy is best served when ordinary citizens are given the maximum opportunity to make the key political decisions directly. That is, the public should be able to choose party nominees; it is not enough that they choose between or among party slates in general elections. In advancing so successfully the case for direct primaries, the Progressives were prompted by patent abuses in the party-based nomination systems they saw around them. There really were party "bosses," autocrats who used all manner of means, including illegal ones, to consolidate their personal power by seeing to it that the only road to elective office ran through their back rooms. Especially in those areas where only one party had a realistic chance to win most of the time, boss control over nominations meant boss control over public office. The Progressives confronted real problems, and their energetic response is a tribute to the vitality of American democratic life.

Still, the Progressives' model of democracy carried them well beyond such problems as corrupt and unresponsive party leaders. They argued that democracy is best served by direct citizen decision making. It would be better, the Progressives held, to have the public choose nominees for the parties than to have party leaders playing the decisive role in choosing them, no matter how able, honest, and intelligent those leaders might be and no matter how competitive the system.

We know that in making their case for direct democracy the Progressives drew on the deepest political values and inclinations of the American people, on that far-reaching political and social individualism that is a defining attribute of the American polity. Rossiter notes this, observing that "we have never been as willing as the British or Swedes or Belgians or even the Canadians to consign to partisan hands the great process of decisionmaking for the nation."[6] We must conclude, I think, that the Progressives, with their many allies and intellectual descendants, could not have failed, given the faithfulness with which they articulated the underlying assumptions of this individualistic system.[7] No democratic institutions can survive and flourish unless they reflect distinguishing values of their host society. Most other countries with successfully operating democratic institutions do so on less individualist assumptions. But American democracy must be an individualist democracy, or it is neither American nor democratic.

Nonetheless, in a large nation-state like the United States, strong intermediary institutions are necessary in politics, along with expansive opportunity for individual participation. By suggesting that a choice had to be made between "the parties" and "the people," the Progressives left an unfortunate legacy. We can still read it in the editorial pages of our newspapers where almost any effort to support parties as intermediary institutions is derisively dismissed, though parties now operate in a most inhospitable terrain. It is very hard today to get the public to listen to the case that paying a little more attention to the institutional needs of parties as representative institutions may be in the public interest and certainly need not entail an abandonment of their general preferences for an individualist polity. The Progressives and their many heirs in our day must be held responsible for playing upon deeply held public predispositions in such a way that most Americans today simply cannot see that some of their deepest dissatisfactions with current politics flow inevitably from the breadth of their disregard for political parties.

The Need for "More Responsible" Parties

The core of the contemporary case for strengthening parties is impressive. It is that even an individualist polity—in one sense, *especially* such a polity—needs vigorous intermediary political institutions, first and foremost of which are political parties. When the party presence in the electoral process is reduced below a certain core level, democratic malfunctions result.

The judgment that such malfunctions are now evident in American electoral politics, and the concomitant argument that political parties need to be strengthened so that they can play a "more responsible" part and thus curb the problems, have gathered a degree of support in American political science that is probably as close to consensus as the discipline will ever get. Most political scientists would agree with E. E. Schattschneider's argument, made in *Party Government* a half century ago, that "modern democracy is unthinkable save in terms of the parties."[8] They would agree with the Committee on Political Parties, organized in the late 1940s by the American Political Science Association, that parties are the "indispensable instruments of government."[9] And they would echo the Committee for Party Renewal's "Statement of Principles," which declares that "without parties there can be no organized and coherent politics. When politics lacks coherence, there can be no accountable democracy. Parties are indispensable to the realization of democracy. The stakes are no less than that."[10]

Some current deficiencies in the U.S. democratic process seem directly attributable to the diminished party presence. One of these involves that strange and confusing electoral arrangement persistent for the last quarter century whereby the two major parties have shared control of the national government.

When George Bush defeated Michael Dukakis on November 8, 1988, it was the fifth time in the last six elections that the Republicans had won the presidency. The GOP has gained 55 percent of the total two-party popular vote over this span. Since winning narrowly in 1968, the Republicans' victory margins have been 23 percentage points in 1972, 10 in 1980, 18 in 1984, and 8 in 1988. The one election the Democrats won in a sense provides the most graphic indication of the Republican ascendancy, for Jimmy Carter and the Democrats managed only the narrowest of victories in 1976, even though the GOP had been decimated by the Watergate scandals that culminated in the forced resignation of a Republican president. The GOP presidential margins of the last quarter century are large by any historical comparison, exceeded only slightly by the Democrats' margin during the New Deal elections (1932–48).

Yet the other half of the elective national government has remained solidly Democratic. The GOP lost control of the House of Representatives in the off-year election of 1954 and has never regained it. The Democratic lead in seats stood at 100 following the 1990 elections—267–167.[11] This contemporary pattern has no precedent in any previous period of American history. Table 1.1 shows that split results were highly uncommon prior to the 1950s.

When they did occur, it was almost always when the public was saying something that took two elections to express; that is, one got split control following midterm elections when the incumbent president was losing favor. Voters could not turn him out at that point, but they could punish his party. In recent elections, in sharp contrast, divided government has occurred routinely; even popular presidents winning reelection handsomely have been unable to carry Congress with them.

Such persistent divided control could not have occurred were Americans profoundly uncomfortable with the results, as French voters so plainly were with "cohabitation" in their brief experience with it between 1986 and 1988.[12] Indeed, many U.S. voters seem to see split control of national government as an almost natural extension of their country's historical commitment to the separation of powers—something they clearly like. Besides this, contemporary opinion research shows an American public highly ambivalent on many of the central questions of public policy. It endorses, for example, very high levels of government protection and services but at the same time insists that government is too big, too expensive, and too intrusive.[13] In wanting somewhat contradictory things from the modern state, segments of the public seem in some respects to welcome pitting the two parties' views of government against each another; the Republican executive pushing one way, a Democratic legislature pushing the other.[14]

However, it is one thing to argue that there are reasons why the American public is comfortable with aspects of divided party control, quite another to maintain that the public has planned or consciously intended it—or that it is happy with the bottom-line results. As to the latter, there is abundant evidence that Americans are frustrated by the performance of the current system, a frustration manifest in a number of ways, including strong criticisms of the institutional performance of Congress.[15] Besides, with the same general underlying views about government, Americans throughout most of the country's history did not choose split control. They gave one party or the other ascendancy in both branches.

Split control has come about in the modern era primarily through the confluence of two developments: (1) growing advantages for incumbents

Table 1.1. Split Results in National Elections, 1800–1990

1800–1950

Stage in election cycle[a]	Number	Number of split results	Percentage of split results
First	29	3	10
Second	25	12	48
Third	11	1	9
Fourth	10	2	20
Percentage of all elections yielding split results = 24			

1952–1990

Stage in election cycle[a]	Number	Number of split results	Percentage of split results
First	7	3	43
Second	7	4	57
Third	3	3	100
Fourth	3	3	100
Percentage of all elections yielding split results = 65			

Source: Based on Bureau of the Census, *Historical Statistics of the United States, Colonial Times to 1970*, pp. 1083–84; *Statistical Abstract of the United States*, 1990, 244.

Note: A split result in a national election occurs when a president of one party is elected with at least one house of Congress controlled by the other party.

[a]The first stage of an election cycle comes when a president first wins election. The second stage is his first mid-term (or that of his vice-presidential successor). The third stage comes, if at all, when an incumbent president wins reelection, and the fourth stage is his second midterm. Franklin Roosevelt's third and fourth terms are treated here like second terms. The election of 1866, when Lincoln's vice president, Andrew Johnson, a War Democrat, occupied the White House, saw Republicans win both houses of Congress. To call this situation either united or split control in the sense these terms are used in the other cases would be misleading; in the above tabulations this election is not counted at all.

in resources relevant to their reelection, including staffs for keeping their names before their constituents in ways vaguely positive and in direct campaign funding, and (2) the weakening of party ties across much of the electorate. In highly visible races such as those for president, governor, and U.S. senator, voters often acquire enough information about the candidates to make up for the declining guidance that party ties historically provided. In elections for school-board members, aldermen, and other local officials, to move to the other end of the spectrum, voters often have enough personal knowledge. But House races and other "intermediate" contests, as for many local government posts, evince a different dynamic. Here party voting is no longer decisive, but substantive knowledge of candidate records, approach to governance, and so on is insufficient to furnish a substitute base. Enjoying huge advantages in resources for self-promotion, incumbents in these contests cannot readily be challenged so long as they avoid scandal. No one planned this.

The public has ample means to end the situation if it makes up its mind to do so, but it finds it hard to make the connection between its institutional dissatisfactions—government seeming unresponsive, out of effective control, "special interests" too strong—and the absence of an effective link between party, policy, and congressional voting. This is all the more the case because incumbent congressmen seem nice enough and in each individual contest are typically much better known than their rivals. Furthermore, since the public has long been taught that parties are really not very important as representative institutions, that they are little more than unavoidable nuisances in the grand game of democracy, it is singularly unprepared to deal with the novel challenge that the persistence of divided government presents.

But a challenge it is. Even if Americans are not wildly unhappy with divided control and to some extent find it satisfying, they would probably find the quality of their representative democracy enhanced much of the time if they gave one party or the other a majority voice in both halves of elective national government. In those instances where they thought a change of direction was in order, it would be helpful if they could kick the "ins" out at both ends of Pennsylvania Avenue and give the other side a chance. Such a system would seem more responsive to popular control, not less.

Writing in the 1960s, Clinton Rossiter took issue with the argument that there was really not much difference between the two major American political parties, rejecting the notion that they were like Tweedledum and Tweedledee. He thought there were differences aplenty, given the requirement that each party assemble a diverse coalition in the interest of gaining majority support nationally. "Look deep into the soul of a Democrat," he wrote, "and you will find plans to build 400,000 units of public housing and to ship 300 tractors to Ghana (whether Ghana wants them or not); look deep into the soul of a Republican and you will find hopes for a reduction in taxes and for a balanced budget."[16] Even less are Republicans and Democrats Tweedledum and Tweedledee today. Studies of congressional voting, such as those done each year by the *National Journal*, show the two parties' congressional delegations more and more coherent ideologically and thus increasingly distinct.[17] But as these partisan differences have become sharper, the workings of the contemporary system of representation have required the two parties to share control of government much of the time.

More Party Responsibility Needed

Americans have long practiced a type of democratic politics in which individual voters play a large role in selecting candidates; hence, the institutional parties—their leadership, committees, conventions—play relatively limited roles. Early in this century, the Progressives successfully championed direct primaries as the principal institutional means for selecting nominees. Nonetheless, until the last several decades, party organizations maintained enough of a role to leave the overall system "mixed." Its mixture of party and direct citizen involvement was evident in the selection of presidential nominees. Primaries were common enough to test meaningfully the popular appeals of contenders in both parties, but the leadership structure of the party still had a control role.

Many analysts are now inclined to look back fondly on "the good old days of the 1950s" when a balance of popular and party roles was still maintained. Today that balance is no more. In presidential electioneering, candidates decide on their own whether to run. There are no enduring party bases to nurture and sustain them, nothing, for example, like the southern party bloc that supported Georgia Democrat Richard Russell in the 1940s and 1950s. Now prospective nominees must "invent themselves" afresh for each campaign. Some have broader national recognition than others, but institutionally they start as essential equals. Each must assemble his own stable of financial backers. No longer does any party body have a role, much less influence, to make meaningful its efforts at planning for a nominee best able to (1) satisfy the party's principal constituencies, (2) assemble the breadth of backing needed to win a national election, and (3) govern ably if elected. This problem is even greater for the party out of power, which lacks the organizing resources of the presidency.

Parties today have a weak, almost nonexistent role in nominee selection. There are a few exceptions. The most significant perhaps is the success the Republican Party has had through its national party committees—the Republican National Committee, the Republican Congressional Campaign Committee, and the Republican Senatorial Campaign Committee—in institutional fund-raising, a significant resource for encouraging candidates to run and assisting them if they do.

The institutional weakness of American parties is in one sense an old story. But the cumulative impact of various developments in the last thirty years has diminished their institutional presence far beyond historical norms. It is precisely because the American system was already highly individualist that a substantial party role could not survive the latest surge of political individualism that burst forth in the 1960s. The historical "mixed system"—public voice and party role—largely vanished.

These developments saw enhanced status for individual candidates and officeholders and a pronounced expansion of the part played by the national communications media. The latter is most apparent in presidential selection. The increased role of the national press in American electoral politics both resulted and was precipitated from the diminished role of the parties. Increasingly, the press has taken over important facets of the political communications functions once performed largely by parties. Two decades ago, journalist David Broder observed that newsmen had begun serving as the principal source of information on what candidates were saying and doing. They were acting the part of talent scouts, conveying the judgment that some contenders were promising while dismissing others as of no real talent. They were also operating as race callers or handicappers, Broder went on, telling the public how the election contest was going. At times they functioned as public defenders, bent on exposing what they considered the frailties, duplicities, and sundry inadequacies of a candidate, and in other instances they even served as assistant campaign managers, informally advising candidates and publicly, if indirectly, promoting his cause.[18] Even more today, we know, self-starting presidential candidacies run a gauntlet not of party but of press-based review.

Doris Graber has discussed the confluence of factors that has ended in such an elevation of the press role and so diminished a place for the parties. Since the "full flowering of the electronic age," Graber writes, "the candidate as a personality has become the prime consideration at the presidential level." When voters focus directly on candidates with little intermediary involvement by political parties, Graber continues,

> the media become more important because they are the chief sources of information about these matters. Correspondingly political parties take on less importance. . . . More than ever before media personnel can influence the selection of candidates and issues. Candidates, like actors, depend for

> their success as much on the roles into which they are cast as on their acting ability. In the television age media people usually do the casting for presidential hopefuls, whose performance is then judged according to the assigned role. Strenuous efforts by campaign directors and public relations experts to dominate this aspect of the campaign have been only moderately fruitful. Casting occurs early in the primaries when newspeople, on the basis of as yet slender evidence, must predict winners and losers in order to narrow the field of eligibles.[19]

It is hard to escape the conclusion that the press's part in nominee selection has become too large and intrusive. Democratic governance would be enhanced if the balance was shifted at least moderately away from nonelected, "nonresponsible" news media to parties whose nominees regularly face the scrutiny of voters. Given the enormous resources now available to communications organizations—accruing from revolutions in communications technology and the consequent jump in audience reach—it is hard to see how media domination of electioneering can be curbed unless ways are found to rebuild the party presence at least modestly.

In choosing candidates, managing electioneering, and organizing voting to facilitate an "up or down" judgment on what government is doing, a larger, more "responsible" role for the parties is needed. American democracy, in this sense, would be enhanced by a more responsible party system. This might suggest that I find much merit in the most publicized of all documents calling for a "more responsible" party system, the 1950 report of the APSA's Committee on Political Parties. In fact, I find the report enormously flawed. It is, of course, possible to conclude that American political parties need institutional resuscitation while disagreeing profoundly with much of the reasoning of the responsible-party school.[20] If there is substantial agreement among political scientists today that parties should be doing more, there is wide disagreement over the "more" proposed by the responsible party advocates. If there is general consensus that American democracy would be enhanced by "more responsible" parties, there is also a considerable dissensus about the conception of democracy and the parties' role therein that guided E. E. Schattschneider and his colleagues.

The report has been criticized from a number of perspectives. Chief among these perhaps is that it lacks a sufficient analytic and empirical base and is instead at its core the statement of a particular, partisan, and ideology-bound political point of view. Samuel Eldersveld observed in 1964 that

> there has been much theory about party organization, a good deal of it revealing our own normative concerns, but there has been little systematic

> analysis of the party as an organizational system. The apotheosis of these developments was perhaps reached in 1950 with the edict of the APSA, again after no systematic study of party organization, that our parties were not democratic, responsible, or effective.[21]

A few years later, in a sweeping indictment of the report that he had signed in 1950 as a member of the Committee on Political Parties, Evron Kirkpatrick concurred in this criticism:

> The Report was not a summary of available knowledge and insights as of the date of its publication . . . and . . . knowledge about parties in 1950 was inadequate on many matters the Committee treated as settled matters of fact. . . . It is not political science, but a campaign document which argues a case, and, like campaign documents, ignores anything contrary to the point of view it is selling.[22]

The Report's Underlying Political Agenda

I understand the political perspective that guided the 1950 "campaign report" somewhat differently than Kirkpatrick does. At its core, that perspective was an articulation of what I will call the New Deal theory of governance—an outlook widely shared in liberal and Democratic circles in the 1940s and 1950s. It held that (1) the United States confronted grave problems which could be resolved only by more expansive and coherent governmental action; (2) leadership in advancing the above could come only from the presidency, the office most reflective of popular wishes and indeed the "great engine" of American democracy; and (3) the only way this presidential leadership on behalf of popular wishes could be exercised, given the American system of separation of powers and our individualist political culture, would be through the vehicle of *disciplined* political parties.

What the responsible-party school wanted most was to transform the majority party, the Democrats, into a more disciplined vehicle for realizing the programs and policies of liberal Democratic presidents. Of course, the Republicans could do their part as a more disciplined opposition. The Committee on Political Parties thus concluded that

> the crux of public affairs lies in the necessity for more effective formulation of general policies and programs and for better integration of all the far-flung activities of modern government. It is in terms of party programs that political leaders can attempt to consolidate public attitudes toward the work plans of government. . . . An effective party system requires, first, that the parties are able to bring forth programs to which they commit

> themselves and, second, that the parties possess sufficient internal cohesion to carry out these programs. . . . Party responsibility means the responsibility of both parties to the general public, as enforced in elections. . . . As a means of achieving responsibility, the clarification of party policy also tends to keep public debate on a more realistic level.[23]

Underlying these assessments was the conviction that the American people had made clear what they wanted government to be and do by repeatedly electing liberal Democrats to the presidency in the five elections preceding the report. But presidential leadership was frequently stymied by an unresponsive Congress, often under the control of an unholy bipartisan alliance of conservative southern Democrats, who dominated powerful committee chairmanships, and Republicans. It was necessary to liberate the general will from these enervating restraints through presidential leadership augmented by party discipline. James MacGregor Burns's *Congress on Trial* (1949) and *The Deadlock of Democracy* (1963) powerfully advanced this case.

The idea that strengthened presidential leadership operating through the mechanism of party discipline would generally sustain more activist and expansionist government seems somewhat amusing today, after a quarter century of conservative presidents. Many liberals now welcome the independence of a Democratic-controlled Congress from Republican presidential leadership. Almost no one sees party discipline as a problem. But in 1950 when the committee issued its report, and even in 1963 when *The Deadlock of Democracy* was published, one could believe that liberal activism found its natural home in the presidency. Arthur M. Schlesinger, Jr., reflected this when he wrote in 1965 that John Kennedy's presidency was based on the belief that

> the chief executive . . . must be "the vital center of action of our whole scheme of government." The nature of the office demanded that the president place himself in the very thick of the fight . . . [that he] be prepared to exercise the fullest powers of his office—all that are specified and some that are not.[24]

Just eight years later, though, Schlesinger was to denounce the presidency as bloated in its powers, imperial in its bearing and style, and dangerously open to personal abuses of power.[25] What a difference a change of regime makes.

Still, this reversal—where conservative presidents now do battle with liberal Congresses—should not obscure the fact that in the late 1940s many who wanted more energetic and activist government were convinced that they would most likely get it by strengthening the president's hand in the American system of governance. Since they were not going to be able to alter the separation of powers in favor of British-style parliamentary democracy, they saw more disciplined parties as the only realistic solution.

The end was more government. We see this throughout the writings of the responsible-parties school, but nowhere is it so forcefully exposed as in E. E. Schattschneider's *The Struggle for Party Government.*[26] This little treatise is an unbroken cry for a larger state. Recent developments had imposed, Schattschneider wrote, enormous new burdens on government for which many Americans were ill prepared intellectually:

> As a nation we have had little opportunity to prepare ourselves for the realization that *it is now necessary for the government to act as it has never acted before.* . . . The essence of the governmental crisis consists of *a deficiency of the power to create, adopt, and execute, a comprehensive plan of action* in advance of a predictable catastrophe in time to prevent and minimize it. . . . The source of difficulties is political, the *failure to mobilize the power of the nation to govern itself,* the failure to organize the power of the majority over the government. . . . It is doubtful if a mere simplification of the structure would in fact create *a government that could meet the need for speedy formulation of comprehensive policies consistently carried out* unless there were organized also a more powerful political base for the system. The central difficulty of the whole system—the difficulty which causes all of the difficulties—is the fact *the government characteristically suffers from a deficiency of the power to govern.* . . . The confusion, friction, and delay which characterized every aspect of the governmental process reflect a political weakness.[27]

Schattschneider goes on and on in this fashion. The need is for more government acting more coherently and more expeditiously, passing more programs.

This is a point of view, but one caught up in intense partisan and ideological controversy. It is also subject to important empirical reservations. Leon D. Epstein notes, for example, that both Pendleton Herring and Don K. Price concluded in the late 1930s that "Britain's disciplined party leadership had produced bad policy results during the 1930s, at a very time that American presidential leadership appeared to have been relatively successful."[28] I have argued elsewhere that Herring's observations are an important reminder of the serious empirical questions whether more party discipline, coherence of action, and so on generally make for better policy. In Britain, Herring maintained,

> it is the whole tendency of the system that distinctive parties govern the nation in accordance with the class basis upon which their strength is organized. . . . The isolation of classes into separate parties prevents that modification of extreme points of view that is possible when different elements join in compromise. The results of the British Conservative party in encouraging German armament because of a fear of Communism are now apparent. Parliamentary government does not provide a place in policy formulation for all of the parties at interest. One party machine rules while the opposition elements stand aside and hope for mistakes that will oust those in power.[29]

Of course, Herring is describing a system distinguished not only by disciplined parties but by a unitary form of government. The American system differs in both regards, with relatively undisciplined political parties and the separation of powers. Still, his analysis is relevant to the question of whether the confidence of the responsible-parties school that a greater coherence of government action achieved through more disciplined parties would make for better policy results was at all well founded empirically. Herring's analysis certainly points in the other direction. He found the American system, with its weak parties and dispersed power, more soundly based: "The chief executive is forced to seek middle ground. He cannot depend on his own party following. His measures are often supported by minority party members." In short, soundness of policy may well come more often from the need to *compromise* than provisions for *coherence*.

The argument that we may have followed our national inclination to an individualist polity too far and now need to find ways to rebuild the party presence—especially in the organization of voting, in candidate selection, and in the conduct of elections—*back to levels such as obtained in 1950* is still a very hard one to make. The Committee for Party Renewal is making it intelligently. Any chance for success in advancing this perspective requires both a determined eschewing of partisan points of view and an equally determined insistence that one not go beyond what can be persuasively demonstrated. By flunking these tests, the 1950 report is a near complete failure.

I have indicated here where I think the necessary, modest partisan agreement and analytic base leads us and leaves us. Public control of government would be enlarged by reviving the articulation that long prevailed between presidential and congressional voting. The present lack of articulation, which manifests itself in split-party control, probably carries the conception inherent in the separation of powers one step too far. It is hard to see how steps to strengthen the party presence in the voting decision and thus restore some measure of articulation in presidential and congressional balloting would be other than helpful by broad standards of democratic governance. The one potentially serious objection involves possible partisan implications. It can be argued that an increase in party voting across presidential and congressional lines would be more likely to increase the Republican presence in Congress than improve the occupancy rate of Democrats in the White House. It can also be argued, as William Schneider has, that the best thing that could happen to enhance Democratic presidential prospects would be for the Republicans to win Congress, which would enable the party to have a real go at governing and thereby expose it to voter wrath as the inadequacies of its approach are exposed.[30] It is hard to do more than speculate on this matter. However this may be, the case that more party voting, a return to that lofty 1950 level, would be an improvement by *democratic* criteria seems on fairly firm ground. Certainly some measure of party voting, hence some greater alternation of party control, is a far more satisfactory democratic response to extreme incumbency advantages and uncompetitive elections than frustration-based proposals such as those for term limitations. Similarly, getting the parties back into the conduct of elections and the selection of candidates would be a democratic improvement over today's hyperindividualist, candidate-centered, media-based electioneering.

But Is It Possible?

Can American political parties ever again be as responsible as they were in 1950? On this the jury is out. The party system of 1950 was consistent with the basic organization of American political institutions and the nation's political culture. Neither is very different now, which suggests that reform efforts toward reviving the kind of party role in place when the 1950 report was issued are not beyond the realm of political possibility.

Assessing steps that might advance this democratic reform is beyond the scope of this chapter, but promising ideas have been advanced in various forums, even if implementing them seems formidably difficult. Parties are losing ground because they occupy a vastly diminished presence in the communication of political ideas. They are resource-poor compared to their principal rivals or competitors: the national communications media whose economic and technological base in national political communication has been so vastly expanded and individual candidates, who get the bulk of campaign contributions and use them largely for self-serving ends. Testifying before the House Task Force on Campaign Finance Reform in May 1991 as executive director of the Committee for Party Renewal, John Kenneth White argued that "money is the crucial ingredient in campaigns. While money itself is not an evil, the system of finance needs repair."[31] How so?

> In making its adjustments, Congress has an opportunity to refurbish a vital institution of government—the political parties. This can be accomplished in five ways. First, limits on individual contributions to parties should be substantially raised for such party-building purposes as voter registration, program development, research, and get out the vote drives. Second, *party* contributors should be allowed to give more than *individual* contributors. Third, the political parties themselves should be able to make unlimited contributions to their candidates for offices at all levels of government. Fourth, any system of public financing should channel campaign funds through party committees. Fifth, there should be full public disclosure of all contributions and expenditures.[32]

Speaking on behalf of the committee, White went on to argue that

> the Congress should mandate significant and free television time for the parties on behalf of themselves and their candidates. . . . The amount of television time should be sufficient so that parties can campaign effectively on behalf of their tickets, sponsor "generic" ads that convey party positions on important voting issues, and provide ample opportunities for individual candidates to reach the voters. The content of these messages should be left completely to the parties and candidates. In addition to the free broadcast time, political parties should be the sole sponsors of televised debates.[33]

Other similarly motivated steps need to be considered. In all this, the end should be kept clear: to rebuild parties modestly in ways consistent with American political institutions and values, and through means that are widely seen as not unduly advantaging one party over the other or advancing any particular programmatic philosophy.

Notes

1. Clinton Rossiter, *Parties and Politics in America* (Ithaca, N.Y.: Cornell University Press, 1960), p. 1.

2. Ibid.

3. The committee was formed in 1975. Its 500 members are, disproportionately, from the ranks of academic political science.

4. Committee on Political Parties, *Toward a More Responsible Two-Party System*, American Political Science Association, supplement to the *American Political Science Review*, September 1950 (hereinafter, CPP).

5. The literature on the Progressive movement is vast. A useful source on Progressive thinking about parties is Richard Hofstadter, *The Age of Reform* (New York: Vintage Books, 1955).

6. Rossiter, *Parties and Politics*, p. 46.

7. The McGovern-Fraser Commission efforts in changing Democratic Party presidential-nomination rules is one example of an effort based implicitly on Progressive thinking about political parties.

8. E. E. Schattschneider, *Party Government* (New York: Rinehart, 1942), p. 1.

9. CPP, p. 15.

10. Committee for Party Renewal, "Statement of Principles," position paper adopted by the Committee for Party Renewal, September 1976.

11. I have discussed aspects of this split-level, split control system in a number of publications going back a decade and a half. See, for example, Ladd with Charles D. Hadley, *Transformations of the American Party System: Political Coalitions from the New Deal to the 1970s*, 2nd ed. (New York: W. W. Norton, 1978); Ladd, "The Brittle Mandate: Electoral Dealignment and the 1980 Presidential Election," *Political Science Quarterly*, (Spring 1981): 1–25; "Politics in the '80s: An Electorate at Odds with Itself," *Public Opinion*, (December–January 1983): 2–6; "On Mandates, Realignments, and the 1984 Presidential Election," *Political Science Quarterly*, (Spring 1985): 1–25; "The 1988 Election: Continuation of the Post-New Deal System," *Political Science Quarterly*, (Spring 1989): 1–18; "Public Opinion and the 'Congress Problem,'" *The Public Interest*, (Summer 1990): 57–67; and "The 1990 Elections: A Clear Message, Unclear Results," *The World and I*, (January 1991): 106–14.

12. "Cohabitation" was the situation in which France had a Socialist president, Francois Mitterrand, and at the same time a prime minister and cabinet from the principal opposing party, the neoGaullist Rally for the Republic.

13. See, for example, Ladd, "Politics in the '80s," p. 206; "The Reagan Phenomenon and Public Attitudes Toward Government," in Lester M. Salamon and Michael S. Lund, eds., *The Reagan Presidency and the Governing of America* (Washington, D.C.: Urban Institute Press, 1984); and Ladd and Karlyn H. Keene, "Attitudes Toward Government: What the Public Says," *Government Executive*, (January 1988): 11–16.

14. For a further elaboration of this argument, see Ladd, "Public Opinion and the 'Congress Problem,'" pp. 66–67.

15. Ibid., pp. 61–65.

16. Rossiter, *Parties and Politics*, p. 149.

17. See Richard E. Cohen and William Schneider, "Partisan Differences," *National Journal*, 19 January 1991, pp. 134–61. They note, for example, that "Southern Democrats and eastern Republicans, the traditional centers of ideological moderation in both the House and the Senate, moved farther apart in 1990. Their shifts (the southern Democrats to the left and the eastern Republicans to the right) were another sign of the increased partisanship in both chambers."

18. David S. Broder, "Political Reporters in Presidential Politics," in Charles Peters and Timothy J. Adams, eds., *Inside the System: A Washington Monthly Reader* (New York: Praeger, 1970), pp. 3–22.

19. Doris A. Graber, *Mass Media and American Politics* (Washington, D.C.: Congressional Quarterly Books, 1989), pp. 197–98.

20. When I refer to the responsible-parties school, I mean that group of political scientists whose foremost spokesmen were E. E. Schattschneider and James MacGregor Burns, and whose analysis and assessments with regards to political parties were articulated in *Toward a More Responsible Two-Party System*. Other notable works of the school are E. E. Schattschneider, *Party Government* (New York: Rinehart, 1942), and *The Struggle for Party Government* (College Park: Program in American Civilization, University of Maryland, 1948); James MacGregor Burns, *Congress on Trial: The Legislative Process and the Administrative State* (New York: Gordian Press, 1966; first published by Harper and Brothers, 1949); *The Deadlock of Democracy* (Englewood Cliffs, N.J.: Prentice-Hall, 1963).

21. Samuel J. Eldersveld, *Political Parties: A Behavioral Analysis* (Chicago: Rand McNally, 1964), p. 14.

22. Evron M. Kirkpatrick, "'Toward a More Responsible Two-Party System': Political Science, Policy Science, or Pseudo-Science?" *American Political Science Review*, (December 1971): 984, 985.

23. CPP, pp. 1,2.

24. Arthur M. Schlesinger, Jr., *A Thousand Days* (Boston, Mass.: Houghton-Miflin, 1965), p. 120.

25. Arthur M. Schlesinger, Jr., *The Imperial Presidency* (New York: Popular Library, 1973).

26. E. E. Schattschneider, *The Struggle for Party Government* (College Park, Md.: Program in American Civilization, University of Maryland, 1948).

27. Ibid., pp. 1–3.

28. Leon D. Epstein, "What Happened to the British Party Model?" *The American Political Science Review*, (March 1980): 10; Don K. Price, "The Parliamentary and Presidential System," *Public Administration Review*, (Autumn 1943): 317–34; and Pendleton Herring, *Presidential Leadership* (New York: Farrar and Rinehart, 1940), pp. 128–46.

29. Herring, *Presidential Leadership*, pp. 129–30. I have discussed his and related arguments in "Party Reform and the Public Interest," *Political Science Quarterly*, (Fall 1987): 363–69.

30. William Schneider, Lecture presentation to students and staff of the Roper Center for Public Opinion Research, University of Connecticut, 3 May 1991.

31. John Kenneth White, statement delivered to the House Task Force on Campaign Finance Reform, Washington, D.C., 28 May 1991.

32. Ibid.

33. Ibid.

2

Party Politics in a Federal Polity

A. James Reichley

The authors of *Toward a More Responsible Two-Party System* were enthusiastic nationalizers in their approach to party reform, as they were, no doubt, in their attitudes on most larger issues of society and government. The party system, they found, "is weighted much more heavily toward the state-local side than is true today [1950] of the federal system of government." The resulting "gap," they claimed, "produces serious disabilities in government."[1]

Decentralization of authority within the parties, they argued, "is probably the principal reason for the frequent difficulty, discord, and confusion" of party operations. "Party organization designed to deal with the increasing volume of national issues," they recommended, "must give wider range to national party leadership."[2]

The drafters of the responsible party government manifesto did not shrink from calling for draconian steps to centralize party control. They proposed that a *party council*, a board of political notables to oversee national party functions, "would be the appropriate agency to interpret" differences on policy issues between the national party and its state and local affiliates "and determine the right position in case of conflict." The party council should be empowered to use "party funds to replace the disloyal leadership" of recalcitrant state organizations, and even to appoint "temporary state officers" to assure national party supremacy.[3]

The drafters understood that they were flying into the face of most American political experience up to that time. Historically and traditionally, American parties had been highly decentralized. Before the 1930s, national party organizations had usually functioned as federations of state and local parties that got together every four years to run candidates for president and vice president. Even in the 1950s, Austin Ranney and Willmoore Kendall could write: "There is perhaps no point on which writers on American politics are so . . . agreed as that our state and local party organizations, taken collectively, are far more powerful than our national party organizations."[4] But if the parties were to survive as effective political forces and serve constructive governmental purposes, the members of the American Political Science Association's Committee on Political Parties were convinced, party organizations would have to be recast as administratively centralized and ideologically unified national institutions.

Since the 1950s, the major parties have evolved structurally much as the Committee on Political Parties would have wanted. National party organizations have substantially increased their financial resources, enlarged their staffs, and expanded their roles in managing state and even local campaigns. Parties have become ideologically more unified. Though still less centralized structurally than most European parties, American parties are now more nationalized than the underlying federal structure of government. Many state and local parties have come to resemble franchises of national business corporations, receiving financial support and strategic direction from a centralized national bureaucracy.

Unfortunately, parties have also become substantially less important factors in American political life. Whether there is some relationship between simultaneous trends toward structural centralization and loss of support for parties among the electorate and whether some return toward greater state and local party autonomy would be both beneficial and achievable are questions that underlie the discussion in this chapter.

Domination by Caucus

In the early years of the Republic it appeared that national party organizations might develop as auxiliaries to contending factions in Congress and the national administration, somewhat as nascent party organizations were growing up in Britain in the closing decades of the eighteenth century to manage election campaigns for rival bodies of Whigs and Tories in the House of Commons.

Almost all the American founders deeply disliked and distrusted parties, which they regarded as socially divisive and politically disruptive. Their aim was that the government of the new nation should be conducted without factions or party divisions. Before the end of George Washington's first term, loosely organized parties had formed in Congress, reflecting conflicts within the executive branch between supporters of Secretary of the Treasury Alexander Hamilton on one side and Secretary of State Thomas Jefferson on the other. Differences over Hamilton's ambitious economic program to promote business growth were the initial cause of the split. These were quickly reinforced by clashing attitudes toward the French Revolution and the war between Britain and France that followed.

In the first few national elections after Washington's retirement in 1796, the congressional caucuses of the two parties, known as Federalists and Republicans, selected slates of candidates for president and vice president. Campaigns for the contending slates were carried on by national structures of party clubs, newspapers, and political jobholders—better organized on the Republican side than the Federalist.

The system of nominating national-party tickets by congressional caucuses broke down in 1824 when the presidential choice of the Democratic-Republican caucus, William Crawford of Georgia, finished third in electoral votes behind Andrew Jackson of Tennessee and John Quincy Adams of Massachusetts, both of whom had been nominated by their state legislatures. The Federalists had grown so weak after 1816 that they had stopped fielding national tickets.

There were several reasons why the domination of national parties by congressional caucuses did not endure. First and probably most important, the federal system of government, at a time when political matters of greatest concern to most citizens were likely to be settled at the state or local levels, caused state party organizations to acquire decisive power. Second, the sheer size of the country, while transportation and communications networks remained preindustrial, made it difficult to maintain an effective national party organization. Third, the constitutional division between the executive and legislative branches in the federal government was bound to induce presidents to look for political bases outside Congress. Fourth, the eclipse of the Federalists after the War of 1812 reduced the motivation for the Republicans to unite behind a single national ticket. For these and other reasons, by the middle of the 1820s state party organizations had emerged as key players in national as well as state and local politics.

An Unbroken Succession

Parties of a kind had existed in some of the colonies before the Revolution. Some of these were not much more than extensions of rival family clans, such as the Wards and Hopkins in Rhode Island and the DeLanceys and Livingstons in New York. But in many colonies these divisions began to take on ideological connotations, with a court party supporting royal authority and a country party promoting increased colonial autonomy. "In every colony," John Adams later wrote, "divisions always prevailed. In New York, Pennsylvania, Virginia, Massachusetts, and all the rest, a court and country party have always contended."[5]

As relations between the colonies and the mother country grew more heated, the country parties, known as Whigs, evolved into fomenters of revolution, and the court parties, Tories, rallied to defend the Crown.

Overthrow of British rule virtually wiped out the American Tory interest, most of whose leaders fled or were expelled. But the victorious Whigs in most of the newly established states soon divided into factions differing over issues such as proposals to defer payment of private debt and efforts to increase the authority of state governors. These factions can be defined in broad senses as *conservative* and *populist*, though neither term was used at the time. Some of these state factions developed rudimentary party organizations. The most advanced organizations were in Pennsylvania where the populists called themselves Constitutionalists because they favored continuation of the radical state constitution of 1776 and the conservatives took the name Republicans, perhaps to distinguish themselves from the state's numerous Tories. In most states neither conservatives nor populists usually achieved absolute majorities, and the balance of power in state legislatures was held by independents who swung back and forth, depending on the issue.[6]

The move to write a new federal constitution in 1787 was spurred by conservative leaders and state parties who feared populists might soon get control in many of the states. In most states, conservatives, calling themselves Federalists, led the fight for adoption of the Constitution, while populists, as Anti-Federalists, were opposed.

There were some crossovers in the parties that formed under the new government. Young James Madison, for example, who had been an ardent and influential Federalist in 1787, later became a leader of the Republican Party that resisted Hamilton's economic program. Jefferson, who had been neutral on the Constitution (he was out of the country serving as ambassador to France), became in 1800 the first president elected on the Republican ticket. In general, however, both Federalists and Republicans traced their roots to differences in the states before the Constitution.

This division continued with the emergence of new national parties in the 1820s. "The two great parties of this country," Martin Van Buren later wrote, "with occasional changes in their names only, have, for the principal part of a century, occupied antagonistic positions upon all important political questions. They have maintained an unbroken succession, and have, throughout, been composed respectively of men agreeing in their party passion, and preferences, and entertaining, with rare exceptions, similar general views on the subject of government and its administration."[7]

The party that formed to support Jackson in his second run for the presidency in 1828 was a truly national party in the sense that it represented a broadly consistent populist ideology. Structurally, however, it was based on state party organizations, each largely autonomous in its political operations. Some of these state parties had by then created political machines in which patronage—distribution of government jobs and favors in return for political services—was a key ingredient.

Van Buren's machine in New York, known as the Regency, was the most highly developed of the state patronage-based organizations. "The Regency," Donald Cole writes, "revolutionized American politics, not only by creating a new type of political machine, but also by popularizing a new theory of political parties."[8] The New York machine used a combination of egalitarian ideology and material rewards to motivate its foot soldiers. One of its operating principles was candidly summarized by Van Buren's political partner, Governor William Marcy: "To the victor belongs the spoils of the enemy."

Other important state party organizations backing Jackson included the Richmond Junto, led by Thomas Ritchie in Virginia; the New Hampshire machine captained by Isaac Hill; and Jackson's state machine in Tennessee. All made extensive use of patronage, espoused egalitarian ideology, maintained close ties with a widely read newspaper, and were dominated by a single strong party leader.

Jackson had again been nominated for president by the Tennessee legislature for the 1828 election. But by 1832, Van Buren and other leaders of Jackson's party, now calling themselves simply Democrats, decided that some nominating mechanism with a national base was needed. Unwilling to return this function to the Democratic caucus in Congress, they called the first Democratic national convention in Baltimore in May 1832. Earlier that same year, the Anti-Masonic party, an ephemeral conglomeration of socially conservative populists, had held the first national party convention, also in Baltimore.

A part of the motive of the Democratic Party bosses in calling a national convention had been to lever Vice President John C. Calhoun of South Carolina off the Democratic ticket and put Van Buren in his place. To placate Calhoun's southern friends, who feared the South was being reduced to a minority within the party, the convention adopted a rule stipulating that a candidate must receive "two thirds of the whole number of votes given" to be nominated—a requirement that was to give any sizable coalition of state delegations veto power over the presidential nomination until it was finally repealed in 1936.

The conservative opposition to Jackson that came together in the Whig party in the 1830s was also chiefly based on state party organizations. In New York, Thurlow Weed constructed a Whig party machine, principally devoted to advancing the political interest of William H. Seward, that for the first time systematically tapped contributions from business to finance election campaigns.[9] Even more than the Democrats, the Whigs conducted campaigns that featured "monster rallies," colorful parades, and barrages of political literature defaming the opposition.

In rapidly growing cities such as New York, Philadelphia, and Baltimore, both parties built machines that did not scruple at boosting their electoral totals through use of "repeaters" and other forms of vote fraud. The Democrats were particularly successful at recruiting masses of recently arrived Catholic immigrants, who were put off by the Whigs' aggressive promotion of Protestant social morality on matters like gambling and drinking. In New York, Tammany Hall, the Manhattan Democratic organization, regularly hauled "cart loads of voters, many of whom had been in the country less than three years," from poll to poll, casting multiple votes for the Democratic ticket.[10]

Perhaps in part because neither major party had a strong unifying national structure, neither was able to deal successfully with the explosive issues of nativism and slavery that erupted in American politics in the 1850s. In the middle of the decade, the American (or Know-Nothing) Party, formed to combat Catholicism and restrict immigration, shook both the Whigs and the Democrats to their foundations and threatened for a time to sweep all before it. Nativism, however, quickly gave way to the even more contentious issue of slavery, which completely finished off the Whigs and divided the Democrats into northern and southern wings. In 1860 each regional segment of Democrats ran its own candidate for president.

Republican State Machines

The newly formed Republican Party, which took advantage of the divided opposition to elect Abraham Lincoln president with only 40 percent of the popular vote, had almost no following in the South but elsewhere had more of a national, as opposed to state-oriented, character than either the pre–Civil War Democrats or Whigs. Lincoln used his control of the federal government payroll and his ability to marshall political support within the Union army to help secure his reelection in 1864 and maintain Republican control of Congress and most northern state governments. "The National Republican Committee," a Washington observer reported in the fall of 1864, "have taken full possession of all the Capitol buildings, and the committee rooms of the Senate and House of Representatives are filled with clerks, busy in mailing Lincoln documents all over the loyal states. . . . Eighty bags of mail matter, all containing Lincoln documents, are daily sent to Sherman's army."[11]

After the chaotic interregnum that followed Lincoln's assassination and Andrew Johnson's succession to the presidency in 1865, the Republican party resumed unified control of the national government in 1868 with the election of Ulysses Grant as president. Under Grant, the federal patronage machine constructed by Lincoln and his associates once more provided reliable sustenance for state and local Republican organizations. Grant allowed control of the machine to be taken over by a quadrumvirate of Republican senators: Roscoe Conkling of New York, Simon Cameron of Pennsylvania, Oliver Morton of Indiana, and Zachariah Chandler of Michigan. John Logan of Illinois joined the Republican high command after his election to the Senate in 1871.

The resources on which the Republican Party fed during the early years of the "Gilded Age" were to a great extent national—not only federal patronage but also contributions from burgeoning business corporations. Under the administration of the Senate bosses, however, operational direction of the party was placed primarily at the state level. Senators, who were elected by state legislatures prior to adoption of the Thirteenth Amendment in 1913, found it essential to maintain control of their state's party machinery. Governors, their natural rivals, were in many states constitutionally limited to a single term or required to stand for election every two years. It was therefore fairly easy for senators with federal patronage at their disposal to dominate most state parties.

In 1876, the corrupt record of the Grant administration and economic depression caused the Republicans almost to lose the presidency. Samuel Tilden, the Democratic candidate, outpolled his Republican opponent, Rutherford B. Hayes, by more than 250,000 popular votes but nevertheless failed to win the White House when disputed electoral votes from three southern states still occupied by Union troops were all counted for Hayes. Though narrowly victorious, the shrewder Republican bosses learned from this experience that their control of federal patronage would probably not last forever. Hayes and most other Republican presidents during the rest of the nineteenth century, moreover, did not give the bosses the unrestricted authority over distribution of federal jobs they had enjoyed under Grant.

Several of the Republican state organizations therefore began basing their operations more on patronage gathered from state and local governments, many of which were expanding rapidly to fill public needs flowing from industrialization and urbanization. This shift by Republican machines to state and local resources necessarily accelerated after passage of the federal civil service act in 1883, and particularly after Grover Cleveland restored the Democrats to control of the White House in 1885.

The most extensive and effective of the Republican state machines was that directed in Pennsylvania by U.S. Senator Matthew Stanley Quay, Cameron's protégé and successor as boss of the state party. Through control of the state payroll and most local governments, including those of Philadelphia and Pittsburgh, and with generous financial support from the state's business interests, Quay's machine was able to maintain a party organization during the 1880s with a work force of 20,000 at an annual cost of about $24 million. Railroads, utilities, traction companies, and other corporate interests, "actually relieved that there was an efficient and effective broker to receive their money, distribute it judiciously, and assure the desired results," fed the coffers of Quay's machine.[12]

In New York state, a similarly structured Republican machine led by U.S. Senator Thomas Platt, Conkling's successor, employed 10,000 party workers at an annual cost of about $20 million. Other Quay-type Republican organizations dominated the politics of Ohio, Illinois, Michigan, and Wisconsin. More loosely structured variants formed in New England and in some of the newer states of the Great Plains and the Far West.

Patronage or the hope of patronage helped motivate many state and local Republican party workers. But enthusiasm for the party among the nonsouthern electorate, which contributed to record voter turnouts never since equaled, was sustained by a common party ideology. The Republican Party was, first of all, the party that had preserved the Union in the Civil War, a fact that Republican orators, wringing the "bloody shirt," never tired of reminding audiences of Union army veterans. Second, the Republican Party was the party, outside the South, of Protestantism, upholding traditional Protestant moral virtues such as piety, temperance, and thrift and offering itself as a barrier against incursions by Catholicism. Many northern Protestant ministers supplemented the plea of Republicans orators to "vote as you shot" with the counsel "Vote as we pray." Finally, the free-market economic ideology, though not contested by the Democrats before 1896, was more closely identified with the Republicans and brought the party not only financial support from business but also electoral backing from many voters who believed that unrestricted capitalism served both their personal pocketbooks and the national interest.

Democrats remained vigorously competitive throughout the Gilded Age in some northern states, particularly New York, Connecticut, New Jersey, Ohio, and Indiana, and occasionally won elections even in Massachusetts, Pennsylvania, Michigan, and Illinois. Democratic Party organization outside the South, however, was generally based on major cities.

Tammany Hall provided a kind of model for what could be achieved politically by mobilizing support from working-class voters, many immigrants and Catholics, to achieve control of municipal governments. During the reign of the notorious William Marcy Tweed as grand sachem in the 1860s, Tammany's operations were so chaotic and corrupt that Tweed and his principal lieutenants were eventually jailed. But under Tweed's successors, John Kelly and Richard Croker, the machine's procedures were rationalized, and corruption was held to a level that business interests and most ordinary citizens regarded as tolerable. Kelly, it was said, "found Tammany a horde and left it a political army." Croker, who took over in the 1880s, proudly defended the machine's function:

> Think of what New York is and what the people of New York are. One half, are of foreign birth. . . . They do not speak our language, they do not know our laws. . . . There is no denying the service which Tammany has rendered to the Republic, there is no such organization for taking hold of the untrained, friendless man and converting him into a citizen. Who else would do it if we did not? . . . There is not a mugwump in the city who would shake hands with him.[13]

The machine helped humanize the city for many. "A bucket of coals and a basket of food," Martin Shefter has written, "a rent payment, funeral expenses, clothing and material benefits were made available to those in need, as were interventions with the law such as providing bail, cutting the red tape to receive a license or permit, or getting charges dismissed." To pay for these services, and reap handsome profits for the boss and his subordinates, the machine ruthlessly levied kickbacks from city workers and extorted payoffs from contractors, saloon keepers, prostitutes, large and small businessmen—almost anyone who was touched by the authority of city government. "Like a business man in business," Croker said, "I work for my own pocket all the time."[14]

Similar Democratic machines, though sometimes less centralized, were established in such cities as Boston, Chicago, Detroit, St. Paul, Jersey City, Hartford, and New Haven. Some of them, such as Chicago's, continued to face formidable Republican opposition in city elections. But they soon dominated Democratic parties in their states and through their abilities to elect congressmen and deliver state delegations at quadrennial Democratic conventions, became players in national politics.

In the other great bastion of the Democracy during the Gilded Age, the South, one-party politics generally prevailed after the end of Reconstruction in the 1870s. The Republican Party in the South became mainly a party of blacks, who, though they continued to vote in substantial numbers until they were virtually disenfranchised by discriminatory state laws passed in the 1890s and 1900s, could not carry state elections. Within the dominant Democratic Party, there were struggles after the 1880s between the old planter class, which had regained control of most state governments after Reconstruction, and populist small farmers who sought economic help from the state.

Some populist leaders, such as Tom Watson in Georgia, experimented in the early 1890s with founding a third party. But they ran up against the fear among most white voters that genuine party competition would give political leverage to blacks. "The argument against the independent political movement in the South," Watson wrote in 1892, "may be boiled down to one word—nigger." He rejoined the Democratic Party and went on to become one of the most virulent of the region's racist demagogues. Southern politics became structured around personalities and impermanent factions. Party organization withered, except in Virginia where the country-squire oligarchy used the Democratic Party as its political instrument.[15]

By the 1890s, many Americans had become convinced that both major parties were tools of corrupt politicians, unresponsive to public needs, and manipulated by predatory economic interests. This mood contributed to the populist movement that swept through many parts of the South and West in the early 1890s. When populism, as represented by William Jennings Bryan's presidential candidacy in 1896, failed at the polls nationally, the impulse to reform if not dismantle existing party structures was taken up by the Progressive Movement, described in the previous chapter. During the first decade of the twentieth century, Progressive politicians such as Robert LaFollette in Wisconsin, Albert Cummins in Iowa, and Hiram Johnson in California, and, on a somewhat different track, the group of publicists, businessmen, and lawyers gathered around Theodore Roosevelt in New York gained control of many state governments. When Roosevelt succeeded to the presidency in 1901, the Progressives had a friend and leader in the White House.

Wherever the Progressives won power, they quickly enacted laws designed to weaken parties. In a belt of western states stretching across the northern half of the country from Michigan to the Pacific and reaching down to include California where the Progressives were strongest, party organizations were statutorily reduced to weakened conditions from which they have never fully recovered. In all these states, enactment of strict civil service laws virtually eliminated job patronage, the lifeblood of traditional party machines.

The Progressives won many of their most significant political victories at the state level and pursued reform of state and local governments, in the sense of making them more efficient and more responsive to middle-class concerns such as education and conservation. Overall, however, the Progressive Era moved American politics toward a more national focus. Roosevelt, in particular, emphasized national themes and promoted expansion of the role of the federal government in economic and social life. The short-lived Progressive Party, on whose ticket Roosevelt unsuccessfully sought return to the White House in 1912, not only expressed a national ideology but was also much more centralized in structure and operational direction than either major party.

Emerging National Parties

During the presidency of Woodrow Wilson, the Republican Party, reacting to its unaccustomed minority status, took the first steps made by either major party to set up a continuing full-time national organization. Will Hays, a live-wire Indiana politician who became Republican national chairman in 1917, established the first national party headquarters in Washington and hired a professional staff. Hays formed a National Council of Republican Women (after adoption of the Nineteenth Amendment, providing votes for women, in 1919), created an advisory committee of party notables that formulated positions on national issues, and sponsored special functions for young Republicans.[16] But the Republican state machines that had escaped demolition by the Progressives in a belt of heavily populated industrial states reaching from Massachusetts to Illinois continued to be principal loci of real power in the party.

The Democrats were slow to match the fledgling national organization that had been set up for the Republicans by Hays. Young Franklin Roosevelt, after running for vice president on the losing Democratic national ticket in 1920, wrote that "the party's [national] machinery was archaic" and "something [should] be done." In 1925, after the Democrats had lost another presidential election, Roosevelt proposed publicly that the party's national organization should be put on a "business-like financial basis" and that a permanent national headquarters should be opened in Washington to operate "every day in every year."[17]

It was not until 1929, however, that John Raskob, the business tycoon whom Al Smith had persuaded to become Democratic national chairman during his losing campaign for the presidency in 1928, at last established a permanent national Democratic headquarters in Washington. Raskob used the national party machinery he had set up and largely financed out of his own pocket to try to prevent Franklin Roosevelt's nomination by the Democrats for president in 1932.

After Roosevelt was nevertheless nominated, James Farley took charge of the skeletal national organization Raskob had put in place and used it skillfully in the fall campaign. Named postmaster general by Roosevelt, Farley supervised distribution of the still substantial horde of federal patronage among the Democratic faithful. In the summer of 1933, Farley complained that he had "only 150,000 jobs" outside civil service to fill applications from "at least 1,500,000 men and women" with political sponsorship.[18]

The decline of traditional city machines is often traced, at least in part, to replacement of the machines' service function by the federal welfare programs instituted by the New Deal. In reality, many city machines wearing the Democratic label—including the Hague machine in Jersey City, the Kelly-Nash machine in Chicago, the Pendergast machine in Kansas City, and the Crump machine in Memphis—fattened during the 1930s on jobs and cash supplied by the new federal programs. In return, the machines gave loyal support to Roosevelt and the New Deal. At the 1936 Democratic national convention that nominated Roosevelt for a second term, about half the 1,100 delegates were federal jobholders.[19]

Over the longer run, it is true, the discovery among working-class voters that they now had legal rights to government benefits that politicians had formerly passed out as favors weakened the hold of the machines. And enactment in 1939 of the Hatch Act, prohibiting most federal employees from participating in political campaigns, sharply curtailed the value of federal patronage to the machines. But the decline of the machines, which began in the late 1940s and accelerated in the 1950s, also had other, in some cases deeper causes.

Passage of restrictive immigration laws in the 1920s cut the flow of recently arrived citizens who had been among the machines' most reliable sources of support. Children and grandchildren of immigrants were less likely to remain in the old neighborhoods or to see the machine as a symbol of ethnic solidarity. Veterans returning from World War II and women who had done war work outside their homes tended to have more independent political attitudes. Voters were becoming better educated and more affluent, and therefore less in need of guidance or handouts from the machines. Introduction of television in the late 1940s made it possible for officeholders and candidates to communicate directly with the electorate, reducing their reliance on party workers to publicize their names and spread their messages. The great migration of blacks from the South to northern cities provided the machines with a fresh bloc of constituents but also soon introduced political tensions between blacks and some of the machines' older ethnic followings.

Most of the political scientists who drafted *Toward a More Responsible Two-Party System* in 1950 and the liberal reformers who generally shared their views were no more fond of the traditional machines than the Progressives had been. Like the Progressives, they wanted a politics focused on substantive issues rather than distribution of government jobs and favors. But they did not share the Progressives' rejection of parties and proposed undoing some of the electoral reforms designed to weaken parties that had been instituted during the Progressive Era. This change in attitudes in part reflected recognition among reformers that machines were losing their dominant positions in party structures and that strong parties therefore no longer need mean machine control and in part the conviction that a truly nationalized party, specifically the Democratic Party, could be a mighty instrument for advancing the cause of liberalism.

The Civil Rights Issue

In the late 1940s, the question of party nationalization was also becoming intertwined with the issue of race. Roosevelt, aiming to hold the support of powerful southern Democrats in Congress, many of whom had been relatively liberal on the economic issues of the 1930s, had not pressed for action on civil rights. But Harry Truman, who succeeded to the White House in 1945, called for enactment of a comprehensive package of civil rights measures to move blacks toward equality in voting rights and employment.

White southern Democratic politicians reacted with almost unanimous fury to Truman's proposal. The administration's civil rights program, said Senator Tom Connally of Texas, amounted to "a lynching of the Constitution." Representative Eugene Cox of Georgia, a leader of the conservative coalition that had developed in Congress in the late 1930s, charged that "Harlem is wielding more influence with the administration than the entire white South."[20]

At the 1948 Democratic convention in Philadelphia, Truman administration operatives tried to work out compromise platform language on civil rights that would be acceptable to southern moderates. But northern liberals led by Hubert Humphrey, the young mayor of Minneapolis, won passage of a civil rights plank endorsing in detail the administration's program. The Mississippi and Alabama delegations promptly walked out of the convention.

A few days later, southern "States Rights" Democrats, commonly called Dixiecrats, assembled in Birmingham, Alabama, and nominated Governor Strom Thurmond of South Carolina for president. In the campaign that followed, several southern Democratic congressmen supported Thurmond, and many others avoided taking sides in the presidential race. Though Truman astonished almost everyone by upsetting Thomas Dewey, the Republican candidate, to win reelection, Thurmond carried the Deep South states of Alabama, Louisiana, Mississippi, and South Carolina. In all of these states the States Rights ticket was listed on the ballot under the Democratic label. In Alabama, electors for Truman were not even given a place on the ballot.

By the beginning of the 1950s, civil rights had become a defining issue for liberalism. The scandal of Democratic parties in most southern states acting as enforcers of racial segregation—in some states officially prohibiting blacks from participating in Democratic primaries—had grown intolerable to liberals (including, it should be said, many southern liberals). Beginning with Truman himself after the 1948 election, liberals began to demand that southern Democratic congressmen who failed to support the national ticket should be stripped of their committee chairmanships. The call by the Committee on Political Parties for stronger national parties therefore had great resonance within the liberal community. When the committee proposed more responsible party government, it had civil rights at least partly in mind as one of the key issues on which the national Democratic party should be empowered to act responsibly.

At the next several Democratic national conventions, there were repeated battles over civil rights and demands by liberals that all delegates be required to pledge to back the national ticket. By 1965, the national Democratic Party, now led by Lyndon Johnson, the first president elected from the South since the Civil War, was firmly committed to total racial equality, and blacks were playing significant roles in most southern Democratic state parties.

The struggle over the obligation of state parties to follow the programmatic leadership of the national party erupted in the Republican Party in 1964. Many conservative midwestern Republicans had long felt uncomfortable with the moderate-to-progressive candidates for president nominated by their party after 1936 but had loyally supported the national ticket in the general election. In 1964 the shoe was on the other foot. Conservatives succeeded in winning the Republican presidential nomination for Senator Barry Goldwater of Arizona, an ardent right-winger. Several progressive and moderate Republican leaders, including Governor Nelson Rockefeller of New York, declined to endorse Goldwater in the fall campaign.

Conservatives were placed in the somewhat paradoxical position of promoting states-rights ideology but castigating state Republican parties that failed to work enthusiastically for the national ticket. After Goldwater's landslide defeat, some conservatives announced plans to make the party more ideologically homogeneous. "We will have no more of these candidates," Ronald Reagan, who had made his first appearance in national politics with a televised address for Goldwater, told the Los Angeles Young Republicans a few days after the election, "who are pledged to use the same socialist goals as our opposition."[21]

Reforming Party Governance

During the 1970s and 1980s, both major parties moved further toward nationalization of structure and centralization of authority than most drafters of the 1950 manifesto on responsible party government probably would have thought possible. Three principal factors were involved: the drive within the Democratic Party to make internal party governance more democratic; the collapse of most of the traditional machines around which strong state and local parties had usually been built; and the efforts, first by the Republicans and then by the Democrats, to establish strong national party organizations.

The drive to reform the governance of the Democratic Party began with the perception that the party's 1968 presidential nomination had been "stolen" for Vice President Hubert Humphrey at the chaotic national convention in Chicago. Opponents of the Vietnam War who had backed the candidacies of Eugene McCarthy and Robert Kennedy—and George McGovern after Kennedy's assassination in June—pointed out that in some states delegates were picked by caucuses composed of party officers elected several years before the convention and that even in some of the states that elected delegates through primaries, such as New York, Pennsylvania, and Illinois, strong party organizations were able through slating mechanisms to assemble controlled delegations. The unit rule, under which a delegation's entire vote was cast for the candidate favored by a majority, used by Texas and some other southern states, was held inherently unfair. And women, blacks, and young people were shown to be demographically underrepresented in most state delegations.

Responding to these complaints and seeking to heal the bitter divisions within the party, the 1968 convention established a commission charged with developing a delegate selection process that would require state parties to make "all feasible efforts . . . to assure that delegates are elected through party primary, convention, or committee procedures open to public participation within the calendar year of the national convention." This commission, headed initially by George McGovern, was the first of a series of similar bodies that completely transformed the process of selecting delegates to Democratic national conventions. Since Democratic-controlled state legislatures altered delegate selection laws to bring them into conformity with national Democratic Party rules, the system of picking delegates to Republican conventions was also greatly changed.

To ensure conformity with elaborate delegate selection guidelines issued by successive national Democratic commissions, most states shifted from selecting delegates by caucus and convention to selecting them through primaries. This had the effect of strengthening the roles of candidate organizations and special interest groups in the selection process and weakening state and local party organizations.

In 1972, the Chicago Democratic organization, led by Mayor Richard J. Daley, defied the new guidelines and put together a delegation of ward bosses as though nothing had changed. The convention, which nominated McGovern for president, refused to seat the Chicago delegation even though it had been elected in full conformance with Illinois state law. In 1975, the Supreme Court upheld the action of the convention against the Chicago delegation on the ground that "the convention serves the pervasive national interest in the selection of candidates for national offices and this national interest is greater than any interest of any individual state."[22]

The change in the system of selecting national convention delegates was only one in a series of blows that continued the erosion of the effectiveness and autonomy of state and local party organizations. Far more serious were the comprehensive extension of state civil service laws and the growth of public employee unions that by the late 1970s had wiped out much of the state and local job patronage from which traditional machines had drawn sustenance. In 1976, the Supreme Court, in another case involving the Chicago Democratic machine, ruled that government employees could not be fired because of their party affiliation.[23] Finally, in 1990, this time acting against the Republican administration of Illinois Governor James Thompson, the Court prohibited consideration of party affiliation in the hiring of most government workers.[24] The patronage system, which from the time of Andrew Jackson had been used by state and local party organizations to motivate their workers and discipline officeholders elected on their tickets, was reduced in the early 1990s to a furtive existence in some cities and a few states such as Indiana and West Virginia. The political support it once gave to parties had been greatly diminished.

In some of the western states where patronage had not been an important factor in politics since the Progressive Era and party organizations had grown woefully weak, some state and local organizations actually staged modest comebacks during the 1980s, attracting workers, though not usually broad support among the electorate, through the appeals of competing liberal and conservative ideologies. In some southern states too, where since the end of Reconstruction party organizations were generally weak and largely irrelevant because of the Democratic one-party system, the arrival of genuine competition between Republicans and Democrats in the 1970s and 1980s produced some invigoration of parties, also based mainly on ideology.

Nowhere in the early 1990s, however, are there state or local party organizations with anything approaching the political effectiveness or mass followings of the great machines that grew up in the Gilded Age and in some places carried on into the 1960s. In the 1970s, partly to fill the gaps left by the decline of state and local organizations, national party organizations, at first mainly on the Republican side, began to broaden their operations and enlarge their roles in campaigns.

When William Brock became Republican national chairman in 1977, the party was still suffering from its identification with the Watergate scandals that had brought down the presidency of Richard Nixon. Some conservatives believed that the party's associations with big business and "country-club" social attitudes were even deeper afflictions. A few Republican strategists even suggested that the party change its name and start over with a new label.[25]

Brock decided, he later said, that party recovery required a strong infusion of energy—and money—from the national level. His first step was to launch a direct-mail fund-raising program far more extensive than those the Republican National Committee (RNC) had been using since the 1950s. For the 1977–78 midterm election campaign, direct mail netted the RNC more than $17 million. In the 1979–80 presidential campaign cycle, the RNC's net from direct mail rose to a stunning $42 million. After three years of operation, Xandra Kayden writes, the overhead of direct-mail fund-raising was "at least ten percent cheaper than all other forms of raising money."[26]

Brock used the increased funds to carry the RNC into areas never before entered by a national party. Beside financing extensive national polling and advertising, it set up a separate division to revive state and local party organizations and recruit candidates for state legislatures. Between 1977 and 1980, more than ten thousand Republicans attended campaign seminars sponsored by the local elections division. In some cases, the RNC gave financial support to preferred candidates in contested primaries—a degree of intervention in local politics that national parties had rarely attempted. In 1980 Brock helped pay the salaries of the executive directors of all fifty Republican state committees, and the RNC gave financial support to more than four thousand state legislative campaigns. "The Republicans," Leon Epstein writes, "have nationalized their party effort by a method analogous to the federal government's grant-in-aid system."[27]

Following the lead of the RNC, the National Republican Senatorial Committee (NRSC) and the National Republican Congressional Committee (NRCC) vastly increased their fund-raising and expenditures on campaigns. The NRCC peaked in fund-raising in the 1981–82 cycle, and the NRSC in 1985–86, after which both declined somewhat. At the beginning of the 1990s, however, all three national Republican political committees continued to raise and spend much more than they did in the 1970s.[28]

The Democratic National Committee (DNC) and the two Democratic congressional campaign committees entered the 1980s raising and spending far less than their Republican counterparts. At the end of the decade, the gap in dollars remained substantial, but the relative size of the Republican advantage had been considerably reduced. In the 1979–80 election cycle, Republican committees outspent their Democratic rivals by a 4.6:1 ratio. In 1987–88, the Republican edge had come down to 2.1:1.[29]

The Democratic Congressional Campaign Committee in particular, under the chairmanship of Representative Tony Coelho of California from 1981 through 1986, was successful not only at raising a substantial campaign war chest but also at persuading business political action committees (PACs) to contribute much more to Democratic candidates for the House than to their Republican opponents, despite the ideological preference of most businessmen for the Republicans. During the 1985–86 election cycle, Coelho reportedly visited more than one hundred business and trade-association PACs, making three points: "Not all Democrats are anti-business; Democrats will retain control of the House for the remainder of this century; and PACs who side with the Republicans shall pay a political price for doing so."[30]

The Cost of Centralization

In the late 1980s some state and local party organizations showed signs of revival, in parts of the South and West coming to life where state and local parties had long been moribund. In some of these, leaders had begun to express resentment toward the tutelage they increasingly received from their national party organizations. Interviewing state and local party leaders in various parts of the country from 1985 to 1989, however, as part of a study of parties, I found that most continued to look to their national organizations for strategic direction, technical expertise, and financial help.

There are several reasons for this. First, state and local organizations in the old machine states have not found adequate substitutes for the vanished job patronage on which they used to depend. Second, party fund-raising is now done more efficiently at the national than at the state and local levels. Third, both major parties have become more ideologically cohesive. There is still a fair amount of ideological and regional diversity within both parties but nothing comparable to the old splits between southern conservative Democrats and northern liberal Democrats or between progressive and conservative Republicans.

Let me now return to the question with which I began: Is there a relationship between the current comparative centralization of party organization and the general weakening of parties, as measured by such criteria as ticket splitting, the large share of voters (about one-third) who now call themselves independents, and declining turnout in elections since 1960?

While no sure response can be given, common sense and impressions gained through studying parties in many parts of the nation during the late 1980s suggest the answer is yes. Parties under relatively centralized direction have become much less organic institutions and more organizations of mercenary technicians put together to promote the election of candidates, much as similar organizations promote sales of automobiles or deodorants.

Nationalized parties do not for the most part reach into the lives of communities as the old machines or local reform clubs once did. Most voters, even if they acknowledge a party preference, do not seem to feel any great bond of pride or affection toward their own party or any particular antipathy toward the opposition. They view parties much as they view competing supermarkets or movie theaters. Voters may develop a degree of customer loyalty but are less likely than before to regard a party as their political home.

There are a number of sources for the changed attitude of most voters toward parties, including the increasingly atomized quality of contemporary social life. But surely one of the most important of these is the shift from a politics based substantially on face-to-face contact between party workers and constituents to a politics carried on mainly through nationally coordinated televised communication and continual polling.

The change in voters' attitudes toward parties is not all bad. American politics has become less rancorous. The fuss over Willie Horton in 1988 was mild compared to the rage with which the national parties combated each other during the New Deal or the pitched battles that used to occur on election days in many localities between adherents of rival machines. Candidates and officeholders who know they will be judged on their merits rather than mainly through their identification with a party are likely to be more attentive to the will of the voters.

However, the decline of voter turnout since 1960, itself a symptom and a further cause of lowered political morale, is probably traceable in part to the fact that campaigns conducted chiefly through television are simply less effective at getting voters to the polls than the old armies of party workers. Moreover, the high levels of alienation toward government and the nation's social "direction" shown by polls may grow from frustration over the unavailability of the kind of direct human contact with government and social power that used to be supplied by the local party committeeman or town leader, whether to hear complaints or arrange favors.[31]

Tendencies toward dehumanized politics are offset to some extent by the increased identification of parties with ideologies. American parties have always been ideological to some degree, going back to the conservative and populist parties in the states before the Constitution. But since the development of two-party competition in the South in the 1960s, and particularly since the election of Ronald Reagan as president in 1980, both parties have projected more distinct and consistent ideological images in all parts of the country than at almost any previous time in the nation's history. Voters can therefore relate to a party's ideology even if they have little direct contact with it as a social institution.

Growing ideological differentiation, however, carries risks of its own. While giving voters a meaningful choice in elections, as the writers of the 1950 report on responsible party government so urgently wanted, identification of parties with distinct ideologies may make practical compromises on contentious issues more difficult and at some future point might deepen social divisions. Strong and operationally autonomous local party organizations could help smooth the rough edges of competing national party ideologies and maintain some of the political pragmatism that has helped keep American society adaptable to changing needs and circumstances.

There now seems to be a fair degree of agreement among politicians and students of politics that some shift back to stronger and more independent state and local party organizations would be socially desirable. But is such a shift attainable? Or has the structural centralization that modern technology and management techniques bring to most social institutions set in inexorably (though after some delay caused by governmental federalism and the inherent resistance to change of democratic politics) among parties?

Certainly we are not going back to the days when local parties functioned almost as secular churches (often with close attachments to churches). Some local party clubs may still serve as the focus of community or neighborhood social activities, but the mobility and distractions of modern life, as well as the tinge of disrespectability that has clung to parties at least since the Gilded Age, makes the party an unlikely instrument in most places for achieving community cohesion.

State and local parties, however, remain at least potentially functional political units. The people running national parties during the 1980s discovered that they could go only so far by means of tightly centralized and heavily financed "high-tech" campaigns. Tasks such as registering voters, operating local phone banks, gathering crowds for visits by candidates, "showing the flag" through yard signs and bumper stickers, distributing absentee ballots (a factor of growing importance as many states relax qualifications for absentee voting), and turning out the vote on election day require local organization. As a result, and because national election laws place fewer restrictions on money spent at the local level, national committees at the end of the decade were channeling increasing shares of their funds to state and local organizations. There was initially some inclination among national managers to couple this growing financial support with even more centralized control of operations. But the federal nature of the governmental structure provides state and local parties with bulwarks and resources to resist centralized control that are not available to their counterparts in the private economy. If they have funds, no matter at what geographic level they are raised, state and local parties will probably soon exert more independence, and in some cases are already doing so.

The plea by the Committee on Political Parties in 1950 for more centralized national parties had some merit when it was made. More cohesive national parties, it could then reasonably be argued, would both provide more effective government and more accountability to the public will. But now the pendulum seems to have swung too far the other way. Parties have grown so centralized that they are obtruding on the values of federalism and failing in one of their primary tasks—mobilizing voter participation in elections. Restoration of a more federal nature to parties requires not so much changes in laws as strategic decisions by party leaderships. Those that move to encourage greater state and local autonomy in their party structures will serve democratic values and should reap substantial practical rewards through raised voter commitment.

Notes

1. Committee on Political Parties, *Toward a More Responsible Two-Party System* (New York: Rinehart, 1950), p. 26 (hereinafter, CPP).

2. Ibid., pp. 33, 46.

3. Ibid., pp. 7, 48, 52.

4. Austin Ranney and Willmoore Kendall, *Democracy and the American Party System* (New York: Harcourt, Brace, and World, 1956), p. 160.

5. Adams, quoted by Clinton Rossiter, *Parties and Politics in America* (Ithaca, N.Y.: Cornell University Press, 1960), p. 66.

6. Jackson Turner Main, *Political Parties Before the Constitution* (Chapel Hill: University of North Carolina Press, 1973), pp. 326–55.

7. Martin Van Buren, *Inquiry into the Origin and Course of Political Parties in the United States* (New York: Augustus M. Kelley, 1967), p. 2.

8. Donald B. Cole, *Martin Van Buren and the American Political System* (Princeton, N.J.: Princeton University Press, 1984), pp. 95–96.

9. Glyndon G. Van Deusen, *Thurlow Weed: Wizard of the Lobby* (Boston: Little, Brown, 1947), p. 77.

10. Gustavus Myers, *The History of Tammany Hall* (New York: Dover, 1971), pp. 90–91.

11. Eric L. McKitrick, "Party Politics and the Union and Confederate War Efforts," in W. W. Chambers and W. D. Burnham, *The American Party Systems* (New York: Oxford University Press, 1967), p. 150.

12. James A. Kehl, *Boss Rule in the Gilded Age* (Pittsburgh: University of Pittsburgh Press, 1981), pp. 32–33.

13. Martin Shefter, "The Emergence of the Political Machine: An Alternative View," in Willis D. Hawley et al., eds., *Theoretical Perspectives on Urban Parties* (New York: Prentice-Hall, 1976), pp. 22–23; Ralph G. Martin, *The Bosses* (New York: Putnam, 1964), p. 33. Mugwumps were middle-class Republican reformers.

14. David R. Mayhew, *Placing Parties in American Politics: Organization, Electoral Settings, and Government Activity in the Twentieth Century* (Princeton, N.J.: Princeton University Press, 1986), p. 310.

15. V. O. Key, *Southern Politics in State and Nation* (New York: Vintage, 1949), p. 19.

16. Ralph M. Goldman, *The National Party Chairman and Committees: Factionalism at the Top* (Armonk, N.Y.: M.E. Sharpe, 1990), pp. 287–303.

17. Ibid., pp. 319–20.

18. James A. Farley, *Jim Farley's Story: The Roosevelt Years* (New York: McGraw-Hill, 1948), pp. 39–49; Cornelius P. Cotter and Bernard C. Hennessy, *Politics Without Power: The National Party Committees* (Atherton, 1964), p. 144. In the 1980s only about 2,000 federal jobs could be filled completely outside the merit system.

19. Sidney M. Milkis, "FDR and the Transcendence of Party Politics," *Political Science Quarterly*, 100 (Fall 1985): 495.

20. Robert J. Donovan, *Conflict and Crisis: The Presidency of Harry S Truman, 1945-1948* (New York: W. W. Norton, 1977), pp. 352–56.

21. Adam Clymer, "A Star Is Born," in *Reagan, the Man, the President*, ed. Hedrick Smith, et. al. (New York: Macmillan, 1980), p. 10.

22. Cousins v. Wigoda, 419 U.S. 477 (1975).

23. Elrod v. Burns, 427 U.S. 347 (1976).

24. Rutan v. Republican Party, 88 U.S. 1872 (1990).

25. In Minnesota, the Republican Party took this advice and changed its name to Independent Republicans.

26. Xandra Kayden, "Parties and the 1980 Presidential Election" in Campaign Finance Study Group, *Financing Presidential Campaigns* (Cambridge, Mass.: Harvard University Press, 1982), p. 11.

27. Interview with William Brock, January 22, 1985; David Adamany, "Political Parties in the 1980s," in *Money and Politics in the United States: Financing Elections in the 1980s*, ed. Michael J. Malbin (Washington, D.C.: American Enterprise Institute, 1984), p. 80; Leon D. Epstein, "Party Considerations and Political Nationalization," *Publius*, 12 (Fall 1982): 86.

28. *Federal Election Commission* news releases.

29. Ibid.

30. Brooks Jackson, *Honest Graft* (New York: Knopf, 1988), pp. 84–85.

31. See, for example, *The Public Perspective*, ed. Karlyn H. Keene and Everett Carll Ladd (May–June 1991), p. 82; *The Wirthlin Group National Quorum Memorandum*, ed. Richard B. Wirthlin (April 1991), p. 2.

3

The Party-as-Organization

Party Elites and Party Reforms in Presidential Nominations and Conventions

JOHN S. JACKSON III

It has been more than forty years since the Committee on Political Parties of the American Political Science Association (APSA) issued its famous report, *Toward a More Responsible Two-Party System.*[1] The report has been soundly criticized and defended in many forums since 1950.[2] Nevertheless, no other report of an academic association in the United States has ever created more sustained intellectual foment and so dominated a discipline's research agenda. The report urges a redesign of American parties to make them more effective instruments in a democratic polity that had undergone extensive change in both the philosophy and scale of governance in the decades since Reconstruction. Especially frustrated by the political failure to complete the New Deal program in the 1930s, the committee saw the problem in the nation's decentralized party system, where power resided primarily in the hands of the state and local party leaders. This confederated party system had dominated American politics since its formation in the first decade under the Constitution.

In its call for a "more responsible" party system, the committee clearly urges a more national and politically more effective party system, as well as one whose organized center of gravity is the party platform or program. The proposal of a party council epitomizes the committee's desire for a more national, centralized, and disciplined party system. At the same time, the committee suggests that an effective party system must rest on a broad base of member participation in party affairs. Having thus banished a decentralized party system by the front door, the committee seems to invite it to return through the back.

This wish for an effective *national* party system that is at the same time broadly participatory at its *base* continues to tease and torment democrats in general and political scientists in particular. The idea of "responsible" parties aside, a more basic question in the American setting is what constitutes a strong party? Is a more centralized, national organization dominated by officials and elites a strong party? Is a more decentralized participatory organization dominated by activists and rank-and-file members a strong party? Must it be both? Can a party organization be both? Is internal party democracy and competition the servant or the enemy of stronger and more competitive national parties? These questions were not settled by the report, and they have plagued the discipline ever since.

The responsible-parties model has not been realized in American politics in the ensuing four decades. The well-known pragmatic, decentralized political parties, dominated by the state and local power centers and best described as confederations, have dominated American politics since the founding of the first American party system in the late 1790s. That system of pragmatic parties has changed, however, and in some dimensions changed substantially since the 1950s. A part of this change is in the direction of the responsible-parties model, although the movement in that direction is neither linear nor uniform. This chapter focuses on the changes that have occurred in the presidential nomination process—in the national conventions and among the national party organizations. These are the areas where some of the most profound changes in the parties have taken place in the decades since 1950.

At the outset, it is important to note that there is some lack of clarity in the APSA report about which dimensions of the political party are being addressed in their critique and recommendations. Since the report, a vigorous debate has developed over the question whether American parties are in a period of decline or resurgence.[3] Here too, the debate is not joined as cogently as it could have been because of a lack of consensus about which part of the party is being assessed.[4] It helps to clarify the debate if one follows the classic delineation of the political party into three basic components, as suggested by V. O. Key.[5] Key separated the political party conceptually into the party-in-the-electorate, the party-as-organization, and the party-in-government. This analytical division is now widely recognized and accepted in political science literature.

Denise Baer and David Bositis, however, have criticized this tripartite concept of political parties as somewhat too limited as a theoretical approach to the analysis of modern American parties. They offer instead a theoretical view that emphasizes political and social group mobilization as it affects political parties, and they define democracy in terms of how much access new movements have to political parties through political elites. They also stress the cohesiveness of elites in the parties and the distinctiveness of elites across the two parties, both being relevant to questions of group and thus mass opportunity for representation in the policy-making process. Baer and Bositis thus advocate the analysis of elite and mass political views within the same research design, a position adopted here in the presentation of the empirical data.[6]

Under the tripartite division, it is possible for the party-in-the-electorate to be in a state of decline, as considerable evidence suggests was the case in the 1960s, 1970s, and 1980s.[7] At the same time, the party-as-organization could be growing stronger and more active, as several scholars contend was the case from the 1960s to the 1980s.[8] These two trends lead to different diagnoses of the political party system as a whole: one that it is healthy; the other that it is not. The tension between the party-as-organization (structure) and the party-in-the-electorate (elites and masses) is endemic to the committee report and frames the discussion that follows.

The Party as Structure

Organizationally, American political parties look much as they did after World War I. The party committees in place since the 1840s are still there. Congressional campaign committees, first formed in the 1860s, and the Senate campaign committees, formed after the ratification of the Seventeenth Amendment, are still in place to complete the triumvirate of national party components. Since the advent of the reform era beginning in the late 1960s, the Democratic Party has become a federal system organizationally with some real power shifting to the national level. During this same period, the Republicans have continued their long-standing practice of operating as more of a confederation; however, there have been functional shifts favoring the national organs of the GOP. Within these broad structural contours, much has changed in the American party system since the APSA report was first issued.

In the realm of the national party constitutions, the Democratic Party's Charter, adopted in 1974 at the Kansas City Midterm Party Conference, is the most notable development. The Charter grew out of the political turmoil that beset the Democrats between 1968 and 1972. It was their attempt to provide for the rule of law and stability in the rules of the game in what had been a very volatile political situation. Few of those on the Sanford Commission that drafted the Charter (Austin Ranney is an exception) and fewer still of those who ratified it knew much explicitly about European parties or the responsible parties model. They were intent on developing an organizational response to the political situation that confronted them. In short, they were engaged in the imperative of organization maintenance and survival to which complex organizations of all types universally respond.

The Charter provides the Democratic Party with a codified set of national laws that essentially has become the party's constitution. The party adopts various bylaws that supplement the Charter and issues "calls" specific to each Democratic National Convention, but the Charter remains the basic law for the national party. The Charter has provided stability and continuity in the way basic constitutions are supposed to function. Indeed, recent intramural debates within the Democratic Party regarding various rules changes have been couched in terms of what the Charter provides and whether the Charter should be amended.

The Republican Party has not adopted a charter comparable to that of the Democrats; however, its national bylaws serve as the functional equivalent. The Republicans have enjoyed a relatively high level of consensus surrounding national rules, and they tend not to have suffered from the kinds of internal party divisions that have plagued the Democrats at the national level. Nevertheless, as the Republicans experience success in winning new converts and to the extent that they attempt to diversify their coalition, they are likely to experience some of the same questions of internal democracy faced by the Democrats. Whether the Republicans can keep their internal divisions from developing into basic disputes about the rules of the game, which is the situation that has plagued the Democrats, remains a question. If such disputes develop in depth, the Republicans will also undoubtedly try to fashion new organizational responses to the challenges that confront them. Again, organizational maintenance is crucial.

There have also been several court cases relevant to the issue of national party law. In each of these cases the power and prerogative of the national parties have been upheld in the face of challenges posed by state laws and constitutions. Indeed, the role of the national parties has been augmented by several Supreme Court cases. In the 1975 case of *Cousins v. Wigoda*, for example, the Court ruled that the national party's associational rights take precedence over state law in controlling the selection of the delegates to national conventions.[9] This case clearly establishes the supremacy of national party rules over state law and state party procedures in delegate selection, one of the most important original objectives of the APSA committee. In another 1975 decision, *Ripon Society v. National Republican Party*, in which the liberal Ripon Society challenged the Republican Party's delegate-apportionment formula as favoring conservative states, the Court upheld the national party's right to define its own delegate apportionment formula.[10] It should be emphasized that while this was a victory for national prerogatives, the Ripon Society wanted the apportionment formula to reflect the party's geographical strength more accurately, an objective also endorsed by the committee. Finally, in *Democratic Party of the U.S. v. LaFollette* (1981), the Supreme Court held that the national party has the right to require closed primaries to select national convention delegates.[11] This meant that national party law held sway over Wisconsin's use of open primaries to select delegates. It should be noted that the use of closed primaries was an objective of the APSA committee. The thrust of these cases is clear. It is in a pro-national-party direction perhaps not entirely anticipated by the committee but certainly compatible with its desire for more centralized national parties.

The national committees. The national committees are the first place to look for substantial changes in the national organizations. The APSA report recommended that the national convention be more active in the selection of the members of the national committees "through a more active participation in the final selection of the Committee Membership." "It is also desirable," the report continued, that "the members of the National Committee reflect the actual strength of the party within the areas they represent."[12] There have been some changes in these two directions, especially among the Democrats. At the time the committee issued its report, the Democratic National Committee (DNC) and Republican National Committee (RNC) consisted of one committeeman and one committeewoman from each state. This meant that each committee had equal representation from each state, following the model of the U.S. Senate. This distribution tended to strengthen the hand of the conservative elements of both parties, and it was to this malapportionment that the APSA committee objected.

As a result of the reforms in the Democratic Party in the 1970s, the DNC was expanded to approximately 350 members, with greater representation given to the larger states and a bonus given to states that voted more heavily Democratic in previous elections. In effect, the Democratic National Convention delegate-apportionment formula was adopted for the DNC. In addition, a long list of other party officials were given automatic membership on the DNC. While technically the national conventions for both parties select the members of the DNC and RNC, in reality they ratify the product of various state selection procedures. The selection procedures vary among the states, but some states authorize the national convention delegations to select the national committee members, while others provide for selection by the state party's central committee, state conventions, or primaries. In the latter selection methods, the national conventions play no more than a nominal role, and there seems to be no sentiment to increase that role in either party.

The Republican National Committee is only about half the size of the DNC. The Republicans use the core of the old system, one committeeman and one committeewoman from each state. But starting in 1968 the Republicans added the party chairs from each state for a base total of 150 plus delegations from D.C., Guam, Puerto Rico, and the Virgin Islands.[13] Thus the RNC formula continues to provide essentially equal representation for each state, which tends to favor the smaller states in national committee representation, a practice clearly opposed by the APSA report.

With respect to the recommendation that the national committees have larger permanent staffs, both parties have made substantial progress. Paul Herrnson documents the increased size and activity of both national committees,[14] and when his findings are compared with the original landmark research on national committees done by Cornelius Cotter and Bernard Hennessy, the growth in size and responsibility of both national committees is remarkable.[15] For example, Herrnson finds that the DNC staff grew from 30 members in 1972 to 130 in 1984, while the RNC staff grew from 30 to 600 in that period.[16] The RNC and DNC staffs have been transformed into the sort of highly professional organizations now routinely associated with congressional staffs, and the transformations of these staffs has taken place in parallel periods. These professional staffs have helped to augment the nationalization of the two parties. These larger and more professional RNC and DNC staffs are clearly congruent with the recommendations of the APSA report.

The functional development of the national organizations. It is also evident that the functional development of the national party organizations is in a direction that if not anticipated by the APSA committee is at least compatible with the report's general recommendations. Here Herrnson's work is the seminal contribution; his study of the Democratic National Committee, the Republican National Committee and the four Capitol Hill campaign committees shows fairly conclusively the significant expansion in the functions of those national party organs, especially during the 1980s.[17] It is worth noting, first, that the three GOP committees are housed together near Capitol Hill in the very impressive Eisenhower Center and that the three Democratic committees are now housed together in the new Democratic National Committee Building in Washington.

Furthermore, Herrnson shows that the national party organizations have come to play a much more active and intrusive role in the congressional campaigns than previously. Jointly, they help recruit candidates, supply them with campaign intelligence in the form of opposition research and public opinion polls, provide them with a full array of campaign management services if needed, and most importantly give the candidates direct financial support. In addition, these national committees are increasingly acting as go-betweens, or "brokers," linking their preferred candidates to political action committees (PACs) likely to support their candidacies.

Rather than PACs being a competitor with the parties, as is ordinarily assumed, the national committees have been able to co-opt the PACs and use them and their resources to complement the national party's strategic plans in congressional campaigns. The Republican Party's national organization has led the way in expanding the functions of these groups, although the Democratic Party has made progress in its drive to catch up with the opposition. Herrnson takes note of the responsible-parties model advocated by the APSA committee. He explicitly rejects the proposition that the United States has seen the development of full-fledged responsible parties, noting that the structural impediments of federalism and separation of powers, together with the political imperative of getting reelected for officeholders, tend to form great barriers to unified party government.[18] On the other hand, the political campaign developments are notable for the extent to which they have strengthened the national parties. Herrnson concludes:

> Regardless of how much or how little party behavior comes to resemble that envisioned under the responsible party model, it is clear that the institutionalization of their national organizations has strengthened the parties' role in congressional elections. . . . The political parties are alive and well, and the parties' national organizations are more powerful than ever before. The United States may be embarking on a new era of party politics, one characterized by strong and highly active national parties.[19]

Party councils. The Committee on Political Parties recommended the creation of a party council of some fifty members for each national party. This is probably the most important and innovative proposal in the report. This party council is patterned on a similar body recommended earlier by Charles Merriam and one actually adopted by the Republicans in 1919.[20] The party council is intended to give greater policy coherence to the executive and legislative branches and provide for integration of the state and national levels of party organization. In short, what the separation of powers and federalism divide the party council is designed to put back together. In the words of the committee report:

> Such a Party Council should consider and settle the larger problems of party management, within limits prescribed by the National Convention; propose a preliminary draft of the party platform to the National Convention; interpret the platform in relation to current problems; choose for the National Convention the group of party leaders outside the party organizations; consider and make recommendations to appropriate party organs in respect to congressional candidates; and make recommendations to the National Convention, the National Committee or other appropriate party organs with respect to conspicuous departures from general party decisions by state or local party organizations. . . . In presidential years, the council would naturally become a place for the discussion of presidential candidacies, and might well perform the useful function of screening these candidates in a preliminary way.[21]

This is the kind of centralizing and coordinating body the committee hoped could overcome the decentralizing influences built into American government and the party systems, which, it believed, made policy coherence difficult if not impossible to achieve. No such council has been put into place since the 1950 report was written. The early draft of the 1974 Democratic Party Charter provided for such a council, but it was not part of the final Charter. Despite the 1919 Republican precedent cited by the APSA committee, the GOP has not moved to reestablish such a council in the years since the 1950 report. There are simply too many political obstacles—too much attachment to the status quo, too much fear of the unknown, too much threat to established power bases—in so drastic a change as the creation of a really viable party council represents. Party reforms are generally driven by the perception among elites of a political threat to which they must respond to ensure organizational maintenance and survival. The political crises that have propelled other organizational changes have not been deep enough or of sufficient magnitude to cause the elites to support so radical an approach.

Party Elite and Mass Participation

The party as a vehicle for political participation for both elites and masses constitutes the second component of a political party as defined by V. O. Key. In this section, which follows Baer and Bositis in assessing elite representation of mass values, the focus is on the national parties' most prominent function, the nomination of their presidential candidates. The two parties go a long way toward determining who the president of the United States will be by structuring the choices offered to the American voters into a choice between one of two candidates who will win that most powerful office. In the four decades since the APSA report was issued, the party-in-the-electorate has come to play an increasingly important role in the presidential nomination process.

The increased importance of the party-in-the-electorate has produced a profound change in the national conventions. The national conventions still adopt the party platform and nominate the presidential and vice-presidential candidates. But since the 1960s the major political focus for presidential nominations has shifted to the primaries.[22] It is the primaries and the media attention they garner that determine who the presidential nominees will be. No national convention has gone to a second ballot since 1952, and the nominee of both parties is often known well in advance of the national conventions. Many observers have criticized the national conventions as too long, too expensive, and generally superfluous. Nevertheless, the conventions continue as the instrument for making the nominations official and conducting official party business. The conventions also serve other salutary political functions—launching the campaign and making the parties "combat-ready" for the November elections.

The APSA committee recommended the use of more preprimary conventions but also recommended more primaries in the presidential nomination process. The latter has certainly come to pass.[23] In 1968 only fifteen states held presidential primaries. By 1988, that number had grown to thirty-five. In 1992, there will be as many as forty presidential primaries, a new record.[24] Mass participation in the presidential primaries grew to historic highs during the 1970s and 1980s and promises to go higher in the 1990s.

The APSA committee's advocacy of primaries flies in the face of the conventional wisdom in the parties' literature, which suggests that caucuses and conventions strengthen party organizations more than primaries. Nevertheless, the committee apparently felt strongly that primary elections would improve the representativeness of the delegates.[25] Whether the "representativeness" of the national convention delegates has been enhanced by the primaries is a matter of some contention,[26] but it is indisputable that presidential primaries grew significantly in both numbers and importance in the presidential nomination process during the 1970s and 1980s. Consequently, the nomination system has shifted decidedly in the direction of greater mass participation.

The use of presidential primaries is now so pervasive and widely supported that there is again serious discussion of moving to a single national primary to nominate American presidents. This change too was advocated by the APSA committee. While a national primary has not been adopted, public opinion polls consistently show it to be a popular proposal. Moreover, the growth of regional primaries, like the southern "Super Tuesday" of 1988, may be a tentative step in the same direction. These unplanned and ad hoc political developments seem to be producing changes recommended by the committee.

The committee also urged that national conventions be held every two years and that they serve as instruments for developing party positions and policies. Interestingly, the Democratic Party's Charter adopted this recommendation in the form of a "Mid-Term Conference" to be held in the off year between presidential nominating conventions. Democratic Party conferences were held in 1974, 1978, and 1982 but discontinued thereafter because party leaders considered the off-year conference too contentious, exacerbating the Democratic Party's image as too faction-ridden. The conferences were also expensive, and some feared that they diverted attention and resources away from the off-year congressional races. Regardless, the 1982 midterm party conference in Philadelphia was the last held by the Democrats. The Republicans have not adopted anything like a midterm conference and have shown little interest in doing so.

Another recommendation of the committee was that the conventions have fewer delegates and alternates, but the movement has clearly been in the opposite direction. The committee report cites the 1948 national convention delegate numbers as 1,234 for the Democrats and 1,094 for the Republicans.[27] The national conventions have increased steadily in delegate numbers as the political pressures to reward the faithful mix with the self-interest of candidate organizations to produce a constant demand for more seats. In 1988 the Democrats had 4,161 delegates, the Republicans 2,277 delegates. This means that the number of delegates has more than tripled for the Democrats and more than doubled for the Republicans since the 1950 report. The report recommends a reduction in the size of the convention so that it might be a more "deliberative body." The increasing importance of primaries in the presidential nomination process has all but eliminated the deliberative functions of conventions. As the size of the conventions has increased and the early commitment of delegates to candidates has grown, the ability of the conventions to debate issues and develop party positions has diminished.[28] Obviously, the size of the conventions prohibits their functioning in anything like the deliberative policy-oriented body the APSA report envisions.

In some respects, the committee's position in favor of reducing the size of national conventions was at odds with its recommendation that the convention delegates be more representative of the "party's grass-roots strength in the individual states."[29] In the real world of politics it is always more feasible to add than to subtract, and creating more delegate seats is one way to accomplish the goal of greater representation for the party's grass-roots strength—a goal of the APSA committee. Indeed the Democratic Party's apportionment formula builds on the Electoral College base for each state, but it also rewards Democratic votes in preceding elections as a way to recognize Democratic voting strength. This approach is generally consistent with the committee's recommendations regarding the apportionment of the delegations. As the *Ripon Society* case indicates, the Republican apportionment formula has been controversial among some Republicans. In sum, the overall direction of change in the national conventions has been mixed with respect to the recommendations of the APSA committee.

The platforms. The role of the party platforms has always been one of the weakest links in the political chain of party government. Developing a national party platform and then having it translated into public policy by the Congress is a challenge that founders and breaks apart on the barrier of separation of powers and the dynamics of American political campaigns. Most of the specific recommendations of the committee have not been realized. The early draft of the Democratic Charter did follow the recommendation that a party council adopt a platform every two years, involve members of Congress more actively in platform writing, and interpret the platform for the party. Not much has come of these original Charter provisions, which would have made the platforms a more integral instrument of party government.

One of the interesting developments in the area of platforms is de facto movement in the role of the national platforms as reasonably coherent statements of the parties' policy positions. Gerald Pomper has shown that national party platforms constitute important philosophical and policy-oriented statements about what the party is likely to do if elected.[30] Some consistency in party platforms is the natural concomitant of an activist-driven party realignment, discussed more fully below. Such elite-level realignment may force more consistency in platform positions, which is generally in the direction recommended by the committee. Overall, however, the platforms are still not the kind of binding policy statements on officeholders envisioned by the framers of the report.

The party elites. The political values and opinions of party elites matter in shaping the party's program and its image, as well as in the policy-making process. The elites are crucial because they shape the responses of the party organization to political challenges and crises. They are particularly concerned about organizational maintenance and adaptation to external challenges. Since approximately 1964, significant change has been under way in the elites of the parties. Put simply, Democratic elites have become substantially more liberal, and Republican elites have become substantially more conservative. In essence, there has been an important ideological polarization of the parties at the elite level and an internal ideological "purification" of the two parties. During the past three decades, the Democratic Party has lost most of its conservative (largely southern) wing, and the Republican Party has lost most of its liberal (largely northeastern) wing. This elite-level clarification has produced a limited version of the party realignment much discussed and long predicted in the literature.[31] The ideological realignment at the elite level, however, is a truncated realignment, in the sense that mass partisanship has not undergone the basic transformation necessary to complete the classic definition of realignment.

At the mass base, the important transformation is the remarkable extent to which the images of the two parties have become clarified and polarized in the minds of the electorate. Pomper contends that the 1964 contest between Lyndon Johnson and Barry Goldwater was a turning point in the march from "confusion to clarity" in the minds of the voters.[32] In the 1960s and 1970s, the mass of voters came to view the Democratic Party as the liberal alternative and the Republican Party as the conservative alternative, with real policy differences offered by the parties.[33] Certainly the 1980 and 1984 elections of Ronald Reagan continued and reinforced this clarification process.

In addition, the work of Earl and Merle Black, among others, shows conclusively the significant realignment of partisanship in the South over the past three decades.[34] Beginning especially in the early 1960s, the national Democrats adopted the cause of civil rights in response to external pressure from the civil rights movement and the demands of one of their core constituencies. This stance produced a realignment of southern whites, transforming them from a strong Democratic identification into a strong Republican identification in the years since Lyndon Johnson's election.

This transformation is one of the most significant facts of modern political life in the United States. It is also one of the key explanations for the Republican Party's remarkable string of successes in presidential politics, beginning with Richard Nixon's first victory in 1968. The Republican leadership saw an opportunity to encourage the migration of conservative white southerners to their banner, and they grabbed it. The Republican elites acted as good entrepreneurs in seizing this opportunity to strengthen their mass base. From much speculation about the demise of the GOP in the wake of Goldwater's defeat in 1964, the Republicans have rebounded to win every presidential election but one, and the realignment in the South has been crucial. These two trends—substantial ideological realignment of the two parties at the elite level and secular readjustment of party images and loyalties at the mass level—are necessary but not sufficient conditions for the development of "responsible" party government.

Elite-level views and values. There are two landmark studies in how well elite views represent the mass base of the parties. The first is Herbert McClosky's classic work on the 1956 delegates; the second is Jeane Kirkpatrick's work on the 1972 delegates. They bracket the transition period neatly. Warren Miller and Kent Jennings add data for the years to 1980. McClosky found an ideological continuum for party elites ranging from the Republican leaders on the conservative right to the Democratic leaders on the liberal left.[35] He emphasized, however, that the Republican leaders were so conservative and so far removed from their own partisan base as well as mass opinion as to constitute a fairly extreme case of ideological separation from the mainstreams of their party and the electorate. Indeed McClosky found that the Democratic elites were closer to and more representative of the Republican voters than the Republican elites.

In her massive study of both 1972 national conventions, Kirkpatrick documented that the left-right continuum still existed, with Republican leaders on the right and Democratic leaders on the left and the mass voters in the moderate middle. But Kirkpatrick found that the Democratic elites were the "odd man out" because they were so much more liberal than their party's identifiers and the mass public.[36] She contended that Democratic Party elites had become far removed from the mainstream as a result of the McGovern-Fraser party reforms and George McGovern's presidential candidacy. Indeed, she warned of the perils of a Democratic Party captured by a left-leaning group of political amateurs only weakly attached to the political party, qua organization.

Much subsequent research has been built on the McClosky-Kirkpatrick bases. Miller and Jennings build directly on the Kirkpatrick data.[37] Their research covers party elites in 1972, 1976, and 1980, and they find that this period marks a fundamental transition in the two parties wherein the party elites came to differ markedly from each other ideologically. In addition, contrary to Kirkpatrick's projections, the newly mobilized party elites had developed rather strong attachments to their parties. Miller and Jennings conclude:

> Not only did the interparty differences remain intact over the decade, they actually expanded among our band of activists. . . . The increasing ideological distance was achieved by both circulation and conversion processes,

with much of the shift being fueled by the increasing conservatism of Republican activists.[38]

My studies of party elites, which began in 1974 and continued through 1988, encompass a broader range of groups, including members of the national committees, state chairs, and a sampling of county chairs in both parties, as well as national convention delegates.[39] Findings on self-identified ideology for 1988 are reported in table 3.1, which also includes the distribution of ideology in the general public.

Table 3.1. 1988 Party Elites' Self-identified Ideology

	Liberal	Moderate	Conservative
1. Democratic Delegates	53%	42%	5%
2. DNC/State Chairs	66	28	6
3. Democratic County Chairs	45	47	9
4. Democratic Identifiers	37	35	28
5. National Public	23	31	45
6. Republican Identifiers	10	21	69
7. Republican County Chairs	2	24	74
8. RNC/State Chairs	0	26	74
9. Republican Delegates	5	31	64

Source: The data for the party identifiers and the national public were collected in the 1988 National Election Study by the Center for Political Studies of the University of Michigan.

Note: For the mass public, the original scale scored 1–7 with 1 = extremely liberal, 2 = liberal, 3 = slightly liberal, 4 = moderate, 5 = slightly conservative, 6 = conservative, 7 = extremely conservative. Here, 1 through 3 were collapsed into liberal; 4 = moderate; 5 through 7 were collapsed into conservative. For the party elites, a 5-point scale was used originally: 1 = very liberal, 2 = liberal, 3 = moderate, 4 = conservative, 5 = very conservative.

As might be expected, Democratic elites identify themselves as liberal to moderate, with the party's convention delegates, national committee members, and state chairs most liberal and county chairs more moderate. Republican elites are mostly conservative and quite homogeneous across the board in their ideological self-identification. The mass public, however, tends to locate itself ideologically somewhere between the elites of the two parties, though Democratic identifiers and Republican identifiers tilt in the directions of their party elite. Moreover, though not shown in table

3.1, this picture of the ideological dispositions of the two party elites and the mass public has held for all presidential elections in the 1980s.[40]

Table 3.2 provides the results of an issues-oriented question regarding the provision of governmental services as opposed to decreasing public spending. This question seems to capture the liberal-conservative debate in the United States, the results forming a clear and unequivocal pattern. The Democratic elites are very strongly in favor of providing governmental services rather than cutting spending; the Republican elites favor the opposite position. The Republican and Democratic identifiers fall in between the elite groups, but a majority of each party's identifiers favor each party's characteristic position. Overall, the national public is rather evenly divided on the issues with a 39 to 32 percent plurality in favor of the provision of governmental services over cutting spending. Thus, the party leaders are providing some fairly consistent policy alternatives for the consideration of the American public. We included several other domestic and foreign policy issues in this survey, and the results were very compatible with those found in tables 3.1 and 3.2.

Table 3.2. Fewer Services, Decrease Spending vs. More Services, Increase Spending

	More Services	Moderate	Fewer Services
1. Democratic Delegates	81%	11%	8%
2. DNC/State Chairs	85	8	7
3. Democratic County Chairs	73	15	12
4. Democratic Identifiers	52	28	20
5. National Public	39	29	32
6. Republican Identifiers	22	28	51
7. Republican County Chairs	10	16	74
8. RNC/State Chairs	6	17	76
9. Republican Delegates	17	18	64

Note: Originally a 7-point scale with a range of 1–7. After collapsing, 1, 2, 3 = fewer services, decrease spending; 4 = moderate; 5, 6, 7 = more services, increase spending.

While all of this research on party elites is fairly consistent in its findings, one may well ask what its relevance is to the larger thesis, the developments related to the responsible-parties model. Party elites are the official party, holding the important elective and appointed leadership positions. They jointly constitute the operational definition of what V. O. Key calls the "party-as-organization."[41] They help to define the future of the party in such functions as choosing presidential candidates, writing platforms, adopting party policy, and operating the organization on a day-to-day basis. Party elites also help to define the party image held by the mass public. Elites are thus the critical link between the party-in-the-electorate and the party-in-government, and the more accurately elite ideology mirrors that of party voters, the better able they are in translating mass party convictions into government action.

Congressional parties. Party organization in Congress is a significant part of what Key calls the party-in-government. There is a rich literature on congressional party structures, and at least passing note should be taken of it. Overall, it appears that the party organizations in the House and Senate are strong, and some of the trends regarding congressional parties are in directions advocated by the APSA report. The party unity scores in Congress, for example, were at very high levels during the 1970s and 1980s.[42] Republican loyalty to the Reagan agenda was very high through his first term, although it declined significantly in the second term.[43] Partisanship in Congress, moreover, continues to be very strong well into the Bush administration. There was a sharp partisan division in the vote authorizing the use of force against Iraq in 1991, only three Republicans in the House and two in the Senate voting against the Bush position.[44] In addition, the always contentious issues of the deficit and taxes continue to provoke clear partisan divisions.[45] The increased level of party unity in Congress seems related to the increased party homogeneity at the elite level. Undoubtedly, this homogeneity was increased significantly over the past two decades by the loss of much of the southern wing of the Democratic Party, thus reducing the importance of the conservative coalition in Congress.[46]

Donald Baumer's recent work on the Democratic Policy Committee in the Senate shows that it has been used to develop a legislative agenda for the party and to strengthen the leadership. Baumer concludes: "Although responsible party government of the sort advocated by reformers of the late 1940's and early 1950's remains a remote prospect for the contemporary U.S. Congress, there are increasing signs that Democrats are warming up to the possibility of stronger party leadership."[47]

Barbara Sinclair reached essentially the same conclusion about former Democratic Congressman Jim Wright's development of a partisan position and agenda during his term as Speaker.[48] The critical role of the House and Senate leadership works to ensure some policy coherence to the positions taken by the two parties in Congress. These ad hoc political developments are undoubtedly not a master plan to produce party government, but some of the uncoordinated political developments have tendencies in that direction.

Studies also indicate that the party-in-government is highly polarized among the ordinary members of Congress. Rank-and-file Democrats in Congress are much different from their Republican counterparts in ideological and issue positions, as can be seen in the policy positions taken in roll-call voting.[49] For example, Aaron Wildavsky argues that the budget votes and basic positions on spending bills are the most partisan divisions in the modern Congress.[50] He adds: "The basic reason for this is that differences over the budget have increasingly come to define differences between the parties."[51]

Squabbles over the budget contain very important policy differences. Republicans and Democrats in Congress have come to stand for something with respect to budget priorities and programs in general. While there are also considerable areas of overlap, the differences between the parties now seem to be considerably greater than the agreements. When two successive fairly consistently conservative Republican presidents and an unprecedented series of divided governments are added to this mix, the partisan differences are magnified. In addition, the Reagan and Bush administrations have now appointed over 70 percent of all federal judges, which places this third branch of American government firmly under the control of the Republicans—a structural fact that further emphasizes the important partisan divisions in American politics and has important policy ramifications.

Conclusion

Many of the trends noted in this chapter were not specifically advocated by the Committee on Political Parties. These trends are not necessarily the kind of formal, legal, and structural changes in the parties and their organizations anticipated by the committee's report. The thesis here is that the parties' organizations, their elites, have responded to political pressures and opportunities in their external environments. They try to make the changes thought necessary to ensure organizational success and survival. The resultant changes are encouraging for those, like the members of the APSA committee, who see the development of political parties containing some level of ideological and issue-oriented coherence as a good thing. These transformations have produced two political parties populated at the organizational and governmental levels by people homogeneous within their own ranks but with values and policy perspectives quite different from those in the other party. These elites run parties that appear to the voters to offer relatively systematic policy alternatives and to be ideologically distinct.

This transformation, however, has not produced a fully developed responsible-parties system. The structural barriers of separation of powers and federalism and the political barriers of different constituencies and staggered elections producing elected officials emphasizing election-day self-interest still exist, and they drive and divide the party-in-government. At the participatory level, the American voter is still not the programmatically and ideologically oriented voter apparently favored by the the APSA committee. Nevertheless, the two major parties in the last decade of the twentieth century are different, even much different, from the parties encountered by the committee at midcentury. The party elites are decidedly different, and even the mass public has changed. Some of these changes are in directions that would have been endorsed by those visionaries of the 1950s.

There are, however, two models of "responsible parties" implicit in the report. One is a highly centralized national party whose key feature is the party council, a network of state and national party and public officials. This party is likely to be dominated by elites who would set the political agenda for the masses. The second model is mass-based, the elites serving the policy preferences of the masses. How to weld these two models together, how to link elites and masses, remains the elusive challenge. Parties can be responsible *for* something, a program or ideology advocated by elites. Parties can be responsible *to* someone, the grass-roots members. They have a difficult time creating the organizational structures and behavior patterns to do both. Nevertheless, as the framers of the report recognized, political parties are the most likely instruments in a mass democracy for effectuating those two-way linkages between elites and masses vital to a democracy.

Notes

1. Committee on Political Parties, *Toward a More Responsible Two-Party System* (Washington, D.C.: American Political Science Association, 1950); hereinafter, CPP.

2. Austin Ranney, *The Doctrine of Responsible Party Government* (Urbana: University of Illinois Press, 1954); Evron Kirkpatrick, "Toward a More Responsible Two Party System: Political Science, Policy Science, or Pseudo-Science?" *American Political Science Review*, 65 (December 1971): 965–90; David H. Everson, *American Political Parties* (New York: Franklin Watts, 1980).

3. William Crotty and Gary C. Jacobson, *American Parties in Decline* (Boston: Little, Brown, 1980); David Broder, *The Party's Over* (New York: Harper and Row, 1971); Alan R. Gitelson, M. Margaret Conway, and Frank B. Feigert, *American Political Parties: Stability and Change* (Boston: Houghton Mifflin, 1984); Larry J. Sabato, *The Party's Just Begun* (Boston: Scott Foresman, 1988).

4. John S. Jackson III, "Political Science and the Study of Parties'," *Polity* (Summer 1988): 720–26. See also Stephen C. Craig, "The Decay of Mass Partisanship," pp. 705–13; Paul S. Herrnson, "The Importance of Party Campaigning," pp. 714–19, in the same issue of *Polity*.

5. V. O. Key, Jr., *Politics, Parties, and Pressure Groups*, 4th ed. (New York: Thomas Y. Cromwell, 1958), pp. 180–82.

6. Denise L. Baer and David A. Bositis, *Elite Cadres and Party Coalitions: Representing the Public in Party Politics* (New York: Greenwood Press, 1988.

7. Some question just how clear the evidence is. See Warren E. Miller, "Party Identification, Realignment, and Party Voting: Back to the Basics," *American Political Science Review*, 85 (June 1991): 557–68.

8. James L. Gibson, Cornelius R. Cotter, John F. Bibby, and Robert J. Huckshorn, "Assessing Party Organizational Strength," *American Journal of Political Science*, 27 (May 1983): 193–222. See also, by the same authors, "Whither the Local Parties? A Cross-sectional and Longitudinal Analysis of the Strength of Local Party Organizations," *American Journal of Political Science*, 29 (February 1985): 139–60. In addition, see Cornelius P. Cotter, James L. Gibson, John F. Bibby, and Robert J. Huckshorn, *Party Organization in American Politics* (New York: Praeger, 1984).

9. Cousins v. Wigoda, 419 U.S. 477 (1975) 487.

10. Ripon Society v. National Republican Party, 525 F.2d 565 (1975).

11. Democratic Party of the United States of America v. LaFollette, 49 U.S.L.W. 4178.

12. CPP, pp. 5, 39.

13. Gitelson, et al., *Political Parties*, pp. 88–90.

14. Paul S. Herrnson, *Party Campaigning in the 1980s* (Cambridge, Mass.: Harvard University Press, 1988), Ch. 2.

15. Cornelius P. Cotter and Bernard C. Hennessy, *Politics Without Power: The National Party Committees* (New York: Atherton Press, 1964).

16. Herrnson, *Party Campaigning*, p. 39.

17. Ibid., Ch. 2.

18. Ibid., p. 129.

19. Ibid., p. 130.

20. CPP, p. 43.

21. Ibid.

22. William Crotty and John S. Jackson III, *Presidential Primaries and Nominations* (Washington, D.C.: CQ Press, 1985).

23. Ibid., Ch. 3.

24. Rhodes Cook, "When More Democracy Could Aid Democrats," *Congressional Quarterly Weekly Report*, 13 April 1991, p. 346.

25. CPP, p. 10.

26. Gary L. Rose, ed., *Controversial Issues in Presidential Selection* (Albany: State University of New York Press, 1991), Ch. 1.

27. CPP, p. 28.

28. Crotty and Jackson, *Presidential Primaries*, Ch. 8.
29. CPP, p. 37.
30. Gerald M. Pomper and Susan S. Hederman, *Elections in America*, 2nd ed. (New York: Longman, 1980), Ch. 7.
31. Walter Dean Burnham, *Critical Elections and the Mainsprings of American Politics* (New York: W. W. Norton, 1970).
32. Gerald M. Pomper, "From Confusion to Clarity: Issues and American Voters: 1956–1968," *American Political Science Review*, 66 (1972): 415–28; Gerald M. Pomper, *Voter's Choice* (New York: Dodd, Mead, 1975), Ch. 8.
33. Larry J. Sabato, *The Party's Just Begun*, Chs. 1, 4; Warren E. Miller and M. Kent Jennings, *Parties in Transition: A Longitudinal Study of Party Elites and Party Supporters* (New York: Russell Sage Foundation, 1986), Ch. 9.
34. Earl Black and Merle Black, *Politics and Society in the South* (Cambridge, Mass.: Harvard University Press, 1990).
35. Herbert McClosky, Paul J. Hoffman, and Rosemary O'Hara, "Issue Conflict and Party Leaders and Followers," *American Political Science Review*, 56 (1960): 401–27.
36. Jeane Kirkpatrick, *The New Presidential Elite* (New York: Russell Sage Foundation, 1976), p. 315.
37. Miller and Jennings, *Parties in Transition*, Ch. 1.
38. Ibid., pp. 252–53.
39. John S. Jackson III, and Robert A. Hitlin, "A Comparison of Party Elites: The Sanford Commission and the Delegates to the Democratic Mid-Term Conference," *American Politics Quarterly*, (October 1976). See also Denise L. Baer, David A. Bositis, and John S. Jackson III, "The Party Elite Study," *VOX POP: Newsletter of Political Organizations and Parties Section of the American Political Science Association*, 9 (1991): 5–7.
40. John S. Jackson III, Barbara L. Brown, and David A. Bositis, "Herbert McClosky and Friends Revisited," *American Politics Quarterly*, 10 (1982): 159–80. See also Baer and Bositis, *Elite Cadres*, pp. 185–206.
41. Key, *Politics, Parties and Pressure Groups*, pp. 180–82.
42. Roger H. Davidson and Walter J. Oleszek, *Congress and Its Members* (Washington, D.C.: CQ Press, 1981), pp. 193–95; "Party Unity Scores Slip, but Trend Is Up," *Congressional Quarterly Almanac*, (1988): 33-B-38-B.
43. "Presidential Success on Votes, 1953–88," *Congressional Quarterly Almanac*, (1988): 23-B.
44. "Even Votes of Conscience Follow Party Lines," *Congressional Quarterly Weekly Report*, (1991): 190–93.
45. "Partisanship Likely to Drive Any Debate on New Taxes," *Congressional Quarterly Weekly Report*, 29 January 1991, pp. 239–41.
46. "Conservative Coalition Still Alive, but Barely," *Congressional Quarterly Almanac*, (1988): 42-B–48-B.
47. Donald C. Baumer, "An Update on the Senate Democratic Policy Committee," *P.S.: Political Science and Politics*, 24 (1991): 174–79.
48. Barbara Sinclair, "House Majority Leadership in the Late 1980s," in

Congress Reconsidered, 4th ed., ed. Lawrence C. Dodd and Bruce I. Oppenheimer (Washington, D.C.: CQ Press, 1989).

49. Davidson and Oleszek, *Congress and Its Members*, pp. 193–95.

50. Aaron Wildavsky, *The New Politics of the Budgetary Process* (Glenview, Ill.: Scott Foresman, Little Brown College Division, 1988), pp. 197–98.

51. Ibid., p. 198.

4

Mandates Without Parties

JOHN KENNETH WHITE

The hotel ballroom was warm, but the crowd gathered around the podium was impervious to the heat. An electoral landslide had just rumbled across the land. Joining the jubilant partisans was one of the enthusiastic winners. As he began speaking, it was apparent that he was going to say something more than "we won." To him, the ballots contained "a mandate for peace and freedom; a mandate for opportunity for all Americans regardless of race, sex, or creed; a mandate for leadership that is strong and compassionate . . . a mandate to make government the servant of the people in the way our founding fathers intended."[1] Vice President–elect George Bush's 1980 peroration can easily be forgiven as the hyperbole of an enthused candidate savoring an exhilarating moment. But other winners have perceived messages from the voters. Andrew Jackson asserted that his 1832 reelection reaffirmed his veto of a charter for the Bank of the United States. In the words of Leonard White, Jackson's win gave him the "settled conviction [that] the President is an immediate and direct representative of the people."[2] Some years later, James K. Polk elevated Jackson's "settled conviction" to doctrine, telling Congress: "The President represents in the executive department the whole people of the United States." Polk added that the chief executive is responsible "not only to an enlightened public opinion, but to the people of the whole Union."[3]

During the twentieth century, mandates assumed an air of invincibility. Presidents ranging from Republicans Dwight Eisenhower, Richard Nixon, and George Bush to Democrats Woodrow Wilson and Lyndon Johnson have seen in Polk's "enlightened public opinion" a call to expand the limited constitutional authority vested in the office. Woodrow Wilson believed that when the voters gave the Democrats the presidency and control of both houses of Congress in 1912, they were doing something more than changing parties. Wilson believed the electorate had tendered a mandate for his "New Freedoms" program that included a lower tariff, reform of the banking system, and greater federal regulation of the workplace and the environment. In his inaugural address, Wilson declared: "There has been a change of government. . . . No one can mistake the purpose for which the Nation now seeks to use the Democratic Party"—and this from a candidate who won with just 41.8 percent of the popular vote.[4]

Few of Wilson's successors have resisted the temptation to interpret victory at the polls as anything other than a mandate to act in the name of the vox populi. On election night 1964, Lyndon Johnson told supporters in another hot, stuffy hotel ballroom that vanquishing Barry Goldwater was "a mandate for unity, for a government that serves no special interest, no business government, no labor government, no farm government, no one faction, no one group, but a government that is the servant of all the people."[5] Johnson subsequently used his landslide to enact the most liberal domestic program since the New Deal—the Great Society.

Republicans have been no less brazen in seeing victory as a mandate for action. Dwight Eisenhower, a cautious, constitutionally minded president, called his party's victory in 1952 a "mandate for change" and titled his memoirs accordingly.[6] In them Eisenhower relates how he informed Republican congressional leaders that "it was my intention to redeem the pledges of the platform and the campaign," noting that they were "amazed by my uncompromising assertion that I was going to do my best to fulfill every promise to which I had been a party."[7]

Twenty years later, Richard Nixon tried to save his Watergate-battered administration by asserting that impeachment would negate a mandate issued by the voters in 1972: "Last November, the American people were given the clearest choice of this century. Your votes were a mandate which I accepted to complete the initiatives we began in my first term and to fulfill the promises I made for my second term."[8] To Nixon, the presumptive mandate superseded the Constitution itself.

Assertions of mandates by twentieth-century liberal Democratic and conservative Republican presidents would shock the Founding Fathers. In designing the presidency, especially in creating their political Rubik's Cube, the Electoral College, the framers sought to insulate the chief magistrate from the whims of a fickle electorate while elevating the office above the babble of partisan "factions." Alexander Hamilton wrote that in selecting "some fit person as President," the electors should see to it that "the station [is] filled by characters pre-eminent for their ability and virtue."[9] Mandates, be they from the electors or the voters, were to be subordinated by questions of character. Using the Constitution as his guidebook, Vice President John C. Calhoun was appalled when Andrew Jackson claimed a mandate in 1832, rebuking the president in strong language: "He claims to be not only the representative, but the immediate representative of the American people! What effrontery! What boldness of assertion! The Immediate representative? Why, he never received a vote from the American people. He was elected by the electors—the colleges."[10] The quaintness of Calhoun's denunciation is an indication of just how widely accepted is the Wilsonian notion that the president has a responsibility to interpret "the national thought" and boldly insist upon its implementation.[11] But exactly what lies behind the *x*'s marked next to a winner's name?

The Search for Intelligence

The search for meaning behind the balloting is not limited to winning candidates. Politicians, journalists, and political scientists believe they have a responsibility to interpret the electoral tea leaves.[12] Often, contradictory answers are given to the question What does it all mean? Usually, a "second campaign" begins immediately after the balloting, this time to choose which candidate and party will write the final election chapter. The day after the 1988 election, for example, George Bush asserted from Houston that "the American people had spoken," giving him a mandate to "hold the line of taxes." Said Bush: "The American people must have understood that when they voted in rather large numbers for my candidacy."[13] From Boston, Michael Dukakis disagreed, telling reporters:

> I don't see a mandate. Not when the [Congress] has increased its Democratic membership. The American people . . . have expressed a desire to have some continuity in the presidency, [but] I don't think you can look at those results on the congressional side and not say they're also expressing some very strong progressive feelings about what this country has to do.[14]

Dukakis's reference to the ticket splitting that has characterized nearly all national elections since the mid-1950s makes assertions of mandates far more difficult. For forty years, voters have so frequently elected Republican presidents while giving Democrats majorities in Congress that it is often forgotten just how rare divided-party government has been. When Dwight Eisenhower was returned to the White House in 1957, he became the first president since Grover Cleveland in 1885 to inherit a Congress controlled by the opposition.[15] Then Senate Majority Leader Lyndon Johnson maintained that Eisenhower did not have full authority to act but had to share his "qualified mandate" with the Democrats:

A political party at a national convention draws up a program to present to the voters. The voters can either accept it by giving the party full power, reject it by taking the party completely out of power, or give it qualified approval by giving one party the Congress and the other party the Presidency. And when we in the Congress have been given a qualified mandate, as we were in 1956, it means that we have a solemn responsibility to cooperate with the President and produce a program that is neither his blueprint nor our blueprint but a combination of the two. It is the politician's task to pass legislation, not to sit around saying principled things.[16]

In the thirty-six years since Johnson spoke of a "qualified mandate," one party will have controlled the presidency and Congress for a mere twelve years—one-third of the time.[17] Split-party results are not limited to federal elections. In state contests, more voters than ever before have been willing to give one party the governorship while letting another run the legislature. After the 1990 elections, only nineteen states had one party controlling the executive and both houses of the legislature.[18]

When *Toward a More Responsible Two-Party System* was published in 1950, James Sundquist noted that the Committee on Political Parties confined its recognition of divided government to a single subordinate clause consisting of a mere eight words.[19] Elsewhere, the report is filled with staccato phrases like "the party in power," "the majority party," or "the dominant party," and "the opposition party" or "minority party."[20] This language conforms to the disposition of party elites. Sundquist notes that at no time has a major party ever told the American people, "We want only the presidency or only the Senate or the House." Instead, they have always pleaded, "Give us *total* responsibility."[21] Having it all—the presidency and the Congress—was accompanied by an accountability that Democrats and Republicans have happily accepted.

The fact that the electorate now exercises what Everett Carll Ladd calls "cognitive Madisonianism,"[22] consistently splitting party control between the presidency and Congress, makes the task of "finding the mandate" more difficult. One is reminded of Sir Henry Maine's admonition: "The devotee of democracy is much in the same position as the Greeks with their oracles. All agreed that the voice of an oracle was the voice of a god, but everybody allowed that when he spoke he was not as intelligible as might be desired."[23] Even in 1925, when many more voters pulled the party lever, Walter Lippmann doubted that there was much intelligence behind the balloting:

We call an election an expression of the popular will. But is it? We go into a polling booth and mark a cross on a piece of paper for one of two, or perhaps three or four names. Have we expressed our thoughts on the public policy of the United States? Presumably we have a number of thoughts on this and that with many buts and ifs and ors. Surely the cross on a piece of paper does not express them.[24]

Despite the seemingly haphazard nature of ticket splitting, and in spite of Lippmann's doubts, most political scientists believe that mandates can be found if one looks hard enough. But to locate them, one must have political parties as a guide.

Mandates, Parties, and Governing

When the Committee on Political Parties tendered its report, it reflected a commonly held belief that parties had a solemn obligation to frame the issues so that voters could make intelligent decisions: "Popular government . . . *requires political parties which provide the electorate with a proper range of choice between alternatives of action.*"[25] The report declared that "putting a particular candidate into office is not an end in itself," adding: "The concern of the parties with candidates, elections and appointments is misunderstood if it is assumed that parties can afford to bring forth aspirants for office without regard to the views of those so selected."[26]

These assertions reflected the thinking of the committee's chairman, E. E. Schattschneider. In a 1945 *American Political Science Review* symposium on the enormous problems facing the post–World War II economy, Schattschneider wrote that Democrats and Republicans had a solemn obligation to avert another Depression. To do this, each had to structure its campaigns so that the winning party would be able to grasp the levers of power. Schattschneider noted that of all the varieties of political organization, only the political party "submits its claims to the nation in a general election in which the stakes are a mandate from the people to govern the country."[27]

Ever since political science emerged as a separate area of academic inquiry at the turn of the century, its adherents have steadfastly argued that parties are "the indispensable instruments of government."[28] This argument assumed even greater importance given America's split-level tripartite form of government. Adopting a parliamentary model would unify the two levels and three branches, but changing the Constitution is regarded by many as a quixotic venture. Thus, parties were seen as the best hope to give coherence to a government of diverse and dispersed powers. President Herbert Hoover lent his prestige to this view, telling a 1929 audience:

> We maintain party government not to promote intolerant partisanship but because opportunity must be given for the expression of the popular will, and organization provided for the execution of its mandates. It follows that Government both in the executive and legislative branches must carry out in good faith the platform upon which the party was entrusted with power.[29]

The Committee on Political Parties agreed with Hoover. Its members, however, feared that the parties were no longer the effective organizers of opinion they had once been: "*By and large, alternatives between the parties are defined so badly that it is often difficult to determine what the election has decided even in the broadest terms.*"[30] To them, these trends were "ominous" because parties could no longer legitimately claim mandates from the voters, thereby loosening their grasp on the levers of power.

The report's charge that the parties were not presenting clear, crisp alternatives may have been valid. But the real problem with its critique is that parties have rarely presented issues for an up or down vote. Muddying the clear issue-oriented mandate waters envisioned by the committee were the politics of regionalism, ethnicity, and race. Historically, Democrats and Republicans alike have used an "us versus them" politics to arouse an otherwise uninspired electorate to go to the polls. Brooks Adams once quipped that politics is the systemic organization of hatreds.[31] An 1866 speech by Republican Governor Oliver P. Morton of Indiana is illustrative of the hatreds that have echoed from many a campaign rally:

> Every unregenerate rebel . . . calls himself a Democrat. Every bounty jumper, every deserter, every sneak who ran away from the draft. . . . Every man . . . who murdered Union prisoners . . . who contrived hellish schemes to introduce into Northern cities the wasting pestilence of yellow fever, calls himself a Democrat. . . . Every wolf in sheep's clothing . . . every one who shoots down Negroes in the streets, burns Negro school-houses and meeting-houses, and murders women and children by the light of their flaming dwellings, calls himself a Democrat. . . . In short, the Democratic party may be described as a common sewer and loathsome receptacle, into which is emptied every element of treason North and South, and every element of inhumanity and barbarism which has dishonored the age.[32]

Democrats have also engaged in political hyperbole. For decades after Franklin Roosevelt's 1936 campaign in which he branded his GOP opponents "economic royalists,"[33] Democrats portrayed Republicans as nothing more than a bunch of fat-cat, well-to-do country-club types while championing themselves as defenders of the "common man." Quite often, parties did see elections as occasions to promote public policy but used them to incite religious and regional hatreds.[34] Thus, partisanship was more than the banding together of like-minded, issue-oriented citizens. Joining a party was a declaration about who you were or where you were born. Ethnicity, regionalism, and patronage appointments transformed parties into giant social organizations that eventually integrated millions into the "American way of life." Issues, though important, were secondary. For his part, Tammany Hall boss George Washington Plunkitt believed that winning votes had nothing to do with the issues:

> [Let's say] I hear of a young feller that's proud of his voice, thinks he can sing fine. I ask him to come around to Washington Hall and join our Glee Club. He comes and sings, and he's a follower of Plunkitt for life. Another young feller gains a reputation as a baseball player in a vacant lot. I bring him into our baseball club. That fixes him. You'll find him workin' for my ticket at the polls next election day. Then there's the young fella that likes rowin' on the river, the young feller that makes a name as a waltzer on his block, the young feller that's handy with his dukes—I rope them all in by givin' them opportunities to show themselves off. I don't trouble them with political arguments. I just study human nature and act accordin'.[35]

Stitched together, the threads of history, regionalism, ethnicity, and race make it easy to dismiss mandates as illusions.[36] Such a conclusion would be mistaken. In the late twentieth century, voters have responded more to issues. In a twentieth-anniversary reappraisal of *Toward a More Responsible Two-Party System*, Gerald M. Pomper noted that there had been a significant increase in the correlation between policy and party. Using seven issues—federal aid to education; government provision of medical care; government guarantees of full employment; federal enforcement of fair employment, housing, and school integration; and foreign aid—Pomper found that in 1956 a linear relation between issue and party identification existed only for medical care. By 1968, he found, there were correlations on all of the above except foreign aid. Moreover, the proportion who viewed the Democrats as the more liberal party had risen on every question.[37] Pomper concluded that between 1956 and 1968, "considerable political learning" had taken place.[38]

The education of the American voter continues. During the 1980s, polls showed that voters had persistent and different assessments of the two parties. A March 1991 survey conducted by ABC News and the *Washington Post*, reported in figure 4.1, captures several of the mixed public attitudes. It shows the Republicans with strong advantages in maintaining our national defense, increasing U.S. influence overseas, handling foreign affairs, and making U.S. industry competitive overseas. The GOP had more modest leads in handling the nation's economy, controlling inflation, reducing the problem of illegal drugs, handling crime, holding down taxes, and reducing the threats posed by nuclear war and the federal budget deficit. Democrats had strong leads in protecting Social Security, helping the homeless, and assisting the elderly and the poor. The Democrats had smaller advantages when it came to reducing unemployment and helping the middle class. Neither party could claim education, keeping the United States out of a war, or protecting the environment as their own.

New Mandates, No Parties

While the data presented in figure 4.1 suggest that voters perceive distinctions between Democrats and Republicans, there is a growing body of evidence to indicate that both parties are becoming weaker. During the 1980s, fewer Americans than ever before identified with the major parties. In 1952, 74 percent of those polled by the University of Michigan's Social Research Center said they were Democrats or Republicans. By 1988, the figure had declined to 63 percent.[39] The loss of reliable partisans has turned party identification into a fluctuating barometer, reflecting events more than a structure of stable beliefs. An October 1990 ABC News–*Washington Post* poll, taken when Congress and President Bush were struggling with a budget compromise and government closings, showed 51 percent of the electorate identifying with the Democrats and 43 percent with the Republicans.[40] Five months later, after the Gulf War, the figures were nearly reversed: 47 percent called themselves Republicans; 45 percent said they were Democrats.[41] Pollster Geoffrey Garin believes that emphasizing partisan identification is "silly," likening it to asking "How do you feel about the way things are going in the country today?"[42]

Today the electorate relates more to candidates than to parties. When Ronald Reagan asked voters in 1980, "Are you better off than you were four years ago?," he framed the contest between himself and Jimmy Carter in highly personal terms. In effect, the voters plagiarized Oliver Cromwell's admonishment to the Long Parliament in 1653, telling Carter: "You have sat too long for any good you have been doing. Depart, I say, and let us have done with you. In the name of God, go!"[43]

Reagan pollster Richard B. Wirthlin argues that his candidate's 51 percent win was "a mandate for change" that included "a rejection of

Figure 4.1. Issues and Partisan Preferences

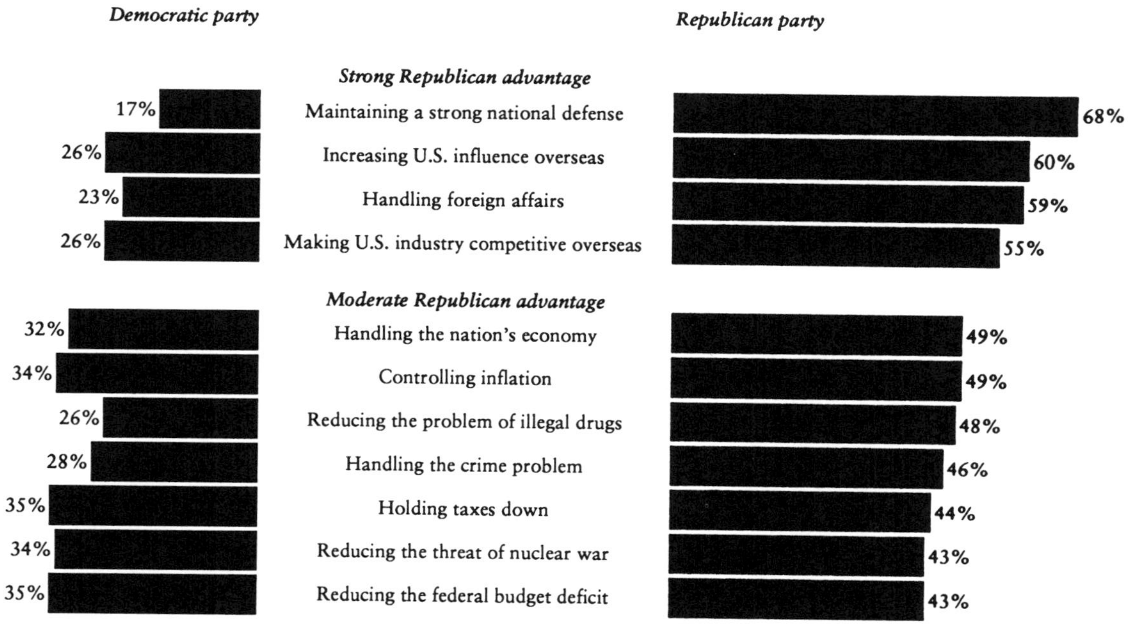
Democratic party
Republican party
Strong Republican advantage
17%
Maintaining a strong national defense
68%
26%
Increasing U.S. influence overseas
60%
23%
Handling foreign affairs
59%
26%
Making U.S. industry competitive overseas
55%
Moderate Republican advantage
32%
Handling the nation's economy
49%
34%
Controlling inflation
49%
26%
Reducing the problem of illegal drugs
48%
28%
Handling the crime problem
46%
35%
Holding taxes down
44%
34%
Reducing the threat of nuclear war
43%
35%
Reducing the federal budget deficit
43%

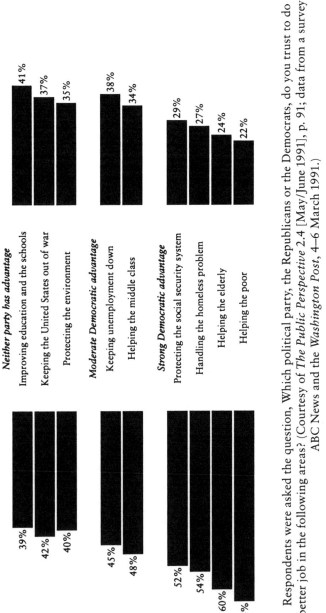

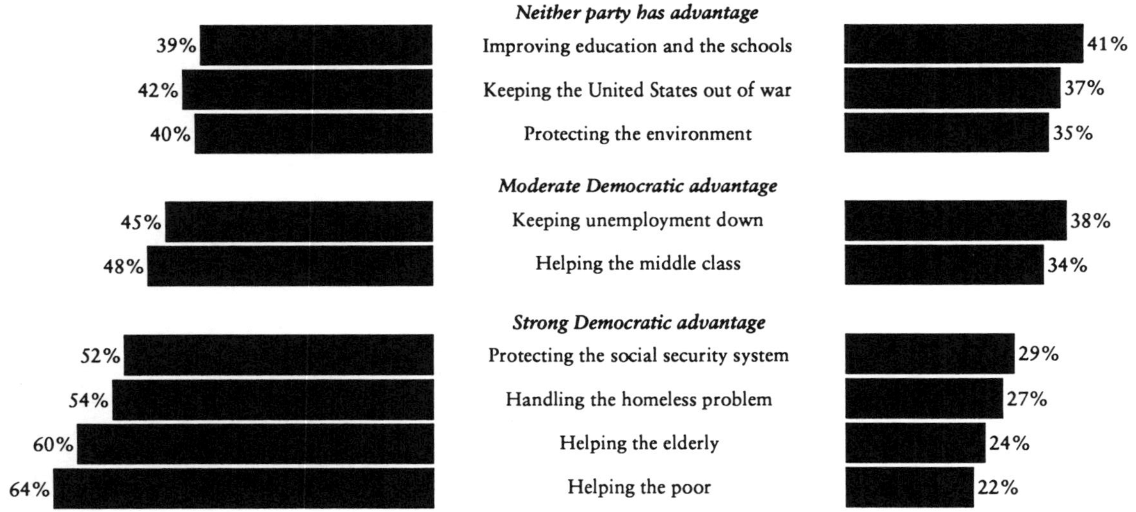

Respondents were asked the question, Which political party, the Republicans or the Democrats, do you trust to do a better job in the following areas? (Courtesy of *The Public Perspective* 2.4 [May/June 1991], p. 91; data from a survey by ABC News and the *Washington Post*, 4–6 March 1991.)

the New Deal agenda that had dominated American politics since the 1930s."[44] In short, voters gave the Republican Party a mandate to bring about wholesale changes in government. The results seemed to bear out Wirthlin's argument. In addition to the presidency, Republicans won twelve more Senate seats—an astonishing rearrangement in an era of incumbency—to become a majority for the first time since 1952. In the House, the GOP added thirty-four new members. While Republicans were not a majority, a coalition of conservative southern "Boll Weevil" Democrats and Republicans gave Reagan de facto control of the lower chamber. Thus, Reagan's win represented something more than a personal victory. David Broder notes that Reagan often told campaign crowds: "If you want these changes [tax cuts, budget cuts, and increased defense spending], then don't just change presidents. We've done that a lot. Vote for so-and-so for the Senate and so-and-so for the House and we will work together to bring about those changes."[45] Moreover, the Republican Party produced several generic television advertisements that reinforced Reagan's message and applied it to all GOP candidates.

But Reagan's tilt to partisanship in 1980 was an aberration. Four years later, the Republican Party was all but forgotten as Reagan did not ask his fellow countrymen to back the GOP, just him. As for the future, Reagan vaguely promised: "You ain't seen nothin' yet." The returns gave Reagan an enormous victory with 59 percent of the vote, 49 states, and 525 electoral votes. But the Republicans lost two seats in the Senate and fifteen in the House. An angry House Republican Minority Leader Bob Michel called Reagan "a son of a buck," adding, "Ronald Reagan really never . . . joined that issue of what it really means to have those [Republican] numbers in the House."[46] Even White House Chief of Staff James Baker thought the election "was a big victory for [Reagan's] philosophy and a victory for him personally, but I'm not sitting here claiming it's a big mandate."[47]

In many respects, 1984 was a typical late-twentieth-century election. An incumbent president seeking renewal of his White House lease calls for a reexamination of his past performance. Thus, the candidate becomes the issue. Two women typify the views often heard in 1984. Janet Patterson, a twenty-four-year-old Reagan supporter from Mississippi, endorsed Reagan, saying: "Reagan represents the American ideals that are most important to me, the true American spirit. That means that America always stands strong as a leader nation, that you can believe in your nation."[48] Lora Potter, a twenty-four-year-old Rhode Island schoolteacher, explained why she backed Walter Mondale: "Reagan is the big reason, his total uncaring attitude about anyone in the lower income brackets. He's cutting the many social services to the point where people who need them aren't getting them."[49]

In each case, Reagan was the man who had become the issue. V. O. Key called this "retrospective voting," explaining: "Voters may reject what they have known; or they may approve what they have known. They are not likely to be attracted in great numbers by promises of the novel or unknown. Once innovation has occurred they may embrace it, even though they would have, earlier, hesitated to venture forth to welcome it."[50] Franklin Roosevelt's first term confirms Key's point. In 1932, he ran on a platform promising a 25 percent *cut* in the federal budget to balance the books. By 1936, after much of the budget-busting New Deal had become law, Roosevelt told campaign advisors: "There's one issue in this campaign. It's myself, and people must either be for me or against me."[51] Two years later, FDR applied the same yardstick to *all* potential candidates, injecting himself into several Democratic primary contests.

While the yardstick that voters must be "either for me or against me" is an old one, the measurements were usually calculated on rulers supplied by the parties. Historically, parties structured campaigns by providing voters with cues about what values they stood for and what kind of America they sought. Thus, the presidents cited earlier in this chapter—Jackson, Polk, Wilson, Hoover, and Eisenhower—took care not to claim mandates for themselves but extended them to their political parties.

Today, presidents and voters have discarded parties in favor of independent, nonpartisan evaluations. This has turned presidential elections into plebiscites whose outcomes mean victory or defeat for the major party candidates but little else. Theodore Lowi likens the president to the Roman emperors and French authoritarians "who governed on the basis of popular adoration, with the masses giving their noisy consent to every course of action."[52]

The Committee on Political Parties prophesied that candidate-centered campaigns would result in an enhanced presidential profile.[53] That prediction has proven accurate. During the 1980s, the presidency became a political Mount Everest as Ronald Reagan towered over the political landscape. When a 1986 poll asked respondents what came to mind when they heard the words "Republican Party," 54 percent answered "Reagan."[54] Surveying the Reagan era, Martin P. Wattenberg writes that responsible party government "can hardly work in an atmosphere where individual candidates dominate the political scene, where political parties have to struggle to maintain a modest degree of relevance, and where control of the presidency and Congress is regularly split between them."[55] But the APSA report warned of just such a result when voters concentrated on candidates rather than parties. Its admonition is worth recalling:

> *When the President's program actually is the sole program . . . , either his party becomes a flock of sheep or the party falls apart.* In effect *this concept of the presidency disposes of the party system by making the President reach directly for the support of a majority of the voters.* It favors a President who exploits skillfully the arts of demagoguery, who uses the whole country as his political backyard, and who does not mind turning into the embodiment of personal government. . . . [Americans] . . . cannot afford to be casual about overextending the presidency to the point where it might very well ring in the wrong ending.[56]

Implications for Governance

Disconnecting presidents from parties has been under way for half a century. In 1940, enthusiastic supporters of Wendell Willkie formed several ad hoc clubs on behalf of the Republican presidential candidate. Dwight Eisenhower established Citizens for Eisenhower in 1952, making it the first formal organization to put candidate above party. In 1972, Richard Nixon perfected the technique by displacing the Republican National Committee in favor of the Committee to Reelect the President. Ronald Reagan did much the same thing, likening himself to a "citizen politician."

As it has become the *candidate's* responsibility, not the party's, to frame the issues on which the voters must render a decision, voters can mark an *X* next to a name without regard to how they would fill in the rest of the spaces on the ballot. In 1988, disgruntled voters could place an *X* next to George Bush's name, thus answering his questions about the Pledge of Allegiance and Willie Horton while supporting other candidates who asked and received responses to their different inquiries. Television's ability to allow politicians with enough cash to enter our living rooms and pose the questions they want answered ensures that the candidate-centered mandate is an enduring quality of the American policy.

This is a long way from the vision of the APSA report. The committee wanted an increase in partisanship. In the forty years since its publication, we have seen a steady decline of partisan identifiers. In this, the committee was prescient: "In a way, a sizable body of the electorate has shifted from hopeful interest in the parties to the opposite attitude. The mass of voters sees itself as the President's or his opponent's direct electoral support."[57]

The decline of parties is the direct result of the American love affair with nonpartisanship. Since the early days of the Republic, Americans have placed a premium on it. A contemporary of a leading Virginia farmer, Edward Pendleton, praised him, saying: "None of his opinions were drawn from personal views or party prejudices. He never had a connexion with any political party, . . . so that his opinions were the result of his own judgment, and that judgment was rendered upon the best unbiased estimate he could make of the publick good."[58]

Not much has changed. In the nearly two hundred years since Pendleton's tribute, "independence" continues to be a valued commodity. John F. Kennedy wrote a Pulitzer-prizewinning book, *Profiles in Courage*, that extolled those who placed conscience above party.[59] In many localities, city managers have replaced elected mayors as voters decide that the "professionalism" of the manager is preferable to the partisanship of officials who must rely upon popular support. E. E. Schattschneider blamed his fellow political scientists for inventing and popularizing nonpartisanship, calling it "a Nirvana in which all good citizens act like college professors who are afraid of losing their jobs."[60] Underneath the idea is the notion, to quote Schattschneider, that "people who do not take sides are morally superior to people who do, that unorganized voters are better than organized voters, that it is more moral to be fatuous than effective."[61]

Still, independence is something Americans value. A 1986 survey found that 92 percent agreed with the statement "I always vote for the person who I think is best, regardless of what party they belong to."[62] Other data echo this finding. When Richard Wirthlin asked why people supported Ronald Reagan or Walter Mondale in 1984, just 5 percent of the Reagan backers and 15 percent of the Mondale supporters cited "partisan allegiance."[63]

Races for Congress have become hallmarks of nonpartisanship. In an era when reelection is based on a member's ombudsmanship, judging the quality of services rendered all but displaces partisanship. Thus, it is not surprising that a 1990 postelection poll conducted by the Republican Congressional Campaign Committee found 55 percent agreeing that it made little difference whether a Democrat or a Republican represented them in Congress.[64] In fact, the last time Congress became an overtly partisan issue was in 1948 when Democrat Harry Truman blasted the "do-nothing" Eightieth (Republican) Congress.

The result is that mandates are diminished because they lack the institutional grounding once provided by the parties. A durable partisanship is a necessary prerequisite for the issue-based mandates envisioned by the APSA report: "The very idea of party implies an association of broadly like-minded voters seeking to carry out common objectives through their elected representatives."[65] But the word *mandate* was mentioned only twice in the document, each time in passing.[66] The report assumed that the intentions of the voters would be clear once the mechanisms of parties were refurbished. Lacking the constraint of party, presidents can casually jettison their mandates whenever it is convenient. In October 1990, George Bush abandoned his "no new taxes" pledge and asked congressional Democrats to help him reduce the gargantuan federal deficit. A bipartisan coalition proposed a series of new levies, including a ten-cent increase in the gasoline tax and an increase in Medicare premiums.

Divided government makes mandates even less secure. Essential to the committee's conception of mandates is the right of the electorate to reassess a party's performance and, if necessary, remove it from power. Coalition government makes it politically attractive for Democrats and Republicans to "blame the other guy," thereby limiting the liability of both. David S. Broder writes that "when voters won't make the hard choice of which party should govern, the only government you can get is government by improvisation."[67]

Such ad hoc policy-making trades the decisiveness of partisanship for the mushiness of bipartisanship. Bipartisanship was once the hallmark of American foreign policy. Today it has become the hallmark of domestic policy as well. An anecdote is illustrative. In his inaugural address, George Bush expressed a willingness to extend his hand to the Democratic Congress, declaring: "The American people await action. They didn't send us here to bicker. They asked us to rise above the merely partisan. In crucial things, unity—and this, my friends, is crucial."[68] At that, those in the rear of the crowd started to clap, and the wave of applause grew so loud that even the dignitaries seated next to the new president were forced to clap.

One of those dignitaries, Democratic Senator Sam Nunn, told the *New Republic* in 1991, "I can't think of any major problem that can be solved with partisanship."[69] Nunn's above-the-fray attitude extends to the House of Representatives where Speaker Tom Foley has been criticized for his above-politics demeanor. A liberal House Democratic aide notes that Foley deals with Congress in the same manner he relates to his constituents—minimizing his Democratic party affiliation and attracting Republican support.[70]

The unfortunate consequence is that problems are not addressed. Since voters have, in the words of the committee, "dispose[d] of the parties as intermediaries between themselves and the government," parties have come to stand for even less.[71] Kevin Phillips has pronounced them "brain dead."[72] Moreover, leaders in both parties are often unwilling to expose themselves without the shield parties once offered. In a 1989 cover story, "Is Government Dead?" *Time* magazine writer Stanley T. Cloud concluded: "Abroad and at home, challenges are going unmet. Under the shadow of a massive federal deficit that neither political party is willing to confront, a kind of neurosis of accepted limits has taken hold from one end of Pennsylvania Avenue to the other."[73]

Political parties may never be restored to what they once were. The old-time boss is dead, along with his patronage. But it is also clear that no matter how much Americans dislike them, political parties are not about to become extinct. What *must* happen is that the two major parties adopt positions on issues that are clear, relevant, and distinctive. There is some evidence that this is happening. Jesse Jackson argues that the Democrats cannot win the presidency in 1992 "by offering a pale imitation of the Republican Party, staging elections in which there are two names for one party, with one set of assumptions and one set of solutions."[74] Others agree with Jackson, but the Democrats remain divided on tactics and strategy. Members of the Democratic Leadership Council, for example, prefer to mute their party's ideological and cultural liberalism. Republicans continue to emphasize their conservative economic policies and foreign policy nationalism while championing cultural conservatism. The electorate's persistent refusal to endorse either party fully by giving one control of the presidency and the Congress leaves both with plenty of tactics in search of a strategy for governance.

Notes

1. Quoted in Stanley Kelley, Jr., *Interpreting Elections* (Princeton, N.J.: Princeton University Press), p. 217.

2. Quoted in Robert A. Dahl, "Myth of the Presidential Mandate," *Political Science Quarterly*, 105 (1990): 356.

3. Ibid., p. 357.

4. Woodrow Wilson, Inaugural Address, Washington, D.C., 4 March 1913.

5. Lyndon B. Johnson, "Radio and Television Remarks at the Close of Election Day, 4 November 1964," *Public Papers of the Presidents, Lyndon B. Johnson, 1963–1964* (Washington, D.C.: U.S. Government Printing Office, 1965), p. 1585.

6. Dwight D. Eisenhower, *Mandate for Change, 1953–1956* (Garden City, N.Y.: Doubleday, 1963). Eisenhower's party won not only the presidency but both houses of Congress, marking the last time the Republicans controlled the legislative branch.

7. Eisenhower added parenthetically, "More than once I was to hear this view derided by 'practical politicians' who laughed off platforms as traps to

catch voters. But whenever they expressed these cynical conclusions to me, they invariably encountered a rebuff that left them a bit embarrassed." Eisenhower, *Mandate for Change*, pp. 194–95.

8. Quoted in Dahl, "Myth of the Presidential Mandate," p. 361.

9. Alexander Hamilton, *Federalist* 68, in Alexander Hamilton, James Madison, and John Jay, *The Federalist Papers*, ed. Clinton Rossiter (New York: New American Library, 1961), p. 414.

10. Quoted in Robert J. Spitzer, *The Presidential Veto: Touchstone of the American Presidency* (Albany: State University of New York Press, 1988), p. 34.

11. See Woodrow Wilson, *Constitutional Government in the United States* (New York: Columbia University Press, 1908), pp. 54–61. The Committee on Political Parties agreed with Wilson, saying of the president: "In him alone all Americans find a single voice in national affairs." See Committee on Political Parties, *Toward a More Responsible Two-Party System* (New York: Rinehart, 1950), p. 2 (hereinafter, CPP).

12. This task has been made somewhat easier since the advent of exit polling.

13. "Transcript of Bush News Conference," *Washington Post*, 10 November 1988, p. A-41.

14. T. R. Reid and Edward Walsh, "Dukakis: Bush Can't Claim A Mandate," *Washington Post*, 10 November 1988, p. A-37.

15. From Andrew Jackson to Dwight Eisenhower, only four presidents had to confront either a House or a Senate controlled by the opposition party: Zachary Taylor in 1848, Rutherford B. Hayes in 1876, James Garfield in 1880, and Grover Cleveland in 1884.

16. Quoted in Doris Kearns, *Lyndon Johnson and the American Dream* (New York: New American Library, 1976), pp. 146–47.

17. Only Democrats have been able to unite the government, controlling the presidency and Congress 1961–69 and 1977–81.

18. Of these, sixteen were Democrats, three Republicans. See *The American Enterprise*, (January–February 1991): 95.

19. James L. Sundquist, "Needed: A Political Theory for the New Era of Coalition Government in the United States," *Political Science Quarterly*, 103 (1988): 625. The subordinate clause Sundquist referred to is this: "For more than ten years now the press has carried news about regular meetings between the President and the Big Four of Congress—the Speaker of the House, the Majority Leader of the House, the Vice President and Majority Leader of the Senate, *when the four are of the President's party*" (emphasis added). See CPP, p. 8.

20. See CPP, pp. 1, 18, 34, 35, 41, 51.

21. Sundquist, "Needed," p. 616.

22. Everett Carll Ladd, "Public Opinion and the 'Congress Problem,'" *The Public Interest*, (Summer 1990).

23. Quoted in Kelley, *Interpreting Elections*, p. 134.

24. Walter Lippmann, *The Phantom Public* (New York: Harcourt, Brace, 1925), pp. 56–57.

25. CPP, p. 15.

26. Ibid.

27. E. E. Schattschneider, "Party Government and Employment Policy," *American Political Science Review*, 39 (December 1945): 1151. This was a symposium titled "Maintaining High-Level Production and Employment" coordinated by Fritz Morstein Marx, a key figure on the Committee on Political Parties.

28. See CPP, p. 15. Another political scientist, Giovanni Sartori, called the political parties "*the* central intermediate structures between society and government." Sartori, *Parties and Party System: A Framework for Analysis* (Cambridge, Mass.: Harvard University Press, 1976), p. ix.

29. Quoted in Kelley, *Interpreting Elections*, p. 127.

30. CPP, p. 30.

31. Quoted in James MacGregor Burns, *The Deadlock of Democracy: Four Party Politics in America* (Englewood Cliffs, N.J.: Prentice-Hall, 1963), p. 51.

32. Quoted in Milton Viorst, *Fall From Grace* (New York: Simon and Schuster, 1968), p. 64. In 1884 the Reverend Dr. Samuel Dickinson Burchard, campaigning for the Republican presidential ticket made a speech in which he referred to the Democratic Party as one "whose antecedents have been rum, Romanism and rebellion"—tough language that many believed cost Republican James Blaine the presidency. Quoted in Stefan Lorant, *The Presidency* (New York: Macmillan, 1951), p. 388.

33. Quoted in James MacGregor Burns, *Roosevelt: The Lion and the Fox* (New York: Harcourt, Brace, and World, 1956), p. 274.

34. There are numerous contemporary examples of the same phenomena. In 1976, Republican vice-presidential candidate Bob Dole termed World War II, Korea, and Vietnam "Democrat Wars," noting that Republicans had a greater affinity for peace. In 1980, Ronald Reagan denounced Jimmy Carter for opening his reelection campaign in Tuscumbia, Alabama, a city Reagan called "the parent body of the Ku Klux Klan." See Lou Cannon, *President Reagan: The Role of a Lifetime* (New York: Simon and Schuster, 1991), p. 69n. Four years later, Democratic vice-presidential candidate Geraldine Ferraro branded Reagan as "un-Christian."

35. Quoted in William L. Riordan, *Plunkitt of Tammany Hall* (New York: E. P. Dutton, 1963), pp. 25–26.

36. Robert Dahl, in fact, does this. See *Myth of the Presidential Mandate*.

37. Gerald M. Pomper, "Toward a More Responsible Two-Party System? What, Again?," *Journal of Politics*, 33 (1971): 929–32.

38. Ibid., p. 936.

39. See Martin P. Wattenberg, *The Decline of American Political Parties, 1952–1988* (Cambridge, Mass.: Harvard University Press, 1990), p. 140.

40. ABC News–*Washington Post* survey, 10–14 October 1990. These party identification figures include those independents who said they "leaned" to the Democrats or the Republicans.

41. ABC News–*Washington Post* survey, 1–4 March 1991. These party identification figures include those independents who said they "leaned" to the Democrats or the Republicans.

42. "Interview with Geoffrey Garin," *The Public Perspective*, 2 (May–June 1991): 9. There are numerous other examples of fluctuation in party identification. A December 1983 survey of white Alabamians found that 53 percent said they were Democrats; 24 percent called themselves Republicans. By election day 1984, the figures were nearly reversed: 29 percent were Democrats; 41 percent said they were Republicans. This represented a net shift of 41 points in less than twelve months. According to Mondale polltaker Peter D. Hart, "The single most dramatic factor of 1984 was movement in party ID." See "Moving Right Along? Campaign '84's Lessons for 1988," *Public Opinion*, 62. Richard Wirthlin's polls showed enormous fluctuations in party identification during the Iran-Contra Affair. In June 1986, Wirthlin's polls showed the parties at parity with Democratic identifiers at 41 percent and Republicans at 40 percent. After the Iran-Contra Affair became public, Democratic identifiers increased to 50 percent while Republicans fell to 39 percent. Thus, a 1-point difference in June became an 11-point difference eight months later.

43. Quoted in Gerald M. Pomper, "The Presidential Election," in Gerald M. Pomper, ed., *The Election of 1980: Reports and Interpretations* (Chatham, N.J.: Chatham House, 1981), p. 65.

44. "Moving Right Along? Campaign '84's Lessons for 1988: An Interview with Peter Hart and Richard Wirthlin," *Public Opinion*, (December–January 1985): 8.

45. Quoted in David S. Broder, "Bush Could Take the Hill, Too . . .," *Washington Post*, 7 April 1991, p. D-1.

46. David S. Broder and George Lardner, Jr., "Did Anybody See a Mandate Go By?", *Washington Post National Weekly Edition*, 19 November 1984, p. 10.

47. Ibid.

48. "Younger Voters Tending to Give Reagan Support," *New York Times*, 16 October 1984, p. A-1.

49. Ibid.

50. V. O. Key, Jr., *The Responsible Electorate: Rationality in Presidential Voting, 1936-1960* (New York: Random House, 1966), p. 61.

51. Quoted in Burns, *Roosevelt: The Lion and the Fox*, p. 271.

52. Theodore J. Lowi, *The Personal Presiden: Power Invested, Promise UnFulfilled* (Ithaca, N.Y.: Cornell University Press, 1985), p. xi.

53. CPP, pp. 93–94.

54. Survey conducted by William R. Hamilton and Staff for Larry Sabato and AMPAC, cited in *The Polling Report*, 20 October 1986, p. 3.

55. Martin P. Wattenberg, *The Rise of Candidate-Centered Politics* (Cambridge, Mass.: Harvard University Press, 1991), pp. 163–64.

56. CPP, p. 95.

57. Ibid.

58. Quoted in Richard Hofstadter, *The Idea of a Party System: The Rise of Legitimate Opposition in the United States, 1780–1840* (Berkeley, Calif.: University of California Press, 1969), p. 13.

59. John F. Kennedy, *Profiles in Courage* (New York: Harper and Brothers, 1956).

60. E. E. Schattschneider, *The Struggle for Party Government* (College Park: University of Maryland Press, 1948), p. 6.

61. Ibid.

62. Cited in Wattenberg, *Rise of Candidate-Centered Politics*, p. 34.

63. "Moving Right Along?" p. 10.

64. Cited in Edward J. Rollins, "*The Republicans*: Prescription for the GOP," *Public Perspective*, 2, p. 5.

65. CPP, p. 66.

66. Mandates are mentioned on pp.30, 37, CPP.

67. Quoted in Wattenberg, *Decline of Political Parties*, pp. 164, 166.

68. George Bush, Inaugural Address, Washington, D.C., 20 January 1989.

69. Sidney Blumenthal, "The Mystique of Sam Nunn," *New Republic*, 4 March 1991, p. 23.

70. See Robert Kuttner, "Congress Without Cohabitation," *The American Prospect*, (Winter 1991): 33.

71. CPP, p. 95.

72. Kevin Phillips, "George Bush and Congress—Brain-Dead Politics of '89," *Washington Post*, 1 October 1989, pp. D-1–2.

73. Stanley W. Cloud, "The Can't Do Government," *Time*, 23 October 1989, p. 29.

74. Jackson argues that this is exactly the path Democrats chose in 1988. See Jesse L. Jackson, "For the Democrats, a Strategy of Inclusion," *Washington Post*, 22 May 1991, p. A-21.

5

Programmatic Liberalism and Party Politics

The New Deal Legacy and the Doctrine of Responsible Party Government

SIDNEY M. MILKIS

The American Political Science Association (APSA) report *Toward a More Responsible Two Party System*, published in 1950, gives prominence to the doctrine of responsible party government. It calls for a party system composed of national policy-oriented organizations capable of carrying out platforms or proposals presented to the people during the course of an election. According to the APSA committee, political parties are perhaps the most archaic institutions in the United States. The American party system continued to operate essentially as it had before the Civil War, as two loose coalitions of state and local organizations with very little national machinery and very little national cohesion. Such a system may once have been adequate in American politics, but the parties developed in a period when local interests were dominant and the national government had not assumed the role it was to play later. The growth of the federal government's responsibilities during the twentieth century rendered traditional party organizations inadequate to the demands of American society. The expansion and growing complexity of public problems indicated that it was "no longer safe for the nation to deal piecemeal with issues that can be disposed of only on the basis of a coherent program."[1]

The need for a more systematic government regulation of society, the committee argues, requires a more "effective" party system, meaning, first, that the parties be able to create programs to which they commit themselves and, second, that they possess sufficient internal cohesion to carry out these programs. But the "ineffective" American party system was ill equipped to organize its members in the legislative and executive branches into a government held together and guided by a party program. For this reason, there is little correspondence, the committee argues, between what happens at the polls and eventual government action. The Committee claims that the responsibility of parties centered on their conduct of government policy-making, and in the absence of a link between party program and public policy, party responsibility at the polls tends to vanish.[2]

In considering this report anew, roughly forty years after its publication, it is important to place its message in historical context. The report of the APSA committee is presented as though it contains a novel statement on the state of the American party system. Yet this is misleading, for the doctrine of party responsibility was widely known by the time of the report's publication. It was not invented by the committee in 1950. Woodrow Wilson, in thought and practice, had advanced the doctrine of responsible party government, conceiving the idea that it was possible to strengthen the party system by remodeling the presidency somewhat after the pattern of the British prime minister. Wilson's presidency, in turn, had a strong influence on Franklin Roosevelt whose extraordinary party leadership both anticipated and influenced the critics of the party system of the late 1940s and 1950s. Indeed, E. E. Schattschneider, who chaired the APSA committee, notes in his seminal *Party Government* (1942), a volume which contains many of the ideas that would inform *Toward a More Responsible Two-Party System*, that Roosevelt's attempt to reform the Democratic Party, particularly the so-called purge campaign of 1938, represented "one of the greatest experimental tests of the nature of the American party system ever made."[3]

The New Deal test of the nature of the American party system is the central focus of this chapter. Roosevelt's party leadership and the New Deal mark a critical historical moment in the development of the American party system, namely, the culmination of efforts, which begin in the Progressive Era, to loosen the grip of partisan politics on the councils of power with a view to strengthening national administrative capacities and extending the programmatic commitments of American government. The American party system was forged on the anvil of Jeffersonian principles and thus wedded to constitutional arrangements such as legislative supremacy and a strict construction of the national government's authority that were designed to constrain state action. The origins and organizing principles of the American party system had established it as a political force against the creation of a modern state. The New Deal commitment to building such a state meant that party politics had to be reconstituted or destroyed. Paradoxically, New Deal politics both reconstituted and weakened partisanship in the United States. On the one hand, Roosevelt's efforts to infuse the Democratic Party with, as he put it, a commitment to "militant liberalism" established the foundation for a more national and programmatic party system.[4] On the other hand, the New Deal facilitated the development of a "modern" presidency and administrative apparatus that displaced party politics and collective responsibility with executive administration.

Because of this twofold effect, there has been much scholarly debate about FDR's goals and accomplishments as party leader. To some, including Schattschneider, Roosevelt's leadership of the Democratic Party reinvigorated partisan politics and facilitated a realignment that addressed more clearly the fundamental political issues of the twentieth century, those related to industrial conflict in the United States.[5] Others, however, construe Roosevelt's actions as party leader as a failure because he emphasized a personalized presidential politics more than partisanship. His presidency, therefore, was one of "broker" leadership that failed ultimately to bring about a truly reformed party system; that is, the New Deal electoral realignment did not create a partisan politics structured by strongly disciplined and ideologically committed party organizations.[6]

In fact, Roosevelt was both very serious and somewhat unsure in his efforts to alter the basis of the American party system. Although FDR wanted to change the character of the Democratic Party and thereby also influence a change in the American party system, he concluded ultimately that the public good and practical politics demanded that partisan politics be deemphasized rather than restructured. In particular, once the presidency and executive department were "modernized," some of the burden of party loyalty would be alleviated, freeing the chief executive, as leader of the whole people, to effect more directly the development of society and economy.

In this respect, New Deal party politics, more than any other critical period of party development, reveals the possibilities and limits of party government in the United States. Furthermore, the New Deal directed the Progressive animus against decentralized parties in a way that eschewed party government and paved an alternative road to a stronger national government. The New Deal dedication to concentrating policy responsibility in a revamped executive resulted in institutional changes that rendered the struggle for party government a moot issue, at least for a time.

Programmatic Liberalism and the American Party System

In the introduction to the 1938 volume of his presidential papers and addresses, written in 1941, Roosevelt explains that his efforts to modify the Democratic Party were undertaken to strengthen party responsibility to the electorate and commit his party more fully to progressive reform:

> I believe it to be my sworn duty, as President, to take all steps necessary to insure the continuance of liberalism in our government. I believe, at the same time, that it is my duty as the head of the Democratic party to see to it that my party remains the truly liberal party in the political life of America.
>
> There have been many periods in American history, unfortunately, when one major political party was no different than the other major party—except only in name. In a system of party government such as ours, however, elections become meaningless when the two major parties have no differences other than their labels. For such elections do not give the people of the United States an opportunity to decide upon the type of government which they prefer for the next two or the next four years as the case may be. . . .
>
> Generally speaking, in a representative form of government, there are generally two schools of political belief—liberal and conservative. The system of party responsibility in American politics requires that one of its parties be the liberal party and the other the conservative party.[7]

Roosevelt's party politics, then, were based on constitutional and policy considerations that would later be expressed in the report of the APSA committee. Like the authors of that report, FDR believed that democratic government requires a more meaningful link between the councils of government and the electorate; furthermore, he reasoned that the clarification of political choice and centralization of authority would allow for more advantageous conditions to bring about meaningful policy action at the national level. He wanted to overcome the state and local orientation of the party system, which was suited to congressional primacy and poorly organized for progressive action by the national government, and to establish a national, executive-oriented party that would be more suitably organized for the expression of national purposes.

In this endeavor, FDR was influenced by the thought and actions of Woodrow Wilson, the first American writer to advance the doctrine of responsible party government. According to Wilson, the major flaw of American political parties is their link with an interpretation of the Constitution that emphasizes a decentralization of power. The decentralized structure of parties had served the country well enough during the nineteenth century, providing a useful context for facilitating consensus and coordinating the limited national purpose in government action. But Wilson thought that further progress in American society required the development of party organizations that could be vessels of a stronger and more permanent expression of national purpose:

> Party organization is no longer needed or the mere rudimentary task of holding the machinery together or giving it the sustenance of some common object, some single cooperative motive. The time is at hand when we can safely maximize the network of party in its detail and change its structure without imperilling its strength. This thing that has served us so well might now master us if we left it irresponsible. We must see to it that it is made responsible.[8]

To make parties more responsible, Wilson initially proposed major institutional reforms that would establish closer ties between the executive and the legislature in an arrangement akin to the British cabinet system. He never abandoned his view that the constitutional system of checks and balances should be replaced by an American version of the parliamentary system, but his focus did shift from Congress to the presidency as the institution through which to realize this end. Impressed by the presidency of Theodore Roosevelt, Wilson concluded that the president, as leader of national opinion, could fuse the executive and legislative branches in his person and that the party system should be modified so that it would serve the president.

In practice, Wilson found it difficult to reconcile Progressivism with the demands of party leader. To be sure, he established himself as the leader of public opinion in a way that helped to transform the presidency. Indeed, his ability to bring the pressure of public opinion upon Congress and assert dominance over the party caucuses in both legislative chambers made Wilson the principal spokesman for the Democratic Party. At the same time, Wilson was persuaded by his postmaster general, Albert Burleson, a veteran of Congress, to accept traditional partisan practices concerning legislative deliberations and appointments. This strategy, combined with his ability to mobilize public opinion, gave Wilson nearly absolute mastery over the Democratic party and its members in Congress, but at the same time it failed to strengthen the Democratic Party organization or its commitment to Progressive principles.

Franklin Roosevelt was less committed than Wilson to working through existing partisan channels; but more importantly, the New Deal was a more fundamental departure from traditional Democratic politics than was Wilsonian Progressivism. Until the 1930s, the patron saint of the Democrats had been Thomas Jefferson, and it was widely understood that this impled a commitment to individual autonomy, states' rights, and a limited role for the national government.[9] The Jeffersonian party system, designed to keep power close enough to the people for republican government to prevail, advanced a public philosophy that supported a strict interpretation of the national government's powers. After Jefferson's triumph in 1800, the party took as its principal task the dismantling of Hamilton's program for a strong executive. Indeed, the purpose of presidential party leadership in the Jeffersonian mold was to capture the executive office to contain and minimize its potential. This system, in its appeals and organization, as James Pierson observes, created a tension between politics and government because the decentralized process of party politics was "hostile" to governmental centralization and bureaucracy.[10]

With Jefferson, American political parties were organized as popular institutions, but they were formed when popular rule meant limiting the power of national government. Before the New Deal, presidents who sought to exercise executive power expansively, or perceived a need to expand the national government's powers, were thwarted, as Stephen Skowronek notes, "by the tenacity of this highly mobilized, highly competitive, and locally oriented democracy."[11] Even Woodrow Wilson's program for extending the role of the national government remained in its essentials committed to the Jeffersonian principle of decentralized power. Indeed, Herbert Croly, whose Progressivism resurrected Hamilton and envisioned a "new nationalism" with the federal government as "steward of the public welfare," lamented Wilson's victory in 1912 as the triumph of "a higher conservatism over progressive democracy." Croly supported Theodore Roosevelt, the standard-bearer of the Progressive Party who was the only candidate in this campaign to advocate "the substitution of frank social policy for the individualism of the past."[12]

The decisive break with the American tradition of limited government, anticipated by Theodore Roosevelt's Progressive Party campaign in 1912, came with Franklin Roosevelt in the 1930s and his deft reinterpretation of the "liberal" tradition in American politics. Liberalism had always been associated with Jeffersonian principles and the natural rights tradition of limited government drawn from Locke's *Second Treatise* and the Declaration of Independence. Roosevelt pronounced a new liberalism in which constitutional government and the natural rights tradition were not abandoned but linked to programmatic expansion and an activist national government. As the public philosophy of the New Deal, this new liberalism, in its programmatic form, required a rethinking of the idea of natural rights in American politics.

Roosevelt first spoke of the need to modernize elements of the old faith in the Commonwealth Club address, delivered during the 1932 campaign and appropriately understood as the New Deal manifesto. The theme was that the time had come—indeed, had come three decades earlier—to recognize the "new terms of the old social contract." It was necessary to rewrite the social contract to take account of a national economy remade by industrial capitalism and the concentration of economic power, a new contract to establish a countervailing power—a stronger national state—lest the United States steer "a steady course toward economic oligarchy." Protection of the national welfare must shift from the private citizen to the government; the guarantee of equal opportunity required that individual initiative be restrained and directed by the national state.

> Clearly all this calls for a reappraisal of values. Our task is not discovery or exploitation of national resources or necessarily producing new goods. It is the soberer, less dramatic business of administering resources and plants already in hand, of seeking to reestablish foreign markets for our surplus production, of meeting the problem of under consumption, of adjusting production to consumption, of distributing wealth and products more equitably, of adapting existing economic organizations to the service of the people. The day of enlightened administration has come.[13]

The creation of a national state with expansive supervisory powers would be a "long, slow task." The Commonwealth Club address was sensitive to the uneasy fit between energetic central government and the Constitution. It was imperative, therefore, that the New Deal be informed by a public philosophy in which the new concept of state power would be carefully interwoven with earlier conceptions of American government. The task of modern government, FDR announced, was "to assist the development of an economic declaration of rights, an economic constitutional order." The traditional emphasis in American politics on individual self-reliance should therefore give way to a new understanding of individualism in which the government acted as a regulating and unifying agency, guaranteeing individual men and women protection from the uncertainties of the marketplace.

Most significant in this shift from natural rights to programmatic liberalism is the association of constitutional rights with the *expansion* (rather than the restriction) of the role of the national government. The defense of Progressive reform as an extension of rights in the Constitution was critical to the development of a positive understanding of government responsibility in the United States. The use of the term *liberalism* by Franklin Roosevelt, moreover, gave legitimacy to the nationalist principles of Croly's Progressivism, embedding them in the parlance of constitutionalism as an extension, rather than the transcendence, of the natural rights tradition.

The need to construct an economic constitutional order, first articulated in the Commonwealth address, was a consistent theme of Roosevelt's long presidency. The 1936 platform was, at FDR's insistence, written as a pastiche of the Declaration and emphasized the need for a fundamental reexamination of rights since the natural rights tradition had to be enlarged to include programmatic rights if the national government was to meet its new obligations. With respect to the 1935 Social Security legislation, the platform claims:

> We hold this truth to be self-evident—that the test of representative government is its ability to promote the safety and happiness of the people. . . . We have built foundations for the security of those who are faced with the hazards of unemployment and old age; for the orphaned, the crippled, and the blind. On the foundation of the Social Security Act we are determined to erect a structure of economic security for all our people, making sure that this benefit shall keep step with the ever-increasing capacity of America to provide a high standard of living for all its citizens.[14]

As FDR would later detail in his 1944 State of the Union address, constructing a foundation for economic security meant that the inalienable rights secured by the Constitution—speech, press, worship, due process—had to be supplemented by a second bill of rights "under which a new basis of security and prosperity can be established for all—regardless of station, race, or creed."[15]

These new programmatic rights were never formally ratified as part of the Constitution, but they became the foundation of political dialogue, redefining the role of the national government. The new social contract heralded by FDR marks the beginning of what has been called the rights revolution—a transformation in the governing philosophy of the United States that has brought about major changes in American political institutions.[16]

Roosevelt's reappraisal of values is important to understanding the New Deal, but it is also important in understanding FDR's impact on the Democratic Party. Under the leadership of Roosevelt, the Democrats became the instrument of greater national purpose. Ultimately, this purpose was directed to the creation of an administrative state that would displace partisan politics with "enlightened administration." This attempt to *transcend* rather than *reform* the American party system bespeaks the limited prospects for establishing party government in the United States.

For New Dealers, the idea of the welfare state was not a partisan issue. It was a "constitutional" matter that required eliminating partisanship about the national government's obligation to provide economic security for the American people. Nevertheless, this displacement of partisan politics required in the short run a major partisan effort to generate popular support for the new economic constitutional order. To a point, this made partisanship an integral part of New Deal politics, for it was necessary to remake the Democratic Party as an instrument to free the councils of government, particularly the president and the bureaucracy, from the restraints of traditional party politics and constitutional understandings.

Party Responsibility and the New Deal

Roosevelt was less diffident than Wilson about overcoming the limits of constitutional government, and he was more intent upon transforming the principles and organization of the Democratic party. As president-elect, he prepared to modify the partisan practices of previous administrations and soon after his election began to evaluate the personnel policy of Wilson with a view to committing his own administration to more progressive appointments. Josephus Daniels, Wilson's secretary of the navy for whom FDR served as assistant secretary, wrote a letter to Roosevelt in December 1932 noting that President-elect Wilson had promised to "nominate progressives—and only progressives." The "pity," Daniels complained, was that Wilson adhered to traditional patronage practices and "appointed some who wouldn't recognize a Progressive principle if he met it in the road."[17] A few weeks later, FDR expressed to Attorney General Homer Cummings his desire to avoid Wilson's betrayal of the pledge to appoint reformers to the executive branch. According to Cummings, Roosevelt was determined to proceed along different lines with a view "to building up a national organization rather than allowing patronage to be used merely to build Senatorial and Congressional machines."[18]

During his first term, FDR generally followed traditional partisan practices, allowing the Democratic Chairman James Farley to coordinate appointments in response to local organizations and Democratic senators, but the recommendations of organization people were not followed so closely after 1936. Beginning especially in 1938, Roosevelt's assault on the traditional party apparatus became more aggressive, and patronage practices began to circumvent the traditional organization altogether. White House aides, notably Thomas Corcoran, became more influential in dispensing patronage. Ed Flynn, who became Democratic chairman in 1940, recalls the growing tension between Farley and Roosevelt:

> By reason of the coolness between the two, the President turned more and more frequently to the so-called New Dealers who were then surrounding him. Under the leadership of Corcoran, these people became more and more pressing in their urging of appointments. In a sense, this short-circuited the National Committee over which Farley presided. As a result, many of the appointments in Washington went to men who were supporters of the President and believed in what he was trying to do, but who were not Democrats in many instances, and in all instances were not organization Democrats.[19]

From a political point of view, this departure from conventional patronage practices resulted, as Paul Van Riper notes, "in the development of another kind of patronage, a sort of intellectual and ideological patronage rather than the more traditional partisan type."[20] In bypassing the state party leaders and the national committee in selecting personnel, the administration was in a sense politically nonpartisan, but careful attention was given to the political commitments and associations of appointees, thus resulting in a loosely knit, albeit well-defined group of individuals whose loyalties were to the New Deal rather than the Democratic Party.

FDR's attempt to make the Democrats into a more national party focused not only on the national committee, which was dominated by state and local party leaders, but also on Congress, which registered state and local policy interests at the national level. Whereas Wilson was careful to associate himself with legislative party leaders in the development of his policy program, Roosevelt relegated the party in Congress to a decidedly subordinate status. Though he used Farley and Vice President John Nance Garner, especially during the first term, to maintain close ties with Congress, party leaders complained that they were called into consultation only when their signatures were required at the bottom of the page to make the document legal. Moreover, FDR offended legislators by his use of press conferences to announce important decisions before he communicated them to a coordinate branch of government.

Thus, by the end of Roosevelt's first term, Congress was "chafing at its subordinate position," and much more than after the first four years of Wilson's presidency it was looking for an opportunity to rebuke this popular president who threatened to relegate it to the position of a "rubber stamp."[21] Wilson's cultivation of party leaders in Congress reflected his interest in giving constitutional form to a parliamentary system, or at least an approximation of that system.[22] In contrast, Roosevelt saw the party as a limited means to strengthen administration and reconstruct the nation's political economy. He supported a stronger role for parties, at least in the short run, to crystallize public opinion and demarcate issues. With respect to government, however, Roosevelt tended to view traditional party politics as an obstacle to be overcome more than an institution to be reformed.

Roosevelt therefore made little use of the congressional party caucus. He rejected as impractical the suggestion of Congressman Alfred Phillips, Jr., "that those sharing the burden of responsibility of party government should regularly and often be called into caucus and that such caucuses should evolve party policies and choice of party leaders." FDR politely suggested that this proposal for the use of the caucus as an instrument of party responsibility foundered on the rock of organization. "Frankly, it is a question of machinery—how to do it. . . . After all, there are four hundred and thirty-five Congressman and ninety-six Senators, many of whom have very decided ideas on individual points which they are not at all hesitant to explain at any meeting which might be held."[23]

FDR's refusal to confine his consultation to the party leaders, relying instead on New Deal loyalists regardless of their political affiliation, marked an unprecedented challenge to party responsibility as traditionally understood in American politics. "If Democrats on Capitol Hill have any pride in the New Deal," White House aide Stanley High asserted in 1937, "it is certainly not the pride of authorship. Its authorship goes back to the President himself, and to the assortment of political hybrids with which he was surrounded."[24]

The most dramatic moment in Roosevelt's challenge to traditional party practices was the "purge" campaign of 1938. This involved FDR directly in one gubernatorial and several congressional primary campaigns in a bold effort to replace conservative Democrats with candidates who were "100 percent New Dealers." Such intervention was not unprecedented; William H. Taft and Wilson had made limited efforts to remove recalcitrant members from their parties. But Roosevelt's campaign was unprecedented in its scale, and unlike previous efforts, it made no attempt to work through the regular party organization. The degree to which his action was a departure from the norm is measured by the press labeling it the *purge*, a term associated with Adolf Hitler's attempt to weed out dissent in Germany's National Socialist party and

Joseph Stalin's elimination of "disloyal" party members from the Soviet Communist party.

FDR's campaign focused primarily on the South, a Democratic stronghold since the Civil War whose commitment to states' rights represented, as the journalist Thomas Stokes put it, "the ball and chain which hobbled the party's forward march."[25] The purge was undertaken not only to overcome the obstacle posed by conservative Democrats to completion of the New Deal but also to alter the structure of the party system. Unlike Wilson, FDR always doubted that political parties in the United States could be modeled after the British system of party government. Nevertheless, he realized that if programmatic liberals were to have a place in future Democratic administrations, chief executives had to be made less dependent upon the convention system and the regular partisan apparatus, which was dominated by Congress and state party leaders. An important victory in the campaign for a more national and programmatic party came in 1936 when the Roosevelt administration succeeded in abolishing the Democratic Party's two-thirds rule for presidential nominations. This rule required backing from two-thirds of the delegates to Democratic national conventions for the nominations of president and vice president. The South had long regarded the rule as a vital protection against the nomination of candidates unsympathetic to its problems. Elimination of the rule weakened southern Democrats and removed an important obstacle to the transformation of a decentralized party responsible only to a local electorate into an organization more responsive to the will of a national party leader—the president—and the interests of a national electorate.

Roosevelt's command of the party, as the rise of the so-called conservative coalition in the Seventy-fifth Congress (1937–38) attests, did not overcome factionalism within Democratic ranks. But New Deal programs and party reforms did alter the structure of conflict within the party. Historically a multifactional party dominated by sectional interests, the Democrats after 1936 became a bifactional party with durable ideological and policy divisions.[26]

If the Democrats were to become a national liberal party, conservative southern Democrats would have to be defeated. Roosevelt did not confine his efforts to the South during the 1938 purge attempt, but his most outspoken and unequivocal opposition was directed against his party brethren below the Mason-Dixon line. His fireside chat to the nation in June 1938, which launched the purge campaign, compared recalcitrant Democrats to "copperheads," who, FDR reminded the nation, "in the days of the war between the States tried their best to make Lincoln and his Congress give up the fight, let the Nation remain split in two and return to peace—peace at any price."[27] The president's reference to events of the Civil War and the fact that he most actively sought to unseat incumbent Democrats in the South conjured images of a renewed northern assault upon the region, one that "would precipitate another reconstruction era for us," as the conservative Virginia Senator Carter Glass wrote a friend.[28]

A New Deal reconstruction of southern politics promised an alignment of parties defined by bold party doctrine. As Roosevelt observed in defending his attack on conservative Democrats who were reluctant to go along with the New Deal program:

> My participation in these primary campaigns was slurringly referred to, by those who were opposed to liberalism, as a "purge." The word became a slogan for those who tried to misrepresent my conduct to make it appear to be an effort to defeat certain Senators and Representatives who had voted against one measure or another recommended by me. . . . Nothing could be further from the truth. I was not interested in personality. Nor was I interested in particular measures. . . . I was, however, primarily interested in seeing to it that the Democratic party and the Republican party should not be merely Tweedledum and Tweedledee to each other. I was chiefly interested in continuing the Democratic party as the liberal, forward looking, progressive party in the United States.[29]

Administrative Reform and Party Decline

After the 1938 purge attempt, the columnist Raymond Clapper observed, "No president has ever gone as far as Mr. Roosevelt in striving to stamp his policies upon his party."[30] This massive partisan effort initiated a process whereby the party system evolved from predominantly local to increasingly national and programmatic party organizations. At the same time, the New Deal made partisanship less important. Roosevelt's partisan leadership, though it effected important changes in the Democratic Party, envisioned a personal link with the public that would enable the president to govern from his position as leader of the nation rather than just the leader of his party.[31] In all but one of the 1938 primary campaigns in which he personally participated, Roosevelt chose to make a direct appeal to public opinion rather than attempt to work through or reform the regular party apparatus. His ability to appeal broadly to the nation was enhanced by Progressive reforms, especially the direct primary, that had begun to weaken the grip of party organization on the voters.

Like Wilson, Roosevelt supported the direct primary. In launching the purge, he noted:

> Fifty years ago party nominations were generally made in conventions—a system typified in the public imagination by a little group in a smoke filled room who made out the party slates. The direct primary was invented to make the nominating process a more direct one—to give the party voters themselves a chance to pick their candidates.[32]

The spread of the direct primary enabled the president to make a direct appeal to the public over the heads of congressional candidates and local party leaders and thus was a useful vehicle for an attack upon traditional party politics. Furthermore, radio broadcasting afforded the opportunity to appeal directly to large audiences, which was especially attractive to an extremely popular president with as fine a radio presence as Roosevelt's.

In the final analysis, the "benign dictatorship" Roosevelt sought to impose on the Democratic Party was corrosive to the American party system. Wilson's prescription for party reform—extraordinary presidential leadership—posed a serious if not intractable dilemma: The decentralized character of American politics can be modified only by strong presidential leadership, but a president determined to alter fundamentally the connection between the executive and his party will eventually shatter party unity. Herbert Croly criticizes Wilson's concept of presidential party leadership on precisely these terms:

> At the final test the responsibility is his rather than that of his party. The party that submits to such a dictatorship, however benevolent, cannot play its own proper part in a system of partisan government. It will either cease to have any independent life or its independence will eventually assume the form of revolt.[33]

The report of the APSA committee, published in the wake of the Roosevelt presidency, expresses a similar view, warning that the weakness of political parties in the United States is leading to an "overextension" of presidential power. In language strikingly similar to Croly's, the report asserts that such an aggrandizement of executive responsibility is a dangerous alternative to, rather than a instrument of, party responsibility: "When the President's program actually is the sole program, either his party becomes a flock of sheep or the party falls apart. This concept of the presidency disposes of the party system by making the President reach directly for the support of the majority of the voters."[34] Only the creation of a more responsible party system, the report argues, "which could furnish the President and Congress a political basis of cooperation within the Constitution," can restrain the personal power of the president. Still, the authors offer no solution to the dilemma posed by Wilson's prescription for strengthening party responsibility.

Roosevelt was well aware of the limited extent to which his purposes could be achieved by party government in the American context. Indeed, it is useful to consider further Croly's criticism of Wilson's concept of party leadership because FDR's sensitivity to this criticism sheds light on the long-term objectives and consequences of New Deal reform. To Croly, Wilson's institutional understanding is flawed by its failure to confront the limits of partisanship. Wilson was correct to view nineteenth-century constitutional mechanisms and party politics as impediments to programmatic reform, but the popularity of measures such as the direct primary revealed how centralized and disciplined parties went *against* the looser genius of American politics. To the extent that government became committed to a democratic program that was essentially social in character, the American people would find intolerable a two-party system that stood between popular will and governmental machinery.[35]

At the same time, Wilson's false hope for partisanship caused him to underestimate the degree to which progressive democracy required "administrative aggrandizement," the development of executive agencies as the principal instruments of democratic life. For Croly, progressive democracy's commitment to expanding the programmatic responsibilities of the national government "particularly need[ed] an increase of administrative authority and efficiency." In addition, the growing dependence of elected officials upon public opinion would yield a more flexible and fluid method of representation, thus necessarily imposing an increased burden on the administrative department of government. The American party system, however, was established as an institution to control administrative authority; it "bestowed upon the divided Federal government a certain unity of control, while at the same time it prevented the increased efficiency of the Federal system from being obnoxious to local interests." The consequent weakening of administrative authority, although rooted in the "pioneer" conditions of the nineteenth century, Croly argues, is an essential and incorrigible aspect of the two-party system. "Under American conditions," therefore, "a strong responsible and efficient administration of the law and public business would be fatal to partisan responsibility."[36]

Wilson believed, as apparently the authors of the APSA report on responsible parties did, that it is possible to strengthen simultaneously both parties *and* administration. In effect, a reformed bureaucracy carries out "professionally" the programmatic initiatives coming from a government organized effectively by a majority political party.[37] But

Croly argues that the principal instrument of responsible party politics, strong presidential leadership, will inevitably be enfeebled by the need to win over fellow partisans in Congress. For that, cooperation can come only from the president's acquiescence to patronage and administrative decentralization—the sustaining elements of party politics in the United States. The essential character of the party system, therefore, could not be dislodged without a transcendence of party politics itself. In the final analysis, Croly argues, Wilson's notion that the president could transform the practices that sustain parties is unrealistic:

> The executive has not the power to make an effective fight against the system, because public opinion, on which he depends for his weapons, still fails to understand its real importance. In cleaving to it party leaders in Congress are cleaving to the strongest and most necessary prop of the party system, but by so doing they are making the destruction of that system an indispensable condition of the success of progressive democracy.[38]

As president, Wilson found it necessary to sacrifice administrative reform on the alter of party unity. In the end, his commitment to working within the party system, which impeded the development of a national state to direct social and economic matters, reflected his ambivalence about expanding the administrative power of the national government. The New Nationalism advocated by Theodore Roosevelt in 1912 represented a much more ambitious commitment to Progressive reform than did the New Freedom program of Wilson whose tendency, Croly observes, was to emphasize those aspects of Progressivism, such as antitrust policy, that could be "interpreted as the emancipation of an essentially excellent system from corrupting and perverting parasites."[39]

In Croly's view, the triumph of a new nationalism necessarily requires, as the Progressives' bolt from the Republican ranks in 1912 foreshadowed, the rejection of the American party system. Indeed, the Progressive Party's support for a more direct government—organized by measures such as the direct primary as well as the initiative, referendum, and recall—reflects the willingness of its members to dispense with the two-party system. As Barry Karl has written of the Progressive Party of 1912, it "was as much an attack on the whole concept of political parties as it was an effort to create a single party whose doctrinal clarity and moral purity would represent the true interest of the nation as a whole."[40]

The debate within the Progressive tradition about the role of party is a critical precursor to New Deal partisanship. FDR patterned his leadership after Woodrow Wilson's *and* Theodore Roosevelt's, thus seeking to reconcile the strengths of these two leaders and the programs they represented. Unlike Croly, he was not willing to abandon the two-party system. He believed party leadership, at least for a time, was necessary to organize public opinion into a governing coalition. FDR was persuaded, however, that strengthening the state required the decline if not demise of traditional partisan politics. He shared the view of New Nationalists that the traditional party apparatus was for the most part beyond repair, so wedded was it to the fragmented institutions of American politics.

Even if the intransigent localism of the party system could be eliminated and a more national party system formed, there would still be the Constitution's separation of powers to overcome. These institutional arrangements, even with nationalized parties, would still encourage the free play of rival interests and factions, thus making ongoing cooperation between the president and Congress unlikely. This skepticism about party government—about the possibility of parties providing a political basis for cooperation between the president and Congress within the Constitution—helps to explain why the purge campaign was limited to a few Senate and congressional contests, for the most part in the South, rather than undertaken as a comprehensive nationwide strategy to elect New Dealers.

The failure of the purge to imprint the New Deal indelibly upon his party majority only reinforced FDR's disinclination to seek a fundamental restructuring of the party system. The purge campaign was successful in only two of the twelve states targeted, Oregon and New York, and it galvanized opposition throughout the nation, apparently contributing to the heavy losses the Democrats sustained in the 1938 general elections. Former Wisconsin governor Philip LaFollette, one of several Progressives who went down to crushing defeat in 1938, concluded: "The results of the so-called purge by President Roosevelt showed that the fight to make the Democratic party liberal is a hopeless one."[41]

E. E. Schattschneider, chairman of the APSA Committee on Political Parties, drew a different conclusion. In a 1948 lecture, he asserted that the failed purge campaign did not render the struggle for party government a moot point. "The outcome of the purge of 1938," he argued, "does not prove that a more serious attempt supported by the whole body of national party leaders could not bring overwhelming pressure to bear on the local party leaders who control congressional nominations."[42] But neither FDR nor any president since has risked a similar effort, let alone a more expansive one, to hold his fellow partisans to a national party program. The purge campaign and its aftermath suggests that resistance to party government under presidential leadership is not merely built into the Constitution and laws but is deeply rooted in a political culture that gives preference to a different way of governing.[43]

The Roosevelt administration's rejection of party government thus developed for reasons both practical and principled—for constitutional reasons that are at once excruciatingly American and a severe challenge to the traditional concept of government responsibility in the United States. The "economic constitutional order" conceived of New Deal programs like Social Security as rights. In principle, these programs were to be permanent entitlements, like speech and assembly, beyond the vagaries of public opinion, elections, and party politics. Once established, as one New Dealer put it:

> We may assume the nature of the problems of American life are such as not to permit any political party for any length of time to abandon most of the collectivist functions which are now being exercised. This is true even though the details of policy programs may differ and even though the old slogans of opposition to governmental activity will survive long after their meaning has been sucked out.[44]

Thus, the most significant institutional reforms of the New Deal did not promote party government but fostered instead a program that would enable the president to govern in the *absence* of party government. The president would be the manager of the people's rights. This program, as embodied in the 1937 executive reorganization bill, was based on the Brownlow committee report.[45] It proposed measures to expand significantly the staff support of the executive office and to extend greatly presidential authority over the executive branch, including the independent regulatory commissions. The strengthened executive that emerged in this report would also be delegated authority to govern, so that as Luther Gulick, a member of the Brownlow committee, anticipated, laws would be little more than "a declaration of war, so that the essence of the program is in the gradual unfolding of the plan in actual administration."[46]

Party politics would be displaced by an executive-centered administrative politics generated by the activities of a dominant and dominating presidency. Whereas a reconstituted party system would strengthen ties between the executive and legislature, the administrative design of the New Deal combined executive action and public policy, so that the president and executive agencies would be delegated authority to govern, thus making unnecessary the constant cooperation of party members in Congress and the states. Louis Brownlow, in a 1943 memorandum to Roosevelt, reflected on this objective of executive reorganization: "We must reconsider critically the scholarly assumption, which has almost become a popular assumption, that the way to produce unity between legislature and executive is to take steps toward merging the two." Thus, commenting specifically on a book proposal that the United States abandon its presidential system in favor of a parliamentary system, Brownlow added:

> In view of the extreme improbability that such a measure would receive organized support, it is worth mentioning only because it carries to a logical conclusion the common proposals (1) to have the Congress establish by statute a cabinet or administrative council for the president; (2) to give department heads or "Cabinet" members seats in Congress, the right to take part in Congressional discussions, or the duty to defend their administration before the Congress; (3) to set up a joint legislative-executive committee, or committees, to plan policy and supervise administration; and (4) to create a committee of congressional leaders to advise the President. . . . *In direct opposition to this assumption and these proposals, it may be suggested that the objective to be sought is not to unify executive and legislature, but to unify governmental policy and administration.*[47]

Roosevelt and his administrative management committee believed that the development of responsible party government was contrary to American political traditions. They looked instead to presidential government as a means to achieve an activist state in the United States. To be sure, political parties were not irrelevant to the task of "state-building." Indeed, the administrative reform program became, at FDR's urging, a party program. Thus, ironically, a policy aimed at making party politics less important became a major focus of party responsibility. So strongly did Roosevelt favor this legislation that House Majority Leader Sam Rayburn appealed for party unity before the critical vote on the executive reorganization bill, arguing that the defeat of this legislation would amount to a "vote of no confidence" in the president.[48]

FDR lost the vote of confidence on administrative reform in April 1938 as the House of Representatives, with massive Democratic defections, voted down the legislation. It was a devastating defeat for Roosevelt, which together with that of the court-packing bill, also closely linked to strengthening administrative power, led FDR to undertake the purge campaign a few months later.[49] The purge failed at the polls, but it scared recalcitrant Democrats, who became more conciliatory toward their president on a few matters after the 1938 election. Administrative reform was one of these, and in 1939 a significant executive-reorganization bill passed the Congress. Although considerably weaker than Roosevelt's original proposal, the 1939 act provided authority to create the White House Office and the Executive Office of the President and enhanced the chief executive's control over administrative agencies. This legislation represents the genesis of the institutional presidency, which was better equipped to govern independently of the constraints imposed by the separation of powers. It set off a new dynamic whereby executive administration, coupled with the greater personal responsibility of the president enhanced by FDR's political leadership and the emergence of the mass media, diminished the role of collective responsibility in American politics in many ways.

The battle for the destiny of the Democratic Party during Roosevelt's second term, therefore, was directly tied to strengthening the presidency and the executive department as the vital center of government action. FDR's success transformed the Democrats into a party of administration, dedicated to enacting an institutional program that would make parties less important. It became a party to end party politics. Theodore Roosevelt and Herbert Croly had conceived of the Progressive Party campaign as an assault on party politics. Unlike his cousin, however, Franklin Roosevelt presided over a full-scale partisan realignment, the first in American history to place executive leadership at the heart of its approach to politics and government. The traditional party system had provided presidents with a stable basis of popular support and episodically during critical partisan realignments with the opportunity to achieve national reform. What was once episodic must now become routine. As the Brownlow report put it: "Our national will must be expressed not merely in a brief, exultant moment of electoral decision, but in a persistent, determined, competent day-by-day administration of what the nation has decided to do."[50]

Thus, the New Deal realignment prepared the ground for the decline of party, a development that FDR explicitly appreciated and supported. Interestingly, he chose the 1940 Jackson Day dinner, a party event, to herald a less partisan future. To establish the right mood, FDR went so far as to invite the Republican leaders to the Democratic celebration, an invitation they declined. In his address, Roosevelt observed that the independent vote was on the increase, that party loyalties were becoming less significant, and that "the future lies with those wise political leaders who realize the great public is interested more in government than in politics."[51] The future of the American political system, then, was predicated on the emergence of a policy-making state; its development meant that party politics and debate were subordinated to a "second bill of rights" and the delivery of services associated with those rights.

For a time, the modern presidency was at the center of this new political universe. With the strengthening of executive administration, the presidency became dissociated from party politics, undermining the latter's importance. As the presidency evolved into a ubiquitous institution, it preempted party leaders in many of their limited but significant tasks: linking the president to interest groups, staffing the executive department, policy development, and most important, campaign support. Presidents no longer won election and governed as head of a party but were elected and governed as the head of a personal organization they created in their own image.[52]

But the purpose of New Deal reforms was not to strengthen presidential government per se. Rather, the presidency was strengthened under the assumption that as the national office, it would be an ally of Progressive reform. Consequently, executive power was refurbished in a way compatible with the objectives of programmatic liberalism, and administrative reform was intended to insulate reformers and reforms from the presidential election cycle. By executive orders issued with authority granted by the 1939 executive reorganization act, most of the emergency programs of the New Deal were established as permanent institutions. Moreover, the Roosevelt administration obtained legislative authority in the 1940 Ramspeck Act to extend civil service protection over the New Deal loyalists who were brought to Washington to staff the newly created welfare state. New Deal civil service reform, therefore, did not replace politics with administration, nor did it replace patronage practices with civil service procedures dedicated to "neutral competence." Rather, it transformed the political character of administration. Previously, the choice was posed as one between politics and spoils on the one hand and nonpartisan, nonpolitical administration on the other. The New Deal celebrated an administrative politics that denied nourishment to the regular party apparatus but fed instead an executive department oriented toward expanding liberal programs.

The New Deal Institutional Legacy and the Doctrine of Responsible Party Government

It might be said that the reforms proposed by the APSA committee, dedicated to forming a "responsible" two-party system, were preempted by the New Deal institutional program, which chartered an alternative path to a more national and programmatic government. This path, the New Dealers believed, was more compatible with the principles and history of American constitutional government. One of the architects of this institutional program, Charles Merriam, observed in 1931 that he did not expect to see the development of a British-style party government in the United States. "There is little probability of a modification of the Constitution either by amendment or custom in such a fashion as to permit the adoption of a parliamentary system," he surmised, "in view of the fact that the trend is strongly in the direction of Presidential government, with constant strengthening of executive power."[53] Merriam's commentary was not simply prescient; as a member of the Brownlow committee, he would play an important part in consolidating the trends he observed. That contribution, however, was made possible by a dramatic though short-lived commitment to party responsibility.

Roosevelt imposed the task defined by the Brownlow committee on the Democratic Party and in doing so strengthened partisanship in the short term and carried out a great experiment on the character of the American party system. But this test of responsible party government transformed the Democratic Party into a way station on the road to administrative government, to a centralized and bureaucratic form of democracy that focused on the president and executive agencies for the formulation and execution of public policy. Concomitantly, this development diminished the role of traditional party politics, Congress, and the state legislatures.

As a party of administration, the Democrats established the conditions for an end to parties unless, or until, a party sprang up that was antiadministration. No such party has arisen in American politics, although the Republicans have slouched toward that role. As programmatic liberalism began to lose support, the Republicans under Richard Nixon and especially Ronald Reagan embraced programs of New Federalism and regulatory relief that challenged the institutional legacy of the New Deal. This bolder conservative posture coincided with the construction of a formidable national Republican organization with strength at the federal level that is unprecedented in American politics. From the perspective of the 1980s, some suggest that the New Deal did not lead to the decline of party but to the development of a more national and issue-oriented one.[54]

Nevertheless, the importance of presidential politics and unilateral executive action suggest that Nixon and Reagan essentially continued the institutional legacy of the New Deal. Thus, Republican presidents, intent upon transforming the liberal political order, have conceived of the presidency as a two-edged sword that could cut in a conservative as well as a liberal direction. The pursuit of conservative policy objectives through the administrative presidency has continued with the accession of George Bush to the White House.[55] Indeed, given that the New Deal was based on a party strategy to replace traditional party politics with administration, it is not surprising that the challenge to liberal policies has produced a conservative "administrative presidency," which has also retarded the revival of partisan politics.[56]

The administrative ambition of Republican presidents is supported by a modern conservative movement whose advocates prefer not so much to limit the state as to put it to new uses. Thus, the Reagan administration, while promising to bring about a "new federalism" and "regulatory relief," was stalled in these tasks by the conviction that a strong national state is necessary to foster economic growth, oppose communism, and nurture "traditional" values.

That the challenge to welfare-state politics has focused on the presidency reinforces the need to strengthen executive power as a means to conservative ends. Ironically, the attempt to change public policy with administrative tools created for the most part during Democratic administrations has been thought useful by Republican presidents faced with a hostile Congress and a bureaucracy intent upon preserving the programs of those administrations. Conservative presidencies have thus deepened the political commitment to executive administration by demonstrating that centralized power can serve the purposes of those who oppose the welfare state.

The conservative administrative presidency has not gone unchallenged. As designed by the Democrats, the modern presidency depends upon broad agreement among the Congress, the bureaucracy, and eventually the courts to expand programmatic rights. Energetic administration, therefore, depends upon a consensus that powers should be delegated to the executive. By the time Lyndon Johnson left the White House, support for unilateral executive action had begun to erode, occasioned by the controversial use of presidential power in Vietnam, and it has virtually disappeared under the strain of "divided government."

The modern presidency was conceived as an ally of programmatic reform. When this supposition was seemingly violated by Vietnam and its aftermath, reformers set out to protect liberal programs from unfriendly executives. The result was a "reformation" of New Deal administrative politics, which brought Congress and the courts into the details of administration. The conception of liberal programs as rights and the evolution of a liberal judiciary combined by the 1970s to establish the courts as the guardians of the liberal order.[57]

Party organization and conflict is certainly not absent from the administrative politics spawned by the New Deal and the opposition it aroused. Indeed, the New Deal—and the erosion of traditional decentralized parties—has made possible a new blending of partisanship and administration, one in which administration has become a vehicle for partisan objectives. Parties have shifted much of their effort from the building of constituencies to the administration of public policy. As such, party politics have come to focus on the management of the economy and which party can best cope with problems in the political economy. Moreover, the concept of rights has become increasingly associated with the expansion of national administrative power—even conservatives in the abortion debate talk of the rights of the unborn.[58] The expansion of rights has further shifted partisan politics away from parties as associations that organize political sentiments into an electoral majority. When rights dominate policy discourse, majority sentiments are commonly viewed as the problem and not the solution. Consequently, as the ongoing disputes between a Democratic Congress and Republican president over judicial appointments and court rulings demonstrate, the Supreme Court has displaced elections as the primary institutional focus of partisan politics. Because administration is so central to current political debates and conflicts, both parties are above all parties of administration: the Republicans the party of administration through the executive branch, the Democrats the party of administration through the Congress.[59]

The authors of *Toward a More Responsible Two-Party System* understood that the development of a more purposeful national government meant loosening the hold of traditional parties on the loyalties and voting habits of citizens. But they failed to appreciate the purpose these parties served as effective channels for democratic participation. American parties, which traced their origins to Jefferson, were critical agents in counteracting the tendency of citizens to shut themselves up in a limited circle of domestic concerns out of reach of broader public causes. By enticing Americans into neighborhood organizations and patronage practices that were beyond their tiny private orbits, traditional party organizations were the primary schools of democracy in which Americans learned the art of association and of citizenship, and formed attachments to government institutions.[60]

With the decline of the traditional party system, a politics of entitlements has arisen that belittles efforts by Democrats and Republicans alike to define a collective purpose with a past and a future, and yields instead a partisanship joined to a form of administrative politics that relegates electoral conflict to the intractable demands of policy advocates. In effect, political parties are much more focused on government than they once were, and to this extent, the new partisanship is consistent with the aspirations of the responsible-party advocates. But a partisanship that emphasizes national administration in support of programmatic rights has little chance to reach beyond the Washington beltway and influence the perceptions and habits of the American people. Contrary to the hopes of the APSA committee, the new form of party politics has been associated with a distressing decline in voting. In V. O. Key's terms, the emergence of parties of administration has strengthened the national party organization and the party-in-government, but at the cost of enervating the party-in-the-electorate.[61] This development does not necessarily mean that Democrats and Republicans consider elections unimportant and have despaired of extending their influence through them. It does suggest that as parties of administration, Democrats and Republicans are hobbled in their efforts to form vital links with the public. The political legacy of the New Deal seems to be a more active and better equipped national state, but one without adequate means of common deliberation and public judgment. This is the novel and pressing challenge for those who would take the idea of party renewal seriously as the American polity approaches the twenty-first century.

Notes

1. Committee on Political Parties, *Toward a More Responsible Two Party System* (New York: Rinehart, 1950), pp. 24–25 (hereinafter, CPP).
2. Ibid., p. 22.
3. E. E. Schattschneider, *Party Government* (New York: Farrar and Rinehart, 1942), p. 163.
4. Franklin D. Roosevelt, *Public Papers and Addresses*, ed. Samuel I. Rosenman, 13 vols. (New York: Random House, 1938–1950), vol. 7, p. xxxi.
5. Schattschneider, *Party Government*, pp. 163–69.
6. Unlike Schattschneider, the proponents of this view do not even consider FDR's party leadership a significant, albeit limited, step toward responsible parties. Instead, his shiftiness and improvisation *detracted* from hard, long range purposeful building of a strong popular movement behind a coherent program. The leading proponent of this view is James MacGregor Burns, *Roosevelt: The Lion and the Fox* (New York: Harper, Brace, and World, 1956).
7. Roosevelt, *Public Papers and Addresses*, vol. 7, pp. xxviii–xxix.
8. Woodrow Wilson, *Constitutional Government in the United States* (New York: Columbia University Press, 1908), p. 220.
9. Merrill D. Peterson, *The Jefferson Image in the American Mind* (New York: Oxford University Press, 1960), pp. 355–76.
10. James Pierson, "Party Government," *The Political Science Reviewer*, 12 (Fall 1982): 51–52.
11. Stephen Skowronek, *Building A New American State: The Expansion of National Administrative Capacities, 1877–1920* (Cambridge, Mass.: Cambridge University Press, 1982), p. 40.

12. Herbert Croly, *Progressive Democracy* (New York: Macmillan, 1914), p. 15.

13. Roosevelt, *Public Papers*, vol. 1, pp. 751–52.

14. "Democratic Platform of 1936," in *National Party Platforms*, Donald Bruce Johnson, ed. (Urbana: University of Illinois Press, 1978), p. 360.

15. Roosevelt, *Public Papers*, vol. 13, p. 40.

16. R. Shep Melnick observes: "The rights revolution refers to the tendency to define nearly every public issue in terms of legally protected rights of individuals. Rights of the handicapped, rights of workers, rights of students, rights of racial minorities, linguistic, and religious minorities, rights of women, rights of consumers, the right to a hearing, the right to know—they have become the stock and trade of political discourse." See his "The Courts, Congress, and Programmatic Rights." *Remaking American Politics*, ed. Richard A. Harris and Sidney M. Milkis, (Boulder, Colo.: Westview Press, 1989), p. 188.

17. Josephus Daniels to FDR, December 15, 1932, Ray Stennard Baker Collection, *Franklin D. Roosevelt File*, Princeton University Library.

18. Personal and Political Diary of Homer Cummings, January 5, 1933, Box 234, No. 2, p. 90, *Homer Cummings Papers* (9973), Manuscripts Department, University of Virginia Library, Charlottesville, Virginia.

19. Edward J. Flynn, *You're the Boss* (New York: Viking Press, 1948), p. 153.

20. Paul Van Riper, *History of the United States Civil Service* (Evanston, Ill.: Row, Peterson, 1958), p. 327.

21. Lindsay Rogers, "Reorganization: Post-Mortem Notes," *Political Science Quarterly*, 53 (June 1938): 170.

22. Wilson to Alexander Mitchell Palmer, 5 February, 1913, *The Papers of Woodrow Wilson*, ed. Arthur S. Link (Princeton, N.J.: Princeton University Press, 1966–1985), vol. 27, p. 100.

23. Phillips to FDR, June 9, 1937; and FDR to Phillips, June 16, 1937; President's Personal File 2666, *Franklin D. Roosevelt Papers*, Franklin D. Roosevelt Library, Hyde Park, New York.

24. Stanley High, "Whose Party Is It?" *Saturday Evening Post*, 6 February 1937, p. 34.

25. Thomas Stokes, *Chip off My Shoulder* (Princeton, N.J.: Princeton University Press, 1940), p. 503.

26. Ralph M. Goldman, *Search for Consensus: The Story of the Democratic Party* (Philadelphia: Temple University Press, 1979), p. 326.

27. Roosevelt, *Public Papers*, vol. 7, p. 395.

28. Carter Glass to Jack Dionne, October 17, 1938, *Carter Glass Papers*, Accession No. 2913, Box 383, Alderman Library, University of Virginia.

29. Roosevelt, *Public Papers*, vol. 7, pp. xxxi–xxxii.

30. Raymond Clapper, "Roosevelt Tries the Primaries," *Current History*, 49 (October 1938): 16.

31. Morton J. Frisch, *Franklin D. Roosevelt: The Contribution of the New Deal to American Political Thought and Practice* (Boston: St. Wayne, 1975), p. 79.

32. Roosevelt, *Public Papers*, vol. 7, pp. 397–98.
33. Croly, *Progressive Democracy*, p. 346.
34. CPP, p. 14.
35. Croly, *Progressive Democracy*, pp. 345–48.
36. Ibid., pp. 346–47.
37. Woodrow Wilson, "The Study of Administration," *Political Science Quarterly*, 2 (June): 197–222.
38. Croly, *Progressive Democracy*, p. 348.
39. Ibid., p. 15.
40. Barry Karl, *The Uneasy State: The United States from 1915 to 1945* (Chicago: University of Chicago Press, 1983), pp. 234–35.
41. Philip F. LaFollette, Elmer Bensen, and Frank Murphy, "Why We Lost," *The Nation*, 3 December 1938, p. 587. In the general election, the Democrats lost eighty seats in the House and eight in the Senate, as well as thirteen governorships.
42. E. E. Schattschneider, "The Struggle for Party Government," in *The Party Battle* (New York: Arno Press, 1974), p. 40.
43. On the limits of party government in the United States, see James Sterling Young and Russell L. Riley, "Party Government and Political Culture" (paper presented at the American Political Science Association annual meeting, San Francisco, September 1990).
44. "Outline for a New York Conference," April 8, 1936, *Papers of the President's Committee on Administrative Management*, Roosevelt Library.
45. The President's Committee on Administrative Management, headed by Louis Brownlow, played a central role in the planning and politics of institutional reform 1936–1940. Theodore Lowi has written that *Toward a More Responsible Two-Party System* "rates second only to the 1937 President's Committee on Administrative Management as a contribution by academics to public discourse on the fundamentals of American democracy." Lowi, *The Personal President: Power Invested, Promise Unfulfilled* (Ithaca, N.Y.: Cornell University Press, 1985), p. 68. Interestingly, these two contributions offer alternative paths to a more "responsible" democracy, reflecting a disagreement that touches on important constitutional issues.
46. Luther Gulick, "Politics, Administration, and the New Deal," *The Annals*, 169 (September 1933): 64.
47. Louis Brownlow, "Perfect Union," 27 January 1943, Appendix to Official Files 101 and 101b, pp. 38–39, *Roosevelt Papers* (my emphasis).
48. *Congressional Record*, 75th Cong., 3rd sess., 8 April 1938, p. 5121.
49. Significantly, the two Supreme Court cases that triggered the dispute between Roosevelt and the judiciary were Humphrey's Executor v. U.S., 295 U.S. 602 (1935) and A.L.A. Schecter Poultry Corp. et. al. v. United States, 295 U.S., 553 (1935), both of which imposed constraints on the executive authority of the president.
50. *Report of the President's Committee on Administrative Management* (Washington, D.C.: U.S. Government Printing Office, 1937), p. 53.

51. Roosevelt, *Public Papers*, vol. 9, p. 28.

52. Although the literature on party development has generally neglected the importance of presidential leadership and the evolution of the presidency as an institution, there are a few exceptions. See, especially, Harold Bass, "The President and National Party Organization," in *Presidents and Their Parties: Leadership or Neglect?*, ed. Robert Harmel (New York: Praeger, 1984); Theodore Lowi, *The Personal President: Power Invested, Promise Unfulfilled* (Ithaca, N.Y.: Cornell University Press, 1985), especially Chs. 3, 4; Lester G. Seligman and Cary R. Covington, *The Coalitional Presidency* (Chicago: Dorsey Press, 1989).

53. Charles Edward Merriam, "The Written and Unwritten Constitution," in *Party Battle*, p. 85.

54. For examples, see A. James Reichley, "The Rise of National Parties," in *The New Direction in American Politics*, ed. John E. Chubb and Paul E. Peterson (Washington, D.C.: Brookings Institution, 1985); Cornelius Cotter and John F. Bibby, "Institutionalization of Parties and the Thesis of Party Decline," *Political Science Quarterly*, 95 (Spring, 1980): 1–27; Joseph A. Schlesinger, "The New American Party System," *America Political Science Review*, 79 (December 1985): 1152–69; Paul S. Herrnson, *Party Campaigning in the 1980s* (Cambridge, Mass.: Harvard University Press, 1988).

55. For example, as was the case during the Reagan era, the Bush administration's efforts to weaken environmental, consumer, and civil rights have come not through legislative change but of administrative inaction, delay, and repeal. Robert Pear, "U.S. Laws Delayed by Complex Rules and Partisanship," *New York Times*, 31 March 1991, pp. 1, 18.

56. The term *administrative presidency* comes from Richard Nathan's seminal work on the employment of executive action by modern presidents to pursue policy objectives. See Nathan, *The Administrative Presidency* (New York: John Wiley, 1983).

57. Richard B. Stewart, "The Reformation of Administrative Law," *Harvard Law Review*, 88 (June, 1975): 1669–1813, Melnick, "The Courts, Congress, and Programmatic Rights."

58. As such, modern conservatives, no less than programmatic liberals, support policies that want to abolish rather than restore the distinction between state and society. For instance, in early 1988, the Reagan administration's Department of Health and Human Services issued a regulation declaring that a program that received federal funds "may not provide counseling concerning the use of abortion as a method of family planning or provide referral for abortion as a method of family planning." Because stays had been issued by lower courts, the regulations were delayed for three years. The restrictions on abortion counseling were declared unconstitutional by the First Circuit in Boston and the Tenth Circuit in Denver on the grounds that abortion counseling and abortion referral were constitutionally protected speech under the First Amendment, and the government could not penalize an individual for exercising his First Amendment rights, even if the penalty was the denial of a government benefit. But in late May

1991, the Supreme Court upheld the regulation in Rust v. Sullivan (No. 89-1391), and the Bush administration proceeded with plans to bar employees of federally financed family planning clinics from providing basic medical information about abortion. Linda Greenhouse, "5 Justices Uphold U.S. Ruling Curbing Abortion Advice," *New York Times*, 24 May 1991, pp. 1, 18–19. Whatever one thinks of the actions taken by the Reagan and Bush administrations in this case, it reflects support among many modern conservatives for the discretionary use of administrative power that hardly challenges the institutional legacy of liberal reform.

59. Robert Eden, "Partisanship and Constitutional Revolution: The Founders View Is Newly Problematic," in *Constitutionalism in Perspective: The United States Constitution in the Twentieth Century Politics*, ed. Sarah Baumgartner Thurow (Lanham, N.Y., and London: University Press of America, 1988).

60. Even when political parties were relatively indifferent to broad moral questions and dedicated to the personal ambitions of their members, Tocqueville found them to be valuable political associations in which individuals learned the art of cooperation and became citizens. Alexis de Tocqueville, *Democracy in America*, ed. J. P. Mayer (New York: Doubleday, 1969), pp. 189–95, 509–13, 520–24.

61. V. O. Key, Jr., *Politics, Parties and Pressure Groups*, 5th ed. (New York: Thomas V. Crowell, 1964). For a discussion of the electorate during the 1980s and the prospects for party renewal, see Walter Dean Burnham, "Elections As Democratic Institutions," in *Elections in America*, ed. Kay Lehman Schlozman (Boston: Allen and Unwin, 1987), pp. 58–60; Martin P. Wattenberg, *The Decline of American Political Parties, 1952–1984* (Cambridge, Mass.: Harvard University Press, 1986); Benjamin Ginsberg and Martin Shefter *Politics by Other Means: The Declining Importance of Elections in America* (New York: Basic Books, 1990).

6

The Party Connection

David E. Price

As Mark Twain cabled from London about reports of his own death, pronouncements regarding the demise of the parties are "greatly exaggerated," at least as far as the party organizations in Congress are concerned. During the past twenty years, despite a steady decline in the hold of the major parties on the electorate, the congressional parties have become more active and their operations more extensive. Party solidarity in roll-call voting has displayed a remarkable comeback from its low point in the Ninetieth through Ninety-Second congresses (1967–72). Of course, party cohesion and control in the House of Representatives fall far short of what is to be found in parliamentary systems or even in many American state legislatures, and in the U.S. Senate the party reins are looser still. But the parties retain a central role in the present functioning of Congress and the periodic efforts to improve its performance.

I will illustrate the party role in Congress by describing my interactions with the Democratic party during my first five years in the House. But I should stress at the outset that not every member's story would be the same. This underscores an important fact about congressional party organizations: While they perform crucial institutional functions and every member must come to terms with them in some fashion, members retain a great deal of independence and discretion in their voting behavior and how they relate to the broad range of party functions and activities. This is mainly because of how members get elected. Parties *outside* Congress have declined in their hold on voter loyalties and their control of critical campaign resources.

Members are increasingly on their own electorally and less dependent on the parties in their constituencies. They face electorates less inclined to vote on party grounds alone and a public largely unaware of and unconcerned about their party regularity once they are in office. They are generally nominated not by party caucuses or conventions but by direct primaries, and the number of districts with party organizations strong enough to control the nomination process has declined substantially. Candidates must raise their own funds and build their own organizations at the primary stage and often for the general election as well. National partisan swings have become less and less determinative of election outcomes in most congressional districts, and ticket splitting has become endemic. Understandably, members are less likely under these circumstances to see their ties to the organized party, either at home or in Congress, as crucial to their electoral fortunes.

Members increasingly relate to their districts directly, in ways unmediated by the party. District service operations have grown, responding to and sometimes stimulating constituents' expanded expectations regarding the role and obligations of government. The growth of television as the dominant medium of political communication in campaign advertising and the daily news also offers manifold opportunities for more frequent and more direct communications with voters than was afforded by traditional friends-and-neighbors or clubhouse channels. The same is true of the computerized mail technologies used in campaigns and most congressional offices. There is very little in all of this that encourages party loyalty in Washington. It is true, as Richard Fenno stresses, that effective servicing of their districts can build members' political capital and give them increased leeway for their activities in Washington.[1] But it is also true that many of these activities, especially roll-call votes, seem more visible now than formerly, particularly when one contemplates the use an opponent might make of them in thirty-second television commercials in the next campaign or in fire-breathing direct-mail solicitations. Such prospects can make the blandishments of party leaders pale by comparison.

The decline of the party-in-the-electorate and traditional party organizations, along with the rise of new modes of political communication, have thus weakened key incentives to party regularity in the Congress. This makes the question of what contribution one will make to the effective functioning of one's party more a matter of individual discretion and responsibility than it was for many members in the past.[2] But it also leaves an important question unanswered: How is it that in the midst of these unmistakable party-weakening forces the *congressional* parties—and particularly the Democratic Party in the House, which has controlled the chamber since 1955—have been able to strengthen their leadership role substantially?

The basic answer is that more and more members have come to regard enhanced party operations as serving their political and policy goals.[3] In the 1970s, increasingly restless members used strengthened party organs to rein in the senior committee chairmen, who had dominated both chambers since the late New Deal. But as old power centers were weakened and authority and resources were dispersed more widely, the impossibility of running a legislature on the premise of "every person for himself" became more apparent. Thus the 1980s have seen the House Democrats, and to a lesser extent the other congressional parties, further expanding their operations and commanding greater loyalty from their members, even as the district-based incentives to party regularity have continued to weaken.

The "New Centralization" in the House

The electoral trends I have delineated—weakened party ties, candidates and incumbents increasingly on their own, seeking media exposure and name familiarity—produced a rising tide of discontent with House operations and eventually, in the 1970s, major organization changes. Members became restless with norms and structures that denied them visibility and leverage until they had accrued years of seniority. Increasing numbers of members also became critical of the conservative bias of institutional arrangements that gave disproportionate power to long-entrenched southern Democratic chairmen. The elections of 1958, 1964, and 1974 in particular brought large numbers of liberal activist Democrats into the House. In the meantime, black enfranchisement and party realignment in the South gradually produced a new breed of Democratic House members from that region who were much closer to the party's mainstream.

These cross currents produced significant shifts in ideology and policy preference in the House's majority party. Members came to see significant advantages in strengthening party organs, not by virtue of party ties outside the chamber but as a means to personal and policy goals within. This is not to say strengthening the party was a dominant goal of congressional reform. Its initial and main thrust was *decentralization*, the dispersal of authority, resources, and visibility throughout the chamber, producing in 1965–78 the organizational phase Roger Davidson called the "rise of subcommittee government."[4]

Congressional reform, however, had a centralizing component from the first. The reformers' main target was committee oligarchs rather than party leaders, and revitalizing the House Democratic Caucus proved necessary to rewrite the rules, depose recalcitrant chairmen, and otherwise effect the desired transfer of power. The leadership, moreover, was the only available counterweight to bastions like the House Rules and Ways and Means committees. Thus, two key early reforms removed the committee assignment function from Ways and Means Democrats and placed it in a leadership dominated Steering and Policy Committee, and gave the Speaker the power to nominate the chairman and the Democratic members of the Rules Committee. For some reformers, such as Representative Richard Bolling (D-MO), the strengthening of party organs was quite deliberate, aimed at giving a true "majority of House Democrats . . . effective control of the House" and enabling them to enact their legislative program.[5] For others it was mainly a means to the end of breaking up oligarchical power. The effect was to strengthen the party involvement of younger members and to enhance the role of the leadership, even as the actual *decisions* of the caucus were helping atomize congressional power.

This atomization, as it proceeded through the 1970s, gave increasing numbers of members a stake in the new order, but it also created new problems for the institution that only strengthened parties could solve. The proliferating pieces of turf from which issues could be publicized and initiatives generated could also become bases for conflict and obstruction when the time came to mobilize the chamber. There was thus widespread support for leadership efforts to overcome organization fragmentation, sometimes through extraordinary devices such as the Ad Hoc Energy Committee (1977)[6] and more generally through increases in the Speaker's referral powers, the development of leadership agendas and the strengthening of whip operations.

The decline in the deference paid committees, the desire for visibility of individual members, and rules changes such as the institution of the recorded teller vote resulted in increased amending activity on the House floor. But many members came to see this as more a threat than an opportunity, as measures they favored were damaged or delayed and members of the opposition party used the amendment process to force politically charged record votes. Thus the leadership began, with widespread member support, to pass more bills under "suspension of the rules" procedures that forbade amendments, to employ more special rules that restricted amending activity, and otherwise to rein in floor activity.[7]

Modern budget politics has also strengthened the role of the congressional leadership. The budget reforms instituted in the mid-1970s had this effect by virtue of the control party leaders assumed over appointments to the new budget committees and because of the necessities for intercommittee and interbranch negotiation the budget process created. Even more determinative was the budget crisis that lasted through the 1980s. "Looming deficits and the need to reach painful decisions about priorities . . . pushed legislative structures and practices toward greater centralization."[8] Budget measures became more complicated, comprehensive, and conflictful, spilling over established timetables, processes, and committee jurisdictions. Working out budget deals yearly with the Republican administration increasingly became a critical leadership function.

Many majority members of the House thus became willing to support an enhanced party role, and of course as the party organization developed, it was able to reinforce these tendencies with a reward structure of its own. Meanwhile, the *costs* of cooperation were decreasing for many members. The political and budgetary climate of the 1980s made for reduced levels of freewheeling policy entrepreneurship.[9] Members had less to lose by being reined in and more to gain as the leadership sought to overcome some of the adverse conditions making legislative action difficult. Nor did the House Democrats have as much trouble uniting under the party banner as they had had in the recent past. Plenty of diversity remained, but the North-South gap that had bedeviled the party and fueled much of the early reform effort continued to narrow. Thus the potential costs of assertive Democratic leadership in disaffection and division were greatly reduced.[10]

It now appears that these trends toward strengthened leadership may well have reached a high point during my first term in the House, the 100th Congress of 1987–88. As Davidson observes:

> Part of the equation was the advent of a new Speaker: Jim Wright (D-TX), who had few inhibitions about exploiting the powers of the office. Even more important, however, were contextual factors that at last made vigorous party leadership feasible. First, after dominating the Washington scene for six years, President Reagan was irrevocably damaged by the 1986 elections and the Iran-Contra scandal that broke shortly afterwards. With both houses of Congress in Democratic hands, the legislative initiative traveled down Pennsylvania Avenue to Capitol Hill. Democrats and their allies at last saw a chance to push their long-deferred legislative agendas. Moreover, Democratic office-holders again found reason to identify themselves with a partisan agenda: not only was the party label worth more than in Reagan's heyday, but Democrats were anxious to compile a record of achievement to carry them into the 1988 elections. Finally, in order to pass a partisan agenda, both committee leaders and the rank and file understood that leadership coordination would be essential.[11]

Speaker Wright saw to it that the first five bills introduced (H.R. 1 through H.R. 5) were those he regarded as lead items on the Democratic agenda. Two of these, the Clean Water Act and an ambitious highway bill, were passed shortly after Congress convened in January 1987; by

April 2, both had again been whipped through over President Reagan's vetoes. The remaining three bills—an omnibus trade measure, reauthorizations of elementary and secondary education, and housing programs—were all passed over the course of the next two years, as were significant welfare reform, Medicare expansion, fair housing, farm credit reform, plant-closing notification, and homeless assistance measures. The 100th Congress could fairly be regarded as the most productive since the Great Society congresses of the mid-1960s, and strong leadership in the House was a critical part of the equation.

The 101st and 102nd congresses found it difficult to maintain this level of productivity, although the falloff was not as great as many commentators suggested. The leading agenda items were neither as obvious nor as easy to pass as the clean water and highway bills had been in 1987. The ethics troubles of Speaker Wright and Majority Whip Tony Coelho deepened quickly as the 101st Congress began, leading to the departure of both by mid-1989. The 1988 presidential elections left Democrats without a clear programmatic thrust and with more than a touch of defensiveness; moreover, the White House vacuum they had moved to fill in 1987–88 was no more. And the long-term constraints imposed by enormous budget deficits and divided party control of government remained.

Still, there has been no major reversal of the trend toward extensive and active leadership operations so evident in the mid-1980s. The new Speaker, Tom Foley, while not as aggressively partisan as Wright, nonetheless became increasingly assertive in defining party goals and using the leadership tools at his disposal. Nor was there any doubt that in so doing he was following the wishes and expectations of most caucus members. Majority Leader Dick Gephardt, who had a relatively high public profile by virtue of his 1988 run for the presidency, emerged as a forceful party spokesman. Whip and caucus operations, under the leadership of Bill Gray (D-PA) and Steny Hoyer (D-MD), respectively, continued largely unchanged. President George Bush proved a formidable adversary, blocking congressional action in areas ranging from civil rights and the minimum wage to civil rights and the protection of Chinese nationals seeking to delay a return home after the Tiananmen Square massacre. But in other areas he proved far more flexible than President Reagan, cooperating with Congress to produce major clean air, handicapped rights, and housing legislation. In either event, under conditions of both confrontation and cooperation, the need for strong party leadership was apparent to and thus generally supported by most Democratic members.

Leadership strength is a relative concept. The House leadership system that in 1988 could plausibly be described as "more centralized and concentrated . . . than at any time since the days of Joseph Cannon" looks considerably less so when compared to its parliamentary counterparts or when whips are scrambling to patch together winning coalitions on difficult issues.[12] The dispersal of authority and resources to 148 subcommittees remains as an enduring legacy of "reform" (and the underlying electoral realities). There is also an unmistakable fragility to leadership strength, which is based less than formerly on "strong parties external to the Congress" and more on the acquiescence of freewheeling individual members.[13] Power relationships could no doubt shift with changes in majority party size, White House control, or the nation's policy agenda. Still, the party role looms large in the contemporary House, a role I will now attempt to elucidate further through a description of my "party connection."

Electoral Support

As a candidate for Congress, I had unusually strong party credentials. I had paid my dues through local party service and as a foot soldier in other Democrats' campaigns. My service as executive director and chairman of the North Carolina Democratic party was the main factor giving me credibility as a congressional candidate. I chose the county Democratic conventions in my district—held simultaneously on April 13, 1985—to announce my candidacy. I did then and still do regard party activists as an essential core of my political base. After surviving the primary, I received substantial support from the Democratic Congressional Campaign Committee (DCCC) and integrated my grassroots campaign with that of county party organizations. My campaigns thus illustrate the role party can still play. But they also demonstrate the limits of that role, even when a candidate has an inclination (which many candidates do not) to run as part of the party team.

The state party chairmanship may actually be emerging was a more promising launching pad for a congressional candidacy. Among the Democratic state chairmen with whom I served, four—Nancy Pelosi of California, Bart Gordon of Tennessee, David Nagle of Iowa, and Chester Atkins of Massachusetts—are now House colleagues. This probably says less about the potency of state parties than about the changing nature of the chairmanship. It has become a far more public role, giving the chairman media exposure, identifying him as a spokesman on key issues, and so forth. Certainly it was the public role I assumed during the Senate and other campaigns of 1984 much more than my behind-the-scenes organizational activity that made others think of me (and me think of myself) as a potential candidate.

Still, neither my recognition among party activists nor my wider exposure as a party spokesman gave me anything approaching a decisive edge in a Democratic primary. That came only as we formulated a television message and scraped together enough money to put it on the air. Relatively little of that money came from party sources. Democratic Party activists are generally able to contribute only modestly. North Carolina party organizations, like others in states with a one-party past where nomination was once tantamount to election, have a tradition of remaining neutral, financially and otherwise, in primary contests. The same is usually true of the DCCC. I called on DCCC leaders during the primary season, knowing that a direct contribution was out of the question but hoping to convince them that I would be a strong, perhaps the best, general election candidate, so that they might informally pass the word to potential contributors that I was good prospect. This happened only to a very limited degree. The fact is that the Democratic nomination was not within the power of local, state, or national party organizations to deliver. I and my fledgling campaign team, including many active local Democrats, were largely on our own in pursuing it.

That changed some, but not entirely, after the primary. The DCCC was targeting four Democratic challengers in North Carolina in 1986—three of us attempting to regain seats that had been lost in 1984 and a fourth, D. G. Martin, trying again for the Charlotte seat he had failed to win by only 321 votes in 1984. Tony Coelho was an unusually active and aggressive DCCC chairman, greatly stepping up fundraising activity and moving from the DCCC's natural tendency simply to shore up incumbents to a strategy of targeting those races where an infusion of funds could have the greatest impact. Martin's Charlotte race, where Coelho strongly disagreed with some of the tactics the candidate was adopting, showed how intrusive the chairman and his aides could be, using their financial support as leverage to try to move the campaign in certain directions. The DCCC leadership apparently had no such problems with my campaign, although we had many quibbles along the way. The committee contributed $39,848 to my campaign which, when added to the state tax checkoff monies funneled through the state Democratic Party, came close to the legal maximum.

The state party, having lost the organizational resources of the governorship in 1984 and having nothing like the Hunt-Helms Senate race to attract contributions and participation in 1986, was not in a position to replicate the state-level voter-contact operations undertaken two years before. Several congressional campaigns were weakened as a result. I was fortunate, however, in having relatively active Democratic organizations in most of my counties and a tradition of extensive phone-bank and get-out-the-vote activity in Raleigh and Chapel Hill. We thus decided after the primary to run our voter-contact operations as part of a Democratic "unity campaign," and our Senate candidate, Terry Sanford, did the same.

While my campaign thus evinced relatively strong participation by both the national campaign committee and local party organizations, it could not, when compared either to parliamentary elections in other western democracies or earlier American practice, be judged a party-centered campaign. We gained numerous foot soldiers and saved scarce campaign dollars by combining forces with other Democratic candidates in our canvassing and turnout operations. But even here we gave as much as we got; party precinct structures were spotty at best, and the cadres of volunteers often needed shoring up. So activists from the Price campaign helped make the party efforts work, as well as the reverse.

In other facets of the campaign, the party role was far less prominent. The state party organized a rally in each congressional district for all the Democratic candidates, and most county parties did the same thing locally. But most of my campaign appearances and fund-raising events were organized by our campaign alone. The state party had an able research director on whom we drew, and the state party chairman sometimes held press conferences or issued broadsides in collaboration with various congressional campaigns, but by and large, in devising a press strategy, formulating a message, in putting together an advertising campaign, and raising the money to pay for it, we were still on our own.

In the two reelection campaigns I have waged since 1986, both against aggressive, well-financed opponents, the party role has slipped somewhat. This is not because of any changed strategy on my part, but reflects changed priorities and capacities on the party side. The DCCC contributed far less in 1988 and 1990 than it had in 1986. Mine was still a targeted race, but the DCCC was strapped for money and perhaps regarded me as better equipped than others to raise my own funds. The state party declined further in the financial resources and campaign services it was able to offer candidates. But we still cooperated actively in county party voter-contact operations and especially in 1990 developed synergetic relationships with other Democratic campaigns such as Harvey Gantt's Senate race, which attracted much participation and enthusiasm, and several targeted state legislative races in my district.

Besides trying to make the most of the party potential in my campaigns, I have tried between elections to keep my local party ties in good repair, attending and speaking at meetings, helping organize and promote events, consulting with party leaders. I value these organizations and believe elected officials can do much to enhance their role. Politicians who complain of the party's weakness and irrelevance and treat the organization accordingly are often engaged in a self-fulfilling prophecy. We do have significant choices about how we relate to party organizations, and the choices we make have a considerable potential to harm or help. I am not suggesting that candidates or officeholders should be expected to sacrifice their basic interests to those of the party. I am suggesting that normally a *range* of viable strategies of campaigning and governance are available, some of which tend to reinforce and others to undermine party strength.

The parties, however, must also help themselves. The national committees, the House and Senate campaign committees, and many state parties have done more than is commonly recognized to remodel themselves—increasing their financial base and their capacity to recruit candidates and to offer a range of supportive services—although these advances now seem to be leveling off. Much depends on the quality of party leadership at all levels. Local parties are not tidy organizations and would lose much of their vitality if they were. Gone forever is the patronage system that bound loyalists to "the organization" and assured tight leadership control. Today's party activists are motivated mainly by issue and candidate enthusiasms, and often give organizational maintenance a decidedly lower priority. Candidates and officeholders who would work with the party must recognize this and adapt to it. At the same time, partisans and their leaders should understand that if they allow the party to degenerate into contending factions, each pushing for its own "pure" policy position or preferred candidate, unable or unwilling to work together after the nomination and platform battles are over, candidates and officeholders will be tempted to distance themselves, seeing in the party tie more hassle than help.

Public policy at all levels also can strengthen or weaken the parties' electoral role.[14] Here I will mention only an area that has concerned me directly both as state chairman and as a member of Congress, the regulation of campaign finance. Campaign finance reform, however necessary or laudable in many respects, has too often handicapped the parties and contributed to their irrelevance, a problem to which Common Cause and other reform advocates are still largely insensitive. What we should be doing is *strengthening* parties as counterweights to more narrowly based groups and as vehicles for healthy and broadly based political participation. At a minimum, this means preserving and expanding the provisions in law for parties to make "coordinated expenditures" on behalf of congressional candidates above and beyond their direct contributions.[15] It also means being very careful in cleaning up the so-called soft money abuses not to penalize or discourage voter registration, get-out-the-vote, and other voter-contact activities on behalf of the entire ticket, federal candidates included.[16] In fact, such activities should be given a protected position in the law. And as we consider reinstating tax incentives for small individual contributions, we should try to encourage support of parties by making available a tax credit or deduction for party contributions separate from what is provided for contributions to candidates.[17]

The Party Network

When newly elected members of Congress come to Washington for the week of organizational meetings before the session begins, they immediately confronts the fact that the chamber is party-led. Members attend orientation sessions organized by the majority and minority leaderships, vote to choose party leaders and adopt caucus rules, and begin to jockey for committee assignments in a process that is party controlled. As I and other new Democratic members lobbied the Steering and Policy Committee for our preferred committee positions, we came to regard party leaders as the gatekeepers of the institution. This continued for me throughout most of my first two terms as I laid the groundwork for my 1991 move to the Appropriations Committee.

New members soon have the opportunity, however, to become part of the party network, at least at its outer reaches. Not everyone chooses do to so, but many do, for party participation is a way of placing oneself in the cross currents of information and influence and for some is a pathway to power within the institution. The leadership ladder is quite crowded these days, with numerous members competing for every appointive and elective leadership post. But any member who wishes can become involved in the work of the caucus and the whip organization. This is a legacy of the 1970s when these organizations were revitalized and expanded, but it also represents a deliberate strategy of inclusion by party leaders, who recognize that members are more likely to be cooperative and helpful when they feel they are being informed and consulted and have a role to play in party affairs.

The House Democratic Caucus meets about every two weeks. Sometimes the purpose is to ratify committee assignments coming from the Steering and Policy Committees or rules changes coming from the Committee on Organization, Study, and Review. More often the caucus is called to discuss a pending legislative battle of major importance, as during the protracted budget battles of 1990 when frequent caucuses let the leadership report on the twists and turns of negotiations but also let the membership communicate a sense of what was politically feasible.

More rarely, the caucus may debate the party's agenda and political strategy, as when the leadership scheduled a series of meetings in 1991 to air member views on long-range strategies for health care, middle-class tax fairness, and other issues.

I came to the House predisposed to be active in the Democratic Caucus. I have served since 1989 on the caucus's Committee on Organization, Study, and Review (OSR) and was appointed in 1990 as coordinator of the caucus's nine issues task forces. I have also participated fairly consistently in the work of the "Message Board," an arm of the caucus that attempts to publicize the party's legislative efforts and put a Democratic "spin" on the day's events. The main aspect of this that involves members like me is the attempt to coordinate and give a consistent theme to members' statements on the House floor, particularly during the period reserved for "one-minute" speeches at the beginning of the day. I have thus joined with colleagues in challenging the president to offer a serious national energy policy, in insisting that we must move beyond presidential rhetoric in improving education, and so forth. The purpose, in part, is to counter House Republicans, who have often been more agressive than we in taking advantage of the national platform the House floor, as telecast by C-SPAN, offers. But the real competition is in the White House, and we are reminded almost daily of the advantages the president has over the majority party in Congress, no matter how energetically led or well coordinated its message, in capturing public attention and framing the day's issues.

The OSR Committee is a housekeeping committee, highly responsive to the Speaker, that screens proposed rules changes for the caucus and renders judgments on requests from members or committees for waivers of rules or the adjudication of rules disputes. The committee emerged briefly from obscurity in 1974 when the highly controversial recommendations on committee reorganization of the Select Committee on Committees were sent to OSR for a thorough reworking. But in normal times OSR operates behind the scenes, a good place for a member to learn the organizational ropes and work with party leaders on internal House matters.

The task force project I coordinated in 1990 was the fifth in a series of election-year efforts begun when Caucus chairman Gillis Long formed the Committee on Party Effectiveness (CPE) in 1981–82. The CPE was an ambitious effort to involve caucus Members, many of them quite junior and from outside the relevant committees, in broad policy discussions, to formulate positions that could inspire agreement among Democrats, and in some cases to nudge reluctant committee leaders.[18] By the time I came to the House, the CPE was not a "committee" at all but a series of caucus-sponsored "Party Effectiveness" luncheons, often with outside experts, on important national issues. I found these sessions quite valuable but also saw the need for more focused discussions aimed at the production of a preelection document trumpeting Democratic achievements and aspirations. I was thus pleased when Caucus Chairman Steny Hoyer asked me to coordinate the task force effort. The fact that I had an able political scientist, Paul Herrnson, on my staff for the year as a Congressional Fellow made me more confident in taking on the assignment.

Our effort was not as far-reaching as Long's Party Effectiveness projects. Our nine task forces contained a mix of members from on and off the relevant committees, and although some committee chairmen cooperated fully in the effort, others displayed disinterest and even some hostility. We kicked off the process at the caucus's annual retreat in February. In the ensuing months, several of the task forces met repeatedly and hammered out consensus positions; in other cases the leaders did little more than order up staff-produced drafts. In any event, after much cajoling and editing, we produced an issues handbook, *Investing in America's Future*, which served as a useful resource in 1990 and laid some groundwork for the 1992 national platform. How useful the task forces were as outlets for their members, however, varied greatly from case to case.

My second party connection has been through the whip organization. I learned very quickly that the most valuable meeting of the week in the House is the Thursday-morning whips meeting where plans for the coming week are discussed and strategy debated in a wide-open fashion. Although I was not formally part of the organization, I began to attend these meetings regularly and to volunteer from time to time for the ad hoc task forces put together by the Whip's office to count votes and mobilize support on specific bills. By 1991, I had been designated an at-large whip and was helping with whip operations on most major bills.

The whip organization and its vote-gathering efforts enlist a good portion of the Democratic membership. Besides the majority whip—currently David Bonior (D-MI), who was elected by the caucus after Bill Gray's resignation in mid-1991—and three chief deputy whips appointed by the Speaker, the organization includes fifteen deputy whips and sixty at-large whips appointed by the majority whip, and fourteen assistant whips (or zone whips) elected by the regional party caucuses. On a bill the organization is whipping, the zone whips normally do the first count, after which the other components of the organization, more directly linked to the leadership, go to work on members whose vote appears problematic or who need shoring up. This further checking and communicating is done by deputy and at-large whips: On particularly important or problematic matters, an ad hoc task force is often appointed which brings into the mix committee leaders and other members particularly influential or interested in the issue. These task forces are essentially open to all comers, and they can be an important avenue of participation for junior members.

My involvement in whip operations has been useful in at least three ways. First, it has let me help mobilize support for measures that I thought were important, such as the 1990 housing bill on which I had worked extensively in committee. Second, it has made me a partner, albeit a junior one, in leadership undertakings. This can be intrinsically satisfying, and it can also bring other rewards. Those who throughout 1990 were trying to position ourselves to gain the next Appropriations Committee seats joked about what a coincidence it was that we so often found ourselves on the whip's task forces. Finally, it has brought me into discussions of floor strategy and the last-minute alterations needed to maximize votes on various bills. Certain committees, most notably Judiciary and Education and Labor, tend to bring bills to the floor that are acceptable to the liberal majorities on those committees but need further work if they are to gain the full assent of a healthy majority of Democratic members. This happens more than it should, and whip task forces are hardly the ideal place to work out accommodations. But on bills like child care in 1990 and civil rights and striker replacement in 1991 the vote counts and feedback garnered by the whip organization have served as a reality check for committee leaders and have given members like myself a means of pushing for needed refinements.

Thus, finding a place in the House, for me and for many other members, has proceeded along parallel tracks, not just in the committee system but also in the sprawling party infrastructure. These party structures are highly permeable, their boundaries frequently unclear. They serve critical functions in the House, disseminating information, gathering intelligence, forging a policy consensus beyond committee enclaves, gathering votes. But they also provide a substantial number of members opportunities for participation and influence.

Party Voting

Party voting in the House has increased steadily and substantially since the early 1970s. About half of the House's roll-call votes now find a majority of one party arrayed against a majority of the other, compared to one-third twenty years ago.[19] More significantly, as figure 6.1 shows, individual members have become more and more inclined to stick with their party on such divided votes. Party voting has reached levels in the 1980s not seen since the party polarization of the Truman years. In part, this is a reflection of another period of national polarization. Ronald Reagan's presidency was a highly ideological one, and both the content of his proposals and his uncompromising style prompted sharp partisan divisions on Capitol Hill. Democrats, by virtue of the political threat Reagan posed and the impact of his policies on their constituencies, were constrained to develop and promote distinct alternatives and unify against a common adversary. They were aided in this by the continued, albeit incomplete closing of the gap between the northern and southern wings of the congressional party.

This growing divergence between and convergence within the congressional parties helped underwrite—indeed created pressures to develop—the elaborate party machinery I have described. That machinery in turn has helped strengthen and solidify the partisan voting trends, although the precise impact is impossible to quantify. Heightened activity by the congressional campaign committees in recruiting and financing candidates, especially on the Republican side, has probably strengthened party identification among incoming members. The increased resources of party leaders (staff positions assigned to leadership offices, not including the campaign committees, now number fifty-eight on the Democratic side and forty-four for the Republicans) facilitate a dominant role for the parties in intra-House communications, help the leaders perform services and do favors for large numbers of members, and give them a strengthened hand in shaping the House's policy agenda and assembling complex budget packages.

The party voting statistics also reflect the enhanced powers of the Democratic leadership in scheduling and structuring floor debate. Firmly in control of the Rules Committee, party leaders may, for example, make "in order" a Republican substitute to a pending bill that they know they can defeat on a party-line vote but refuse to permit the consideration of amendments that would be more threatening and/or might divide the Democratic vote. Such tactics, to be sure, can alienate Democrats as well as Republicans. I can recall instances when I thought a rule should have been granted for an amendment, often proposed by a moderate Democrat, that had merit and deserved an up-or-down vote, regardless of the fact that it had the potential to divide our party or was opposed by the floor manager or the interest groups backing the bill.[20] Moreover, sometimes when bills are reported by committees unrepresentative of the caucus or are fraught with symbolic policies—the perennial "omnibus crime bills" qualify on both counts—members need for both substantive and often political reasons to vote for moderating

Figure 6.1. Party Unity Voting, 81st–101st Congresses

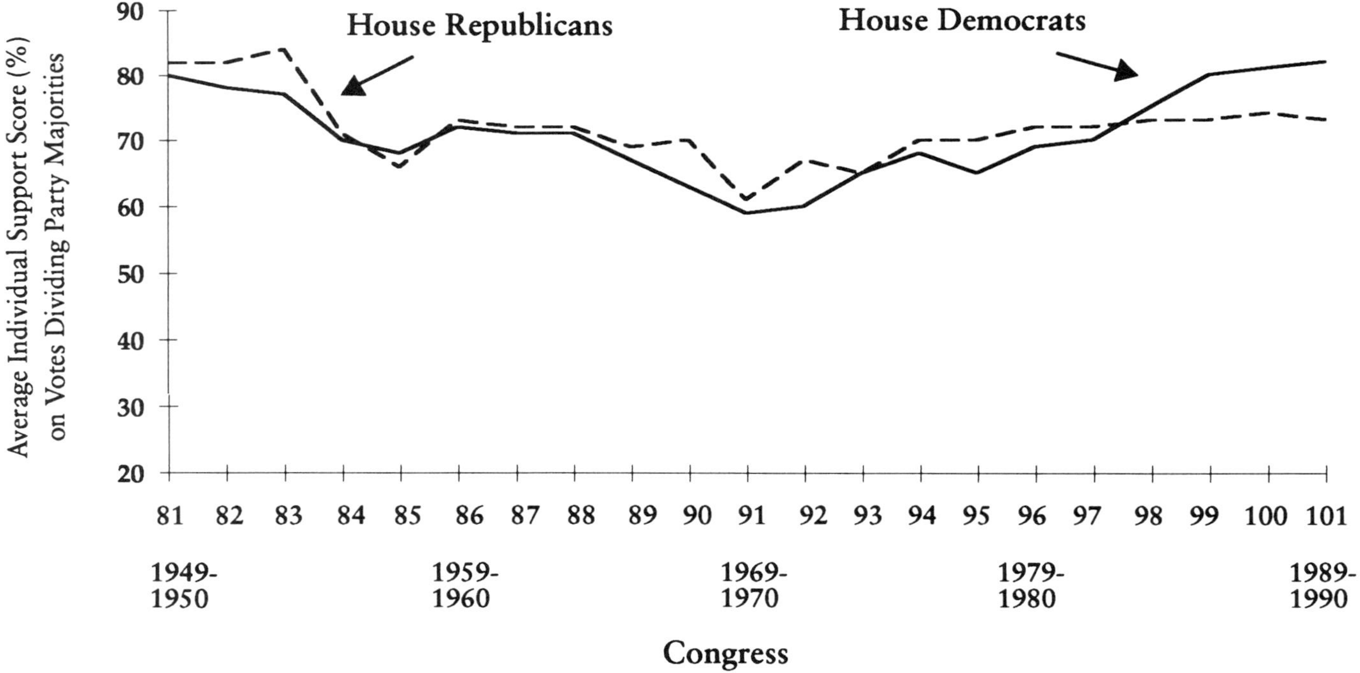

Data from *Congressional Quarterly Almanacs.*

amendments, preferably offered by Democrats. A strategy that denies them that opportunity may backfire, leading Democrats to vote for more extreme Republican countermeasures as the only alternatives.

Thus, members frequently and legitimately debate *how* the leadership's scheduling and structuring powers ought to be used. However, few doubt that they are a useful and necessary instrument of majority control. The trend in figure 6.1 reflects the increasing exercise and acceptance of these powers.

Expanded whip operations have also helped solidify the trend. Whip counts enable the leadership to schedule votes only when a Democratic (and House) majority is in hand. Whip contacts, moreover, help create such results, informing members of the leadership's wishes and intent, providing channels for interpretation and persuasion on pending measures, and generating feedback that helps the leadership avoid trouble, sometimes by making last-minute alterations in content or strategy. This is not to say the whipping process works ideally as an early-warning system. *Late*-warning system is more like it—often picking up problems or grievances that committee or party leaders should have identified and could have dealt with more adequately at an earlier point. Still, the whip system permits the leadership to bring measures to the floor with confidence and maximize the party vote in their favor once they get there.

The leadership is also able to use its control over the Steering and Policy Committee to encourage party regularity (the same is true of the Committee on Committees on the Republican side). But the limitations, deliberate and otherwise, on the use of this power are at least as impressive as the instances of its exercise. For one thing, most members are usually not seeking new committee assignments or other appointments within the authority of the leadership to grant. And the leadership does not always use its leverage to reward party regularity. During the early 1980s, for example, the Democratic leadership fluctuated in its treatment of the "boll weevils," conservative Democrats who were prone to vote with the Reagan administration, sometimes attempting to win their loyalty and cooperation through generous treatment and choice committee assignments but at other times passing over them in favor of their loyalist rivals.[21] This approach was to some extent dictated by the political situation the Democrats faced. They were more accommodating to the conservatives when their House majority was shaky and Reagan was riding high, less accommodating when they had regained the initiative. But the fluctuations also reflected the continuing dilemmas of House leadership. The fluidity of member coalitions from issue to issue and the need to assemble extraordinary majorities in the face of likely vetoes from a Republican president make it risky to write off swing votes or invoke sanctions against them. Sanctions, moreover, are likely to have only a limited impact if members see them as running counter to the imperatives of "voting their district."

These fluctuations between carrot and stick have become less extreme in recent years, partly because nothing like the boll weevil insurrection has confronted House Democrats. But Steering and Policy leverage is still not used in a wholly consistent fashion. When Jim Wright became Speaker, he left little doubt that he intended to reserve choice committee assignments for party loyalists; he once even floated the unheard-of idea of putting members on probation for their first term in new assignments.[22] But two midsession committee appointments in the 101st Congress after Wright's resignation raised questions about the new leadership's intent. A choice Energy and Commerce slot was awarded in early 1990 to a member who had voted against the leadership on the highest-profile party test of the previous fall, a capital gains tax reduction. And the Appropriations slot that opened up in the spring of 1990 was awarded to the only one of the five major contenders who had defected on the most visible vote of that session (in this case the leadership of both parties), the pay-raise/ethics package. As one of those five contenders, I took special note of the discussions that followed these episodes and concluded that the pattern was unlikely to continue. Indeed the leadership's hand was far more evident in the committee assignments made by Steering and Policy at the beginning of the 102nd Congress, and I was at that point elected to Appropriations as part of a slate endorsed by the Speaker.

My party voting score was 84 for my first term in the House, 91 for my second—somewhat above the average scores indicated in figure 6.1 and relatively high for a southern member. These scores for the most part have come "naturally"; they reflect a congruence among Democratic positions, my values and beliefs, and what I take to be the interests of my district. They also reflect the leadership practices and powers I have described: setting agendas, scheduling and structuring decisions, informing and persuading, modifying and accommodating—all designed to facilitate party support among members like myself. My record does contain some defections, mostly on minor matters but occasionally on important ones, as when I found myself at odds both strategically and substantively with Speaker Wright on some key budget votes in late 1987. I had some uncomfortable moments with Wright and Coelho, particularly during my first term when I had little opportunity to play a part in shaping decisions and they no doubt were sending some signals to me. But I have much more often been treated as a member of the team and reinforced in my basic inclination toward party loyalty.

As I stressed earlier, not every member's story would be the same. No two members have exactly the same mix of personal predilections, electoral constraints, and district interests, and we work in a system that gives those individual differences unusually free rein. By world parliamentary standards, the U.S. House, despite its strengthened party operations, would never qualify as a "tight ship." Every member has reason from time to time to take advantage of that freedom, but we also have reason to reflect on the frustrations and failures its excesses bring to the institution. The party structure is the most important mechanism we have to contain those excesses and to impose a measure of collective responsibility upon ourselves. The precise rewards and costs of party loyalty will differ for members differently situated. But for all, I believe, there ought to be a presumption in its favor, for it is the party connection that enables a House of disparate parts to function and that lets the individual member move beyond good intentions to what Edmund Burke called "doing his duty with effect."[23]

Notes

1. Richard Fenno, *Home Style: House Members in Their Districts* (Boston: Little, Brown, 1978), p. 244.

2. See David E. Price, *The Congressional Experience: A View from the Hill* (Boulder: Westview Press, 1992), ch. 10.

3. For useful accounts which root strengthened party operations in the profit-and-loss calculations of individual members (especially liberal Democrats), see Barbara Sinclair, "Strong Party Leadership in a Weak Party Era—The Evolution of Party Leadership in the Modern House" (prepared for delivery at the Carl Albert Center, University of Oklahoma, 12 April 1990); and David W. Rohde, *Parties and Leaders in the Postreform House* (Chicago: University of Chicago Press, 1991).

4. Roger Davidson, "The New Centralization on Capitol Hill," *Review of Politics*, 50 (Summer 1988): 350–51.

5. "Three important goals for the Democrats are to enhance the authority of the Speaker; make sure that Democratic membership on the legislative committees is representative; and to increase the individual responsibility of each Democrat toward his leaders." Richard Bolling, *House Out of Order* (New York: E. P. Dutton, 1965), pp. 236–38.

6. Sidney Waldman, "Majority Leadership in the House of Representatives," *Political Science Quarterly*, 95 (Fall 1980): 383–85.

7. Steven S. Smith and Christopher J. Deering, *Committees in Congress*, 2nd ed. (Washington, D.C.: Congressional Quarterly Press, 1990), pp. 179–89.

8. Davidson, "New Centralization," p. 355.

9. David E. Price, "The House of Representatives: A Report from the Field," in Lawrence C. Dodd and Bruce I. Oppenheimer, eds., *Congress Reconsidered*, 4th ed. (Washington, D.C.: Congressional Quarterly Press, 1989), pp. 424–30.

10. For a survey of postreform Democratic factions and an account of the "considerable increase in Democratic unity and cohesion," see Rohde, *Parties and Leaders*, pp. 45–58.

11. Davidson, "New Centralization," p. 358.

12. Lawrence D. Dodd and Bruce I. Oppenheimer, "Consolidating Power in the House: The Rise of a New Oligarchy," in Dodd and Oppenheimer, *Congress Reconsidered*, p. 60.

13. Sinclair, "Strong Party Leadership," p. 46. Rohde aptly terms this system "conditional party government," reflective both of the goals of congressional reformers and of modern electoral realities: "Unlike in parliamentary systems, party leadership would not make policy decisions which would receive automatic support from the rank and file. Rather, the direction of influence would be reversed and there would be party responsibility *only* if there were widespread policy agreement among House Democrats. When agreement was present on a matter that was important to party members, the leadership would be expected to use the tools at their disposal to advance the cause." *Parties and Leaders*, p. 31; cf. p. 166.

14. For an inventory of possible changes ranging from state law to presidential nomination rules, see David E. Price, *Bringing Back the Parties* (Washington, D.C.: Congressional Quarterly Press, 1984), Chs. 5–8. For a list of party-strengthening campaign finance reforms more ambitious than the ones outlined here, see Ibid., pp. 254–60.

15. This is not to say that limits on party contributions or expenditures should be lifted entirely. Not only would such a change heavily favor well-financed Republican organizations, it could also put parties more completely under candidate control, encouraging their use as mere conduits for funds generated elsewhere. Ibid., p. 258.

16. "Soft money" is money given to parties outside the prohibitions and limitations of federal law. It is most commonly given to state parties under state law, which is generally less restrictive than federal law and in some cases permits direct corporate and union contributions. These funds have often been used, in some cases quite liberally, to benefit federal, especially presidential, candidates.

17. These are essentially the suggestions I made in testimony before the Task Force on Campaign Finance Reform of the Committee on House Administration, Hearings on "Campaign Finance Reform," 30 April 1991, pp. 168–83.

18. See Price, *Bringing Back the Parties*, pp. 280–82.

19. Ibid., p. 55; and relevant numbers of the *Congressional Quarterly Almanac*.

20. One glaring example is an amendment my colleague Martin Lancaster (D-NC) proposed but was not allowed to offer to the Americans with Disabilities Act in 1990. The amendment, which the disabilities lobby opposed but felt it would be difficult to defeat, would have required a disabled individual to inform

the owner of public facilities of his or her disability prior to bringing suit, thus encouraging the resolution of problems short of litigation.

21. See Rohde, *Parties and Leaders*, pp. 47, 78–81. On the particularly instructive case of Representative (now Senator) Phil Gramm, who was able to convince his constituents that his richly deserved party discipline was a badge of honor, see Price, *Bringing Back the Parties*, p. 67.

22. See the episodes recounted in John M. Barry, *The Ambition and the Power* (New York: Viking, 1989), pp. 393, 542–43.

23. Edmund Burke, "Thoughts on the Cause of the Present Discontents," in *Works* (London: George Bell and Sons, 1983), vol. 1, p. 375.

7

Where's the Party?

William M. Thomas

Many of us who participate in the practical art of American politics wonder whether political parties will be relevant to the governing of America in the coming generation. Is there room for organized citizens to play a significant role when politics seems to depend more and more on campaign money from special-interest groups and powerful officeholders? Is there a future for broad-based groups of citizens with the patience and tolerance to make the transition from single-issue causes to building a diverse majority party? Will the next generation of political leaders recognize that successful politics is a "team sport," not just a beauty contest? And perhaps most important, how many citizens of the next generation will be political participants? Can our system attract the energy and commitment of the people in whose name we govern?

These are the challenges that political parties face as they look at American government in the twenty-first century. If we fail in our responses to these challenges, not only will our parties have failed, but perhaps our entire political system will have failed as well. There is no other institution in American society that can take the place of the citizen-based political party as a vehicle for self-government.

But what should the responsibilities of political parties be in the twenty-first century? Political columnist David Broder says they exist "to inform, mobilize, and empower" those very disillusioned citizens who have often given up on politics as a means of effecting change. Parties do this through the candidates they nominate. And the recent Supreme Court decision of *Tashjian v. Republican Party of Connecticut* gives parties the right to decide their method of selecting the candidates they present to the voters. As parties nominate candidates and mobilize citizens to elect them, a more comprehensive agenda of party responsibilities might look like this:

1. Provide a means for citizen activists to influence the political process from the grassroots.

2. Develop citizen leaders over the long term by investing in human capital.
3. Balance priorities among competing special interest groups with an overall view of the national interest.
4. Build stable majority coalitions that rely on principle as well as pragmatism for governing.
5. Maintain competition in American politics.
6. Promote bottom-up rather than top-down decision making about who gets elected to political office.

In many ways, a common denominator of these larger goals is an effort to balance the influence of incumbents with organized citizen power.

I am an incumbent officeholder who believes in strong, viable political parties. My career in politics and my view of parties has been shaped over the years through my involvement in the party structure. During my early years I lived in the city of San Pedro, a working-class suburb of Los Angeles. My father was a Truman Democrat, and my mother a Republican. We moved in my teenage years to Orange County where I attended community college and had a philosophy teacher who was a strong conservative. I went on to San Francisco State University before Dr. Hayakawa's stand against intolerant radicalism made it famous and wound up in 1965 as a professor of political science at Bakersfield College in California's San Joaquin Valley.

In Bakersfield I gained the attention and respect of local Republicans for my issue research and for my use of county-wide maps, each precinct color-coded to reflect its Republican vote percentage in the past election. I was surprised, however, when in January 1973 several former students stopped by to ask if I would consider serving as chairman of the Republican Party of Kern County. A group of local citizens concerned about the way Richard Nixon's 1972 campaign had run roughshod over the local political structure was determined to revitalize the Republican Party in Bakersfield. I accepted.

As it turned out, one of my major tasks was finding a Republican candidate to oppose the local Democrat assemblyman. No one wanted to run. It was 1974, and the country was "wallowing in Watergate." After many unsuccessful conversations, I solved the problem in the best way I could. I agreed to run myself. The race was considered hopeless, but I had worked so hard convincing others that the race could be won, I believed it could be.

We raised and spent $54,000 for the primary and general election combined. That would be just under $150,000 in 1990 dollars. California assembly races today routinely cost $400,000 or more—often much more. But in 1974 you could buy thirty seconds of Monday Night Football in Bakersfield for $100 or Saturday college football for $75. As the campaign progressed, I saw a real opportunity: the annual Oklahoma vs. Texas game, ten days before the election. It was a potent combination, for many Kern County residents had dust-bowl roots. My several commercials late in that game paid off when the game turned out to be extremely close and competitive. That weekend I gained instant name recognition.

My major campaign fundraiser was a $25 event with Governor Ronald Reagan. We raised $12,000 in one day, about one-quarter of my entire budget. I had a small army of volunteers, including friends from the Kern County Republican Central committee and former students who had interned on political campaigns for credit while in my classes years before. They helped distribute fifteen thousand bumper stickers and dug post holes all over the county by hand for four-by-four signs. It *was* a grass-roots campaign!

My message was simple and issues-oriented. I told the people what I believed and that if they believed what I did, they should support me for the assembly. I said that if you do not agree with the person who represents you, you have the ability to control your government by making a change. With 53 percent of the vote, I defeated the incumbent Democrat. I was the only California nonincumbent Republican in any race to defeat an incumbent Democrat in 1974. My base had been the Republican Party of Kern County, and I have never forgotten that.

Four years later, the incumbent congressman in my district passed away unexpectedly after the primary and in the middle of the campaign. Under an obscure provision of California law, a special Republican Party Convention of all elected county and state central committee members from the three counties of the district was convened to nominate a new GOP candidate. Unfortunately, one county with less than 5 percent of the voting population of the district had nearly the same number of central committee members and therefore as many votes as the major county with the bulk of the population. This small county had a favorite-son candidate who was unusually determined. Eight ballots were taken before the convention reached a decision. Finally, however, as the senior Republican elected official in the district, I was nominated. It was this experience perhaps that made me more sensitive to the issue of one-person–one-vote and the importance of a fairly drawn district to voters' ability to select their leaders.

In any case, in 1978 I was elected to Congress. It was there that I got to know Congressman Phil Burton (D-CA), surely one of the most inspired Democratic politicians and strategists of his time. Phil had grown up in the rough-and-tumble world of San Francisco politics. He took few prisoners. When the time came to redraw the boundary lines for California congressional districts, Burton was true to character. In 1981, under lines the courts had drawn in the 1970s, California's congressional delegation had twenty-one Republicans and twenty-two Democrats. Then Burton redrew the lines.

In 1984, despite the Reagan landslide of that year, the newly redrawn political map of California produced twenty-seven Democrats and eighteen Republicans. Republicans spent millions of dollars on lawsuits and four referenda and initiative efforts, but Burton's work survived. It was an artistic monument that stifled true competition for Congress in California for a decade. But the Democratic party's gain was the people's loss. While the 1980s saw Republican George Deukmejian defeat Democrat Tom Bradley for governor and Democrat Alan Cranston defeat Republican Ed Zschau for senator by the narrowest of margins, California congressional voters never had a real choice. Their delegation was virtually handpicked for them. Not until 1990 did demographic trends and scandals at opposite ends of the state result in the defeat of a few incumbents.

During those years, it was my job as the California GOP representative on the National Republican Congressional Committee, to protect and promote the interests of California Republicans in the redistricting process. More than anything else, I saw how the interests of incumbent legislators and the overall interests of a party coalition can conflict during the redistricting process. Legislators want safe districts for themselves regardless of the consequences. But a political party wants competitive districts to maximize its chances to produce a legislative majority.

Burton and his ally, Speaker of the Assembly Willie Brown, had manipulated Republican legislators so skillfully in 1982 that even though their first plan for state legislative districts was rejected by the voters in a referendum, their slightly revised plan for state legislative district lines passed with support from key Republican legislators. The two-thirds vote in favor of the plan made its nullification by referendum a second time impossible under state law. The inability to rescind the legislative plan by referendum doomed any hope of financing a referendum against the Democrat congressional plan even though no Republicans had voted for it. These plans guaranteed Democratic majorities for a decade. Some of those Republicans who voted for their own safe districts are still in office today.

In 1990 a coalition of reformers, remembering the 1980s, placed an initiative on the ballot to remove the redistricting power from the legislature. Supported by Ronald Reagan and the California League of Women Voters, its prospects seemed good. But the California Republican Party, now under the control of some of the very legislators whose votes passed Willie Brown's reapportionment plans in 1982, gave the initiative virtually no support. According to a memo by the initiative's campaign manager, the reapportionment effort was, in effect, sabotaged by party officials.[1] In 1992 Democrats still controlled the California legislature, but because Republican governor Pete Wilson held together enough Republican legislators to support his veto of any gerrymandered plan, the State Supreme Court drew the new districts, and the Court has now adopted a plan without any premeditated partisan advantage.

But the lesson is clear. The interests of incumbent legislators and the interests of those who want to build party majorities are not always the same. Most incumbents of either party want power to flow from the top (themselves) down. They are not really interested in competitive elections. The party grass-roots, citizens who believe in a party philosophy, see things in a different light. Only a strong party can stand up for its interests, even against incumbent legislators. That is one reason why I believe in strong parties.

Yet one may ask, "How do American political parties actually perform in the political arena?" Certainly many observers feel that the influence of political parties has declined in recent years. Interestingly, however, voters who identify with a party have become slightly more loyal to party candidates over the past twenty years. In 1988, for example, voters who identified with a party were loyal to their party's candidates about 76 percent of the time. The 1980 party loyalty average was about 70 percent, the 1968 average about 72 percent. Thus, there was actually a 4 percent increase in party voting between 1968 and 1988. Following the same trend, the number of self-identified "pure" independents who do not identify even weakly with a political party has decreased somewhat over the past twenty years. In 1968, 9 percent of voters who responded in surveys of presidential voting considered themselves independents. In 1980 that figure was 8 percent, and in 1984 and 1988 it was only 7 percent. Percentages for independents in congressional elections showed less change but were also at 7 percent in 1988.[2] This is not much movement, but it is movement in the right direction.

In short, parties still define much of the way American voters view the political process. Unfortunately, the extent of party influence on electoral outcomes is not as certain. The parties' combined share of financial participation in House elections, for example, has declined substantially. In 1976, the percentage of funds spent by parties on behalf of candidates for the House of Representatives was about 8 percent of the funds raised by all House candidates. By 1988, the party percentage had been cut in half to only 4 percent of all House campaign funds.[3] Party spending has obviously become less of a factor in congressional elections as other sources of funding have increased.

During this period, contributions by political action committees (PACs), most sponsored by corporate and union special interests or ideological single-issue groups, soared dramatically. In 1980, PACs contributed about $55 million to candidates for Congress. By 1988, PACs contributed over $147 million to candidates, nearly a threefold increase.[4] PACs were specifically authorized by Congress in 1974. They have served as a valuable method of educating and involving new people in the American political process. Unfortunately, however, too many PACs have been "captured" by incumbents who vote on the issues of interest to PACs. In 1990, for example, the ratio of funds contributed by PACs to incumbents to funds given to challengers was 7:1, a major reason for the lack of competitiveness in congressional elections. Stronger political parties could help balance the current tendency of PACs to favor incumbents and provide candidates with stronger sources of non-special interest funding. Funds donated to candidates by political parties, which raise money from large numbers of donors with diverse interests, are, in my opinion, a healthy complement to the political process.

Part of the reason PACs have eclipsed parties in the campaign fund-raising process is the unlimited potential for proliferation in the number of political action committees, while the number of party committees is limited by the geography of the fifty states and their component cities, towns, and counties. In 1980, there were 2,551 PACs of all types. By 1991, there were over 4,000.[5] During the same period, however, inflation rapidly eroded the contributing power of both PACs and parties. While contribution limits for PACs and direct party contributions have remained the same since 1974, prices have increased 178 percent from 1974 to 1991 and over 60 percent since 1980.[6] In other words, to match the value of a $100 contribution in 1974, one must contribute $278 today. To match the value of $100 given in 1980, today's contribution must be $160.

Special interests representing more than one economic unit can compensate for the erosion in the value of their contributions by sponsoring additional PACs. Parties simply cannot do this.

The inflation multiplier provided in the 1974 law applies only to coordinated party expenditures, not to direct contributions by political parties. The result is that a growing portion of funds contributed by political parties comes from coordinated expenditures that in practice are controlled by the national parties. In 1980, direct party contributions were about 25 percent of the total amount spent to support party candidates, while 1990 direct contributions had shrunk to less than 20 percent of the total.[7] Thus, the 1974 laws not only hamstring local political parties by reducing them to the status of a special interest PAC but also contribute to the centralization of political financial power in the national parties, moving it from the grass-roots, where it should be, to the national level.

A classic example of the way the interests of incumbent officeholders can clash with the interests of the party as a whole occurred during the debate over the pay-raise–ethics package enacted in 1989. Although polls showed that overwhelming numbers of voters opposed the pay raise and that it could be a potent issue in the 1990 elections, a bipartisan deal was struck as part of the agreement on the package. The deal committed both party congressional committees to refrain from financially supporting candidates who made the pay raise an issue in the campaign. This is a clear case of power flowing from the top down rather than from the bottom up in a party institution.

Traditionally, political parties have been expected to provide candidates with volunteers, as well as financial support. But in California the state Republican party resorted to hiring thousands of paid "volunteers" to canvass on election day, a task traditionally done by real volunteers from the local party structure. Party leaders simply decided that the local structure was incapable of fulfilling its responsibility. Ironically, the erosion of a Republican volunteer-based party network in California was exacerbated by a power shift in the party apparatus toward the GOP legislative incumbents in Sacramento. In 1987 and 1988 party rules were changed to ensure that party delegates appointed by incumbents and their allies would have a controlling share of votes on the state central committee. Candidates supported by the incumbent coalition have won by narrow margins over candidates supported by a volunteer group coalition in central committee elections since the rules change. These incumbent allies, moreover, are making party decisions on reapportionment for the 1990 cycle.

Once again, as at the national level, we see an example of incumbents seeking to assert top-down control of local party institutions to promote their own agenda. There are some indications, however, that a combination of factors may bring about a revival of issue-oriented volunteerism in political parties, particularly among young people. In the era of the two-income family, such a renewal of volunteerism in politics may depend heavily on the attitudes of younger citizens. More than any other age group, they have both the time and the physical energy to have a significant impact on races, especially at the congressional and state legislative level.

With voter turnout in off years at a level of barely more than 35 percent of the voting-age population, the potential for volunteers to affect election outcomes through registration and get-out-the-vote (GOTV) activities is enormous. In the art of voter persuasion, there are increased opportunities for volunteers because voters are increasingly saturated by direct mail and less accessible through television advertising. Some voters have abandoned network television or zip and zap their way through commercials with VCRs and remote channel changers. On the other hand, as few as one hundred volunteers walking precincts and talking personally to voters for four weekends before election day and on election day can switch from 2 to 5 percent of the vote in a close race.

In 1988, when less than 2 percent of incumbents were defeated in the general election, there were still twenty-three races for Congress decided by less than 2 percent of the vote and twenty more decided by 5 percent or less. In 1990, when 94 percent of incumbents were reelected, there were eleven races decided by 2 percent and twenty-nine decided by 5 percent or less.[8] Even though these numbers are shockingly low for an electoral system that ought to be competitive and provide voters with meaningful choices, they illustrate the impact that a tiny number of committed volunteer activists could have on American politics. Unfortunately, especially in congressional contests, the challenge of building such a volunteer team for a campaign during its typical nine-month cycle is too great. Fund-raising, the candidate's schedule, and effective media come first, making volunteer organizing a fourth or fifth priority. Put another way, in the current political environment, an investment in new volunteers simply does not yield the kind of short-term returns that come from an investment in a fund-raising network or quality media. Unfortunately, even the sources of campaign funding encourage this tendency to emphasize expensive high-tech campaigning at the expense of grass-roots volunteerism.

The national committees provide much of the funding and even more important the credibility for challenger campaigns. At one time or another in their campaign, many Republican challengers make the pilgrimage to Washington and run the gauntlet of party consultants and political professionals, who determine if they are "serious" candidates. Being "serious," however, boils down to "How big is your budget?" and "Which consultants have you hired?" Unfortunately, the party consultants who evaluate the candidate are often products of the high-priced, high-tech campaign world. The grass-roots campaign is scorned.

Consultants can be understood, if not forgiven, for favoring campaigns with cash in the bank and experienced consultants. Claims of volunteer support and local campaign expertise are hard to verify and all too often exaggerated. And here is where political parties have failed. From a party point of view, an investment in volunteers is not a one-shot purchase. Unlike a television ad or a piece of mail, a new volunteer will be around the day after the election, now perhaps an experienced volunteer leader for the next election. It is parties and the future candidates they represent, not individual candidates, who reap the most benefit from the long-term development of a volunteer force. Yet the parties are not as successful as they should be at volunteer development.

The California Democratic Party's 1990 campaign is a classic case in point. Widely credited with an effective 1988 grass-roots GOTV program, the party sharply curtailed its ambitious plans to expand this network in 1990. Reportedly at the direction of its candidate for governor, Democratic expenditures went to purchase media instead. Some have speculated that the reason for the decision to deemphasize grass-roots organizing in 1990 was a fear of the influence that could be wielded within the party by the leaders of such a grass-roots movement. Donors, lobbyists, and many special interests cannot control volunteers any more than media consultants can. It is safer to build political power in a bank account or a donor file. It is unsafe to put all your volunteers in a room where they might decide to choose a new leader.

Successful party leaders understand that to be a winner, a bigger tent with a larger and more diverse volunteer membership inside is preferable to the smaller and more homogeneous alternative. They also understand that only when the membership has an opportunity to elect the leadership can the kind of volunteer commitment that wins elections over the long haul be developed. Ed Rollins, the outspoken former chairman of the National Republican Congressional Committee, says that what the Republican party needs even more than money is a revitalized network of volunteers. "We've got to get to the grassroots," Rollins insists, "if we want to win."[9] Rollins and other thoughtful strategists know that it was an edge in volunteers that contributed decisively to the narrow victory of Democrat John Olver over Republican Steven Pierce in the recent special election to fill a vacancy in the First Congressional District of Massachusetts.

What political parties need more than ever today are leaders who are committed to rebuilding America's political parties as grass-roots, local-initiative, volunteer-oriented organizations. The question remains, however: "What can we at the national legislative level do to encourage this revitalization?"

Currently I serve as the ranking Republican member of the Committee on House Administration and its Task Force on Campaign Reform. We are in the process of developing legislation to reform the way campaigns for Congress are run. In hearings in Washington and around the country, we have heard testimony about the state of campaign finance laws. There is widespread concern expressed about the lack of competition and the appearance (and in some cases the reality) of excessive influence from special interest money in American politics. Some reformers advocate a fixed limit on spending for political campaigns and an infusion of tax dollars to finance campaigns with public money. In my view, these proposals will reduce competition and participation rather than increase them. No fixed limit can account for the differences in campaign costs in districts around the country. And equal limits for challenger and incumbent totally ignore the money that incumbents can spend on taxpayer-financed franked mail, a tangible election benefit.

Taxpayer financing is simply one more step toward insulating the incumbent completely from any reliance on his constituents for support. With a nearly guaranteed source of money, a built-in head start in taxpayer-financed mail, and an artificial limit on what his opponent can spend, the incumbent will be safer than ever. Citizens will have even less reason to be involved, through parties or in any other way. Once again, power and money will flow from the top down.

I believe there is a better solution: Reempower political parties to level the playing field and restore competitiveness to the electoral process. We should reempower political parties to help counterbalance the influence of special interests and the built-in advantages of incumbency. And most important, we should create a political environment in which the organizing efforts of the local party and citizen activist become as important as the money raised from lobbyists and wealthy special interests around the nation. A few key changes in election law could make an enormous difference in the role parties play in American elections.

First, party contribution limits to candidates for federal office should be increased. There are many ways to do this, but two are obvious:

1. Allow parties to match, in contributions to challengers only, the value of funds carried over by an incumbent from a previous election.
2. Allow parties to match, in contributions to challengers only, the value of unsolicited franked mail sent out by an incumbent in an election year.

These two reforms alone would go far toward giving challengers the ability to offset the built-in advantages of incumbents with accumulated war chests and large taxpayer-financed franking budgets.

Second, we should encourage more individual rather than special interest contributions to political parties. There should be a separate limit for contributions to political parties, one that is not decreased by contributions to candidates. The current limits on contributions to parties are adequate if they do not count against the limit for candidate contributions. On the other hand, political parties that engage in activities to influence a federal election, such as voter registration and get-out-the-vote drives, should not become a conduit for so-called soft money that cannot be contributed legally to the candidate. All party funds for these so-called mixed activities should come from sources that could have been contributed directly to the candidates. In other words, party activities that affect federal elections should receive no corporate or labor union funds. And there should be no more million-dollar presidential-year gifts to political parties by wealthy donors. Strong parties must be built on a broad base of citizen support, not the whims of a few special interests or megadonors.

Third, special attention should be given to developing a stronger role for local political parties as opposed to the state and national parties. It is at the local level that volunteer and donor recruitment are so crucial to the revitalization of our party system that must take place:

1. Local city and county parties should be able to provide unlimited assistance to candidates in their area so long as funds are raised from individuals within the jurisdiction of the local party.
2. Currently, state and local parties are allowed to spend unlimited amounts on voter-registration and get-out-the-vote drives on behalf of candidates for president but not for Congress. Parties should be able to engage in the same kinds of activities for congressional elections as they can for presidential elections.

Fourth and most important, there ought to be a requirement that candidates raise a majority of their campaign funds from individuals in the district the candidate seeks to represent. No other reform I know of would have as dramatic an impact on the way elections are conducted in America.

This reform would reempower the grass-roots voter and contributor because no candidate could raise a dollar in special interest PAC or Washington-lobbyist money until a dollar had been raised from an individual in the district. The average citizen, now a bystander in the media-money-PAC campaign, would have a reason to be involved in politics again. Campaigns would be transformed, focusing on community barbecues and neighborhood precinct walks rather than Washington receptions and PAC breakfasts. Volunteers and small donors would be decisive elements in these campaigns. Political parties, especially local parties, would become vital sources of local volunteers and donors at the beginning of each election campaign. Candidates, unable to rely totally on a flow of money from outside the district, would be forced to spend more time campaigning and soliciting support personally from the constituents they are supposed to represent.

This change, reuniting the fund-raising precinct with the voting precinct, would be the single most important reempowerment of voters and parties at the grass-roots in recent political history. Incumbents out of touch with their districts but in touch with special interests in Washington would lose more often to aggressive local challengers with a strong base in the community.

None of these reforms by themselves, however, can revitalize political parties in America. They can only make it easier for committed citizen activists, perhaps even the readers of this chapter, to make a difference. The challenge for us, as practitioners in American politics, is to keep striving to make that difference.

Notes

1. Memo: Background on Funding Problems With Prop. 119, 7/10/90.

2. Norman J. Ornstein, Thomas E. Mann, and Michael J. Malbin, *Vital Statistics on Congress 1989–1990*, (Congressional Quarterly) p. 65 (Table 2-16: Party Line Voting in Presidential and Congressional Elections 1956–1988).

Sources: SRC/CPS "National Election Studies 1956–86"; calculations for 1956–1978 from Thomas E. Mann and Raymond E. Wolfinger. "Candidates and Parties in Congressional Elections," *American Political Science Review* (September 1980); calculations for 1980, Gary C. Jacobson, *The Politics of Congressional Elections* (Boston: Little, Brown, 1982); calculations for 1982–1986, Peverill Squire and Michael Hagen, the University of California State Data Program; calculations for 1988, Jon Krasno, The Brookings Institution.

3. Ibid., p. 85 (Table 3-9: Funding Sources For Congressional Candidates in General Elections by Party 1974–1988).

Sources: for 1974, Gary C. Jacobson, *Money in Congressional Elections* (New Haven: Yale University Press, 1980), Ch. 3; for 1976, Federal Election Commission, *Disclosure Series No. 4* (National Party Committees), *DS No. 6* (Senate Campaigns), and *DS No. 9* (House Campaigns), September 1977; for 1978, Federal Election Commission, *RFA, 1977–78, Interim Report No. 5* (U.S. Senate and House Campaigns), June 1979, 31–32; for 1980, *Federal Election Commission, Reports on Financial Activity, 1979–80, Final Report* (U.S. Senate and House Campaigns), January 1982, 49–50; for 1982, Federal Election Commission, *Reports on Financial Activity 1981–82, Final Report* (U.S. Senate and

House Campaigns), October 1983, 33–34; for 1984, Federal Election Commission, *Reports on Financial Activity, 1983–84, Final Report* (U.S. Senate and House Campaigns), November 1985; for 1986, Federal Election Commission, *RFA, 1985–86, Final Report* (U.S. Senate and House Campaigns), 37–41; for 1988, Federal Election Commission, "$458 Million Spent by 1988 Congressional Campaigns," press release, 24 February 1989; "FEC Summarizes 1988 Political Party Activity," 26 March 1989.

4. Ibid., p. 99 (Table 3-14: Financial Activity of Political Action Committees, 1972–1988).

Sources: for 1972–1976 and for footnotes, Cantor, "Political Action Committees," 87–88; for 1978, Federal Election Commission, *Reports on Financial Activity, 1977–78, Interim Report No. 5* (U.S. Senate and House Campaigns), June 1979, 94; for 1980, *Federal Election Commission, Reports on Financial Activity, 1979–80, Final Report* (U.S. Senate and House Campaigns), January 1982, 127; for 1982, Federal Election Commission, *Reports on Financial Activity 1981–82, Final Report* (U.S. Senate and House Campaigns), October 1983, 92; for 1984, Federal Election Commission, *Reports on Financial Activity, 1983–84, Final Report* (U.S. Senate and House Campaigns), November 1985, 101; for 1986, Federal Election Commission, "FEC Final Report on 1986 PAC Activity," press release, 5 May 1988; for 1988, Federal Election Commission, "FEC Finds Slower Growth at PAC Activity During 1988 Election Cycle," press release, 9 April 1989.

5. *Federal Election Commission Record*, 17, p. 7.

6. Figures from the Economic Policy Division of the United States Department of the Treasury.

7. Federal Election Commission, Summary of 1989–90 Political Party Finances, 15 March 1991.

8. Sources: 1988 figures are from Federal Election Commission, *Reports on Financial Activity 1987–88, Final Report*, September 1989; 1990 figures are from Federal Election Commission "1990 Congressional Election Spending Drops to a Low Point," press release, 22 February 1991.

9. Ed Rollins, "What My Party has to do to Become a Majority in the House" (speech to the Heritage Foundation, 23 January 1991).

8

Legislating Responsibility

American Political Parties and the Law

Jerome M. Mileur

The call for a more responsible two-party system in America issued forty-two years ago by a committee of the American Political Science Association (APSA) makes a compelling case for the importance in a democratic polity of a party system organized to facilitate voter control over the programmatic direction of government. However one may judge the many recommendations of the committee, there is no denying that in a democracy rightly ordered the people must have a voice in how they are governed and that their voice should speak to the direction of government as well as to its staffing—to the *what* of government as well as the *by whom*.

But the committee, while offering many "concrete lines of approach" for reforming American parties, nowhere says how its proposals are to be achieved. The committee thus has a plan for a better party system but no strategy for its realization. The reason for this is that the committee never asks the question "Why are American parties as they are?" This is an old criticism of the committee's work, one made early and well by Austin Ranney.[1] But it is a criticism of fundamental importance, for with no explanation why American parties are as they are, the committee is reduced to what is at best a truism: "Real change" will come when ordinary citizens and party leaders alike understand and appreciate the need for a more responsible party system.[2]

The usual explanation for the "irresponsible" character of American parties is that our Constitution makes our party system what it is. The historian Richard Hofstadter put it succinctly: We have a Constitution against parties.[3] The committee, however, seems uncertain about this. It acknowledges that federalism contributes to national and state parties that are largely independent of one another but denies that federalism is the cause. The "real problem," it says, is the failure of the parties to achieve a correct balance of power within the federal system, which requires a greater nationalization of party power. It is silent on how this is to be done. Similarly, the committee laments that there is no locus of party leadership in the American system, no figure with authority over party affairs, but it nowhere faults the constitutional separation of powers for this.[4]

Indeed the committee dismisses constitutional reform as impractical and urges the parties to adapt more effectively to the Constitution. It calls upon the parties to explore opportunities for more responsible operation within the existing arrangements and argues that it is logical to discover what is possible before considering what constitutional changes are needed.[5] At the same time, there is no suggestion that the Constitution might be used in some way to achieve a more responsible party system. Ironically, in the same decade that the committee's report was published, the Supreme Court recognized a right of association that would in time give the major parties a new constitutional tool with which, within limits, to shape their being under protection of the Constitution.

The Constitution aside, the committee also has little to say about the effects of state regulation on the parties, especially on the national parties. It acknowledges that American parties have their legal bases in the states but nowhere asks whether or how state law impedes or facilitates the realization of responsible party government. Our party system is unusual among democratic nations in the western tradition for the sheer volume and restrictiveness of its legal regulation—for the most part, a body of state statutes dealing with party organization, membership, and activities across a wide range of matters.[6]

A member of the APSA Committee on Political Parties, Fritz Morstein Marx, in an article on party responsibility in Congress published in the same year as the committee's report, argues that more often than not it is the local and state parties that exercise discipline over their members of Congress and that this "dispersal of control opens the door to irresponsibility in legislation." Marx adds that "the only real menace to the American two-party system arises from incapacity of the parties for representation in the national sense."[7] Oddly, this blunt assessment of the debilitating effects of state and local party control over national legislators—a control that is secured by the principle of federalism and the fact of state party regulation—does not find expression in the committee's report.

The committee's reluctance to ask the strategic question why American parties are as they are and its reticence to face the constitutional and state statutory imperatives for the structure of American parties leaves its work interesting for its recommendations and insights and challenging for its concern with how best to organize the politics of mass democracy in America but nonetheless disappointing in how to realize its objectives. Political parties are products of their environments—legal, historical, and cultural—and their reconditioning requires confronting these factors squarely. This chapter examines only one of these shaping factors—the legal—and argues that the direction of constitutional law over the past two decades, while not directly supportive of the responsible parties ideal, has created a legal environment in which parties in general and national parties in particular are freer to determine their organization, powers, membership, activities, and other matters seen by the committee as key to stronger parties.

The Origin of Parties

Political organizations (social clubs interested in local elections) and partisan divisions (court v. country) were evident in prerevolutionary America. After the Revolution, the new nation saw the formation of strong state legislative parties—the Albany Regency and Richmond Junta among others. Nationally, partylike activities and organizations emerged early under the federal Constitution of 1788, born of the competition between Alexander Hamilton and Thomas Jefferson over the direction of the new nation. But these "national" parties, the Federalists and Democratic-Republicans, like those to follow, were localist in their policy appeals and electoral strategies.

American political parties thus began as voluntary associations, as extralegal and extraconstitutional institutions, and they were from the outset artifacts of an electoral system shaped by the Constitution. Reform of this system began soon after the Constitution was in place, provoked by the nascent party system. Ratification of the Twelfth Amendment in 1804, revising the Electoral College vote for president, was prompted by the rise of political parties in national politics.[8] State registration of voters, which began in 1800 and won constitutional approval in the 1830s, paralleled the growth of a party system and had legal implications for the parties.[9]

For the most part, however, there was little regulation of political parties in the nation's first century under the Constitution. The legal status of parties began to change in the latter part of the nineteenth century as reform movements in the states, aimed in part at correcting the "evils" of the party system, won adoption of the Australian ballot and the mandatory direct primary. Additionally, in the Populist and Progressive years at the end of the nineteenth and beginning of the twentieth centuries, many states passed corrupt practices acts regulating campaign finance and other aspects of the political process.[10]

Together, these reforms brought parties under the law, recognizing their role in the electoral process, conferring certain privileges and advantages upon them, and in return imposing controls upon their organization and activities.[11]

The Australian ballot system, which combined secrecy in voting with an official state-prepared ballot, first won adoption on a statewide basis in Massachusetts in 1888. It spread quickly thereafter and was generally the law throughout the country by the end of the century.[12] This system recognized the political party and gave it both legal standing and privileged access to the ballot for its candidates. In doing so, it defined and differentiated between parties in terms of their electoral support and also subjected all parties to certain restrictions.[13] The effect of these laws was that parties ceased to be merely voluntary associations with complete control over their operations and became part of the legal machinery for state elections.

The direct primary as a system for party nominations was first used by the parties themselves but became a matter of state concern in 1866 when California adopted a plan for state parties if they chose to use it. Most of the early state primary legislation followed the California example and was optional.[14] But by the latter years of the nineteenth century and first decades of the twentieth, state laws ceased to be optional and became mandatory.[15] Among other things, primary laws established tests for party membership and in their advanced form also regulated the organization of political parties with respect to their organization, powers, officers, and internal procedures. The effect of the mandatory primary paralleled that of the Australian ballot in giving parties legal status, but it went further to impose often intricate controls on party activities and to make them hybrid organizations that were at once public agencies and private associations. Austin Ranney calls the direct primary "the most radical party reform yet adopted."[16]

Ballot and primary legislation regulating parties was challenged early in state courts as a violation of the right of voluntary association, but while a few tribunals had reservations on this point, most agreed that state legislatures had the power to regulate political parties either as incident to the party's privilege to certify nominations for the official ballot or as part of the state's interest in protecting the integrity of elections. Charles Merriam and Louise Overacker, writing in the third decade of the twentieth century, describe the prevailing judicial view of party regulation by the states:

> On the whole, the courts have not been much inclined to recognize the "natural rights" or the right of association of political parties, strongly de-

> fended though they have been. The claims of the party as a voluntary association to regulate its own affairs have been completely broken down. The determination of the qualifications for membership in parties, specifications regarding the structure of its official organization, and the minute regulation of its procedure, have all been upheld.[17]

At the same time, Merriam and Overacker note, "the courts were careful to point out . . . that this legislative power to regulate party affairs must be exercised within the bounds of reason and not arbitrarily."[18]

Merriam and Overacker are correct that courts in the first decades of this century did not recognize a right of association for political parties, but they go too far in concluding that "the theory of the party as a voluntary association has been completely overthrown by the contrary doctrine that the party is in reality a governmental agency."[19] While the right of association was not established at this time in either constitutional or statutory law, it was present in common law and custom; and as Joseph Starr notes, the latter gave "the fullest possible recognition of the right of association," one that was "broad enough to cover political parties."[20] Moreover, courts in this early period of party regulation held generally that individuals have the right to organize political parties, that this right is incident to free government, and that legislatures may not deny this right. Further, courts held that parties are not merely creatures of the state but exist independently of the law.[21]

Starr observes that historically political parties had a broad range of powers and that among these were managing their own affairs, making their own rules, nominating their own candidates, and determining their own membership. Legislative regulation, he argues, merely transformed these inherent powers into statutory ones. "The interesting and important question remains," he writes, "as to whether the political party still has any inherent rights—beyond the basic right to exist—which the legislatures are bound to respect."[22] Starr concludes that court decisions leave areas of party activity where the inherent rights of parties survive, but he clearly sees legislation that intrudes upon party freedom as legally superior to the private actions of a party. Parties might fill voids in state regulation but could not on their own initiative displace that legislation.

The question of party as private association or public agency came to the U.S. Supreme Court in a series of judicial challenges to state election laws, known as the *White Primary Cases*. In 1923, the Texas legislature passed a law that excluded Negroes from voting in the Democratic party primary, but the Court ruled it unconstitutional as a violation of the equal protection clause of the Fourteenth Amendment.[23] The Texas legislature next passed a law that gave political parties the authority to set membership qualifications for voting and other purposes. The executive committee of the state Democratic Party thereupon adopted a rule that only whites could vote in the party primary, but this too was declared unconstitutional, the Court holding that the party's action was a state action because its authority to act came from state law.[24]

Undaunted, the Texas legislature next repealed all laws relating to these matters, after which the state convention of the Texas Democrats adopted a resolution that "all white citizens" could be party members and vote in party primaries. The Supreme Court found this action constitutional because the convention's decision was a "party action, voluntary in character," as opposed to one based on the authority of state law. The Court added that denial of a vote in a primary was merely a refusal of party membership with which neither it nor the state need be concerned.[25] This decision clearly assumes that political parties are not merely agents of the state but are essentially private organizations whose members have rights of association.

In 1944 the Court reversed itself once again and declared the party rule excluding Negroes from voting in primaries a state action and therefore unconstitutional.[26] This decision, however, did not turn on the question of associational rights but rested on a change in the Court's view of primaries. Previously seeing them as party elections, the Court had shifted to the view that primaries are an "integral part" of the electoral process in which, as in general elections, the right to vote is protected by the Constitution.[27] The *White Primary Cases* thus did not disturb the principle that parties can act on their own authority in certain areas, but they narrowed that realm and left unclear what its boundaries might be.

By midcentury, at the time of the Committee on Political Parties report, American parties were enmeshed in a web of increasingly restrictive regulation. All of the states had statutes, some quite elaborate, governing party organization and activities; a number of state constitutions included provisions dealing with parties; there was a large body of state court decisions that affected parties and a growing body of federal decisions; and there was some federal regulation of parties, principally the Hatch Acts. The effect of this regulation, Avery Leiserson noted, was "to make the political party in the United States a legal organ of the state for purposes of organizing and conducting elections to an extent hardly paralleled elsewhere in the world."[28] And while parties retained inherent rights as private associations, it was unclear whether this meant anything more than merely the legal right to exist. Austin Ranney and Willmoore Kendall write of party regulation in the 1950s:

"The general rule . . . is that legislatures may regulate and restrain the organization and activities of political parties, but have no constitutional power to destroy a political party outright."[29] But even this rule applied with certainty only to the two major parties. In addition, parties were in a period of organizational decline that went largely unacknowledged until the 1960s and did little themselves to challenge their legal status.[30] It was the nadir of party freedom in America.

Development of the Right of Association

The foundation upon which greater freedom for American parties would eventually be built was laid in a 1958 civil rights case, *NAACP v. Alabama*, in which the Supreme Court ruled that the First Amendment guarantees of free speech and assembly, joined with the Fourteenth Amendment guarantee of "liberty" as embodied in the due process clause, imply a constitutionally protected right of association. In his opinion for the majority, John Marshall Harlan explained the Court's logic:

> Effective advocacy of both public and private points of view, particularly controversial ones, is undeniably enhanced by group association, as this Court has more than once recognized by remarking upon the close nexus between freedoms of speech and assembly. . . . It is beyond debate that freedom to engage in association for the advancement of beliefs and ideas is an inseparable aspect of "liberty" assured by the Due Process Clause of the Fourteenth Amendment, which embraces freedom of speech. . . . It is immaterial whether the beliefs sought to be advanced by association pertain to political, economic, religious or cultural matters, and state action which may have the effect of curtailing the freedom to associate is subject to the closest scrutiny.[31]

Harlan went on to describe the right of association as an "indispensable liberty," equating it with freedom of speech and press, and added that governmental actions violating it, even though "unintended" or "unrelated" to associational rights, are invalid. The right of association, as Harlan described it, is an extension of the *individual's* rights to speech and assembly; it is in no sense a right inherent in the group or association itself. The NAACP case arose when the organization refused to give membership lists to the state of Alabama as a condition of registering as a legal entity, arguing that its right to do so derived from its members' individual rights to privacy in their associations.[32] The NAACP was asserting collectively, as an association, those rights its members possessed individually. As Harlan wrote, the NAACP was "but the medium through which its individual members seek to make more effective the expression of their own views," and "it and its members are in every practical sense identical."[33]

Harlan added that the right of association is subject to the "closest scrutiny," which is to say that while it is not absolute, it may be restricted by government only if the reason for doing so is sufficiently compelling to justify the denial of individual freedoms. Requiring the NAACP to disclose the names of members in this instance, he wrote, "must be regarded as entailing the likelihood of a substantial restraint upon the exercise . . . of their right to freedom of association," adding that the NAACP had made an "uncontroverted showing" that disclosure had previously led to abuse of its members and to an adverse effect on the collective effort to advocate beliefs they embraced.[34] The Court weighed this against the state's interest in obtaining the names of NAACP members and concluded that the latter was insufficient to overcome the constitutional objections of the former. It thus held, in Harlan's words, that "the right of the members to pursue their lawful private interests privately and to associate freely with others in so doing comes within the protection of the Fourteenth Amendment."[35]

Following its 1958 decision, the Court applied the right of association repeatedly in civil rights cases, striking down a variety of governmental intrusions upon First and Fourteenth amendment freedoms and solidifying the judicial foundations of associational rights.[36] At the same time, the Court was developing a parallel line of rulings in cases involving membership in the U.S. Communist Party. None of these was decided directly on the question of associational rights, but they impinged upon it and were the first cases to suggest that members of political parties might be protected by the right of association. In *Sweezy v. New Hampshire*, for example, a case that involved both freedom of speech and the right to privacy in one's associations, Chief Justice Earl Warren, writing for the majority, linked the right of political expression to the right of political association and concluded that "any interference with the freedom of a party is simultaneously an interference with the freedom of its adherents."[37]

By the latter part of the 1960s, the right of association was firmly established as a constitutional principle. Justice Byron White, in a dissenting opinion in *United States v. Robel*, summarized its nature and status:

> The right of association is not mentioned in the Constitution. It is a judicial construct appended to the First Amendment rights to speak freely, to

> assemble, and to petition for redress of grievances. While the right of association has deep roots in history and is supported by the inescapable necessity for group action in a republic as large and complex as ours, it has only recently blossomed as the controlling factor in constitutional litigation; its contours as yet lack delineation. Although official interference with First Amendment rights has drawn close scrutiny, it is now apparent that the right of association is not absolute and is subject to significant regulation by the states.[38]

In the 1970s the Court began to define the "contours" of associational rights with respect to political parties. It did so in a wide range of party-related cases: voter enrollment and party raiding in primaries,[39] ballot access for third-party and independent candidates,[40] and the public financing of campaigns.[41] But the cases of most immediate relevance and importance to political parties related to national party rules governing the selection of delegates to national conventions.

The two major cases of this sort arose from Democratic Party reforms following its 1968 convention and continuing through the following decade and into the 1980s.[42] The first of these, *Cousins v. Wigoda*, grew out of the 1972 Democratic National Convention at which fifty-seven delegates from Illinois who had been properly elected under state law but whose selection violated new party rules were not seated by the convention, which instead seated a delegation chosen in accordance with party rules but not state law.[43] The state of Illinois argued that the lawfully elected delegation should have been seated because the state's compelling interest in protecting the integrity of the electoral process and the right of its citizens to effective suffrage outweighed any claim of associational rights. The Court disagreed and upheld the party's action.

Writing for the Court, Justice William Brennan said the state's claim overlooked a "significant fact," namely, that voting was "to elect delegates to a National Party Convention" and that "the specific function of delegates to such a Convention" weighed against the argument for a compelling state interest. State political parties, he continued, are "affiliated with a national party through acceptance of the national call to send state delegates to the national convention," adding that the "states themselves have no constitutionally mandated role in the great task of the selection of Presidential and Vice-Presidential candidates."[44]

Brennan went on to say that if the qualifications for delegates to national conventions were left to the states, "each of the fifty states could establish the qualifications of its delegates to the various party conventions without regard to party policy," and he concluded that this would be "an obviously intolerable result." It could, he noted, destroy the party process by which its nominees for president and vice president are chosen, and this would violate the associational rights of its members. But Brennan went even further to declare rather sweepingly, "The Convention serves the pervasive national interest in the selection of candidates for national office, and this national interest is greater than any interest of an individual state."[45]

The Court held that the right of association protected national Democratic Party rules governing the selection of convention delegates against the state of Illinois claim of a compelling interest in the integrity of its elections. This led one commentator to note:

> For the first time, the Court recognized a constitutionally protected right of the party to be free from state encroachment in setting qualifications for future delegate selection at the national convention. . . . The Court further decided that the concept of associational freedom also protects the party's right to determine its own criteria for delegate selection.[46]

The *Cousins* decision provided the foundation upon which subsequent party claims to associational rights have been founded and thus led to a significant expansion of the constitutional rights and prerogatives of American political parties and their adherents.

The other important party rules case, *Democratic Party of U.S. v. Wisconsin*, commonly known as *LaFollette*, arose in conjunction with the 1980 Democratic National Convention.[47] National party rules required that convention delegates be chosen by a method in which only those who publicly declared themselves Democrats could participate. The Wisconsin Democrats, however, incorporated their state's open primary law into their plan for delegate selection, which meant that any Wisconsin voter, regardless of party preference, could vote in the Democratic primary at which the *allocation* of delegates to the national convention would be determined for the various candidates seeking the party's nomination. The delegates themselves were *selected* in a separate process that conformed to national party rules.

A national party commission rejected the Wisconsin plan because the results of the open primary bound the state's delegates to the national convention. The state of Wisconsin, joined by the state's Democratic Party, sued the national Democratic Party, arguing that the open primary represented a long-standing state interest in not requiring voters to declare a party preference and that any adverse effects of the law on the national party's right of association was at most minimal. The Wisconsin Supreme Court agreed with the state's position and found the open primary constitutional and binding on both the state and national

Democratic parties. The national Democrats seated the Wisconsin delegation at their 1980 convention, but they also appealed the state court's decision to the U.S. Supreme Court where it was reversed.

Justice Potter Stewart, writing for the majority, based the Court's decision squarely on the associational rights of the national party. He pointed first to the series of Democratic Party commissions authorized by national conventions from 1968 on, noting that each had recommended the selection of delegates by procedures closed to all but Democratic Party members and that each of these recommendations had been approved by national conventions. The will of the party was clear. The Wisconsin court, Potter said, ruled on the wrong question. It found the open feature of the state's primary law constitutional, but the issue was whether the state could compel a national party to seat a delegation to its national convention chosen in a way that violated the rules of the party.

Stewart concluded that this issue had been settled by *Cousins* and said of the *LaFollette* cases:

> Here, the members of the National Party, speaking through their rules, chose to define their associational rights by limiting those who could participate in the processes leading to the selection of delegates to their National Convention. On several occasions this Court has recognized that the inclusion of persons unaffiliated with a political party may seriously distort its collective decisions—thus impairing the party's essential functions—and that political parties may accordingly protect themselves from the intrusion by those with adverse political principles.[48]

To the state claim that its law placed only a minor burden on the national party, Stewart posed the party's counterclaim that the burden was substantial and said that "it is not for the courts to mediate the merits of this dispute," adding that "even if the State were correct, a State, or a court may not constitutionally substitute its own judgment for that of the Party."[49] A party's choice among methods for selecting delegates to its national convention is, Stewart concluded, protected by the Constitution. State interests in the integrity of the electoral process, he said, are in this case insufficient to justify intrusion upon the associational rights of party members.[50]

The *LaFollette* decision, one commentator concluded, "marks another step in ensuring that national political parties have sufficient freedom to make the changes they feel necessary to retain their vitality." "The message," he continued, "seems to be: leave the national parties alone, let them make their own rules and resolve their own disputes."[51] In both

Cousins and *LaFollette*, the Court treats the right of association with such deference as to shift the burden of proof in cases of conflict between party rules and state law (at least as they involve a party's ability to define its membership and advance its beliefs) away from the party and toward the state. In *LaFollette* the Democrats' *claim* of state intrusion upon their associational rights seems to suffice as *proof* thereof. The Court does not ask the party to show that an open primary in fact burdens its associational rights more than a closed one.[52] Moreover, the Court in *LaFollette* clearly wants no part of weighing the relative burden of state restrictions on parties. It is unconcerned that the effect of state law on the associational rights of the Democrats was less direct in *LaFollette* than in *Cousins*.

At the same time, the strict scrutiny test became more stringent and difficult to pass, as it requires a state to show both a compelling interest in its restriction on associational rights and that this restriction is narrowly designed to serve its purpose and poses minimal interference with associational freedoms.[53] The strict scrutiny test seems increasingly to be controlling in these cases, and its application clearly gives important legal advantages to political parties in First Amendment decisions.[54] Indeed, one observer suggests that the Court may have given the national parties a "special status: in these controversies—that neither minor parties, candidates, nor voters share—by holding the state to a higher test of compelling interest and to a more difficult proof of minimal abridgement of rights in national party cases than in others."[55]

Extending the Right of Association

In the 1970s the courts opened a new realm of associational rights for political parties and their members. The 1980s saw a series of cases that began to map this terrain and to explore the new frontiers of party freedom. The first of these cases arose in Massachusetts where in 1979 the Democratic State Convention adopted a charter that in addition to defining the general organization and powers of the state party, provided for a party-endorsing convention for statewide offices. The charter required that to gain access to the party's primary ballot a candidate had to receive at least 15 percent of the convention vote on at least one ballot for the office being sought.[56] This "15 percent rule" was approved by a two-thirds vote of the convention, and the full charter including this provision was likewise approved by a two-thirds vote.[57]

State law governing candidate access to the primary ballot in Massachusetts includes two general requirements: (1) a candidate must be registered as a member of the party whose nomination is sought; (2) a minimum number of signatures must be collected from voters registered as either party members or independents. Legislative attempts to incorporate the 15 percent rule into state law prior to the 1982 election failed. Indeed the legislature acted to the contrary; it voted to amend state law to preclude the possible applicability of the 15 percent rule.[58] Before signing this legislation, however, Governor Edward J. King asked the Massachusetts Supreme Judicial Court for an opinion on its constitutionality.

Acting just a month before the state Democratic Convention, the court declared the 15 percent rule constitutional and binding. Its opinion was grounded in the right of association:

> A determination of who will appear on a general election ballot as the candidate endorsed by an identified political party is a critical decision for that party. The party, therefore, has a substantial interest, implicit in its freedom of association, to ensure that party members have an effective role in that decision.[59]

Noting that state law permits independents to sign candidate nomination papers and to vote in the party primary, the court reasoned that in the absence of the 15 percent rule, it is possible for a candidate to win the Democratic nomination with little or no support from the regular party membership. It saw the charter provision as adding to the statutory requirements and in doing so having the double effect "of limiting the number of candidates on the primary ballot, thereby eliminating the confusion that may result from too many candidates, and of limiting the candidates to those with significant party support, thereby giving the party members an effective role in choosing the party's candidate in the general election."[60]

The court's opinion acknowledged that the state has a compelling interest in the overall regularity of the election process but argued that it is not served by elimination of the 15 percent rule and "does not constitutionally justify elimination of party control over who the party's candidate in the general election will be."[61] The proposed legislation, it concluded, would override the party rule and thereby "abridge the constitutional rights of the Democratic party and its members to associate by allowing candidates to be placed on the Democratic State primary ballot in contravention of the party's charter."[62]

When the Massachusetts Democratic Convention met in late May, two amendments to the charter were introduced, one to repeal the 15 percent rule, the other to postpone its effective date until after the state primary. Both were defeated overwhelmingly, and the convention proceeded to make endorsements of candidates for statewide offices. Several of the hopefuls did not receive the required 15 percent of the votes cast on any ballot. Subsequently, when notified by the Secretary of State that their names would not appear on the primary ballot, one of those denied a place, Frederick Langone, a candidate for lieutenant governor who met statutory requirements for the ballot, filed suit claiming that his First and Fourteenth amendment rights, as well as those of his supporters, had been abridged.

In ruling on the case, the Massachusetts Supreme Judicial Court concluded that the 15 percent rule was constitutional and construed state law as not excluding but accommodating it.[63] The court's reasoning paralleled that in its earlier opinion. It saw the 15 percent rule as intimately related to the party's right of association and quoted the views of Harvard University law professor Laurence Tribe approvingly:

> A political party has a legitimate—indeed, compelling—interest in ensuring that its selection process accurately reflects the collective voice of those who, in some meaningful sense, are affiliated with it. Freedom of association would prove an empty guarantee if associations could not limit control over their decisions to those who share the interests and persuasions that underlie the association's being.[64]

The court again found the state's interest in the regulation of election insufficient to overturn the party's constitutional right of association and argued that it was constitutionally preferable to treat the party rule as an extension of state law since the statute was "not expressly preemptive" and this construction posed no constitutional difficulties. Moreover, the court found that neither Langone's rights nor those of his supporters had been denied unfairly. Langone appealed to the U.S. Supreme Court where he was joined in a separate appeal filed by state Attorney General Francis Bellotti. Langone challenged on two grounds: the state court's ruling on his constitutional rights and its conclusion that state law did not preempt the 15 percent rule. The attorney general challenged only on the second of these grounds. In 1983 the Supreme Court dismissed both cases, thereby upholding the state court's decision.[65]

The Massachusetts case opened a door of opportunity for state political parties to strengthen themselves organizationally through the right of association in ways consistent with state law. The state court decision avoided a constitutional confrontation by reading the statute governing party primaries as accommodating the 15 percent rule and by viewing the rule as furthering state interests in simplifying the ballot and avoiding voter confusion.[66] In this way, the court was able to recognize the party's right of association and the state's interest in the regulation of elections without having to invalidate any state laws governing either parties or elections.

A second case, from Connecticut, went a step further to uphold a party rule contrary to state law. In 1984 the Republican state convention in Connecticut adopted a rule to permit independents to vote in the party primary for U.S. Senate, Congress, governor, and other statewide offices, but not for the state legislature or local office.[67] This rule was in conflict with state law, which provided for a closed primary. The Republicans tried to amend Connecticut's primary law to accommodate their new party rule but were defeated by Democratic majorities in both houses of the state assembly. Frustrated legislatively, the Republicans turned to the courts, claiming that the party's constitutionally protected right of association permitted it to select candidates for public office in accord with party rules and asked that the state be prevented from enforcing its closed primary law against the party.[68] The state replied by claiming broad constitutional discretion with respect to political parties because parties are integral to the selection of candidates for public office and the state has a compelling interest in the integrity of elections.[69]

The federal district court upheld the Republican claim and rejected the state's assertion of a compelling interest in the regulation of the primary. The court concluded that the state-mandated closed primary burdened the Republican Party's right of association excessively because it allowed the state legislature to "substitute its judgment for that of the party on the question of who is and is not sufficiently allied in interest with the party to warrant inclusion in its candidate selection process."[70] Connecticut appealed the decision, but both the circuit court and Supreme Court upheld the lower court decision. "The Party's determination of the boundaries of its own association, and of the structure which best allows it to pursue its political goals," Justice Thurgood Marshall wrote in his majority opinion, "is protected by the Constitution."[71]

Fifteen states joined Connecticut in its appeal to the Supreme Court, arguing that the district court ruling "calls in question virtually any attempt by a state to regulate the primary process." The logic of the decision, they added, is that state laws governing primaries could be invalidated "any time a political party were to adopt a party rule inconsistent with such statutes."[72] Clearly the Connecticut decision goes beyond the Massachusetts case in extending the powers of self-governance to parties. There has been no rush to liberate parties from the clutches of state regulation, but a third right-of-association case, from California, has added significantly to the arsenal of party powers.

Where the right of association in party cases has for the most part been a defensive weapon used to protect party prerogatives, it became an offensive one in California as several party committees, party members, and other interested parties combined to challenge the constitutionality of certain state laws governing the organization and activities of political parties. Election law in California has been among the most extensive and restrictive of any state. The Progressive Movement in the early part of this century broke the power of an entrenched and corrupt party system in California and replaced it with a weak and tightly regulated one. The state not only adopted the direct primary and the initiative and referendum but went further to enact statutory and constitutional rules governing in detail the organization and activities of its political parties. Subsequently, California extended its regulation of parties to include a prohibition against making endorsements in primaries and even more restrictive rules governing party structure.[73]

A case, billed informally as a "party deregulation" suit, was brought in the federal district court for northern California in late 1983 to test on right-of-association grounds the constitutionality of a number of these provisions.[74] It challenged two sets of state restrictions: (l) the prohibition against party endorsements—or support or opposition—of candidates in primaries and in nonpartisan city, county, and school-board elections; (2) the regulation of internal party affairs, including membership, dues, meetings, and other matters. The suit advanced three claims: that the state's denial of party authority to make endorsements violated the First Amendment rights of party members to free speech and association; that denying members control over the rules and regulations governing their party violated their rights of association and assembly; and that by not denying these to other political organizations, the state had violated the Fourteenth Amendment right of party members to equal protection of the law.

The state argued that it had a compelling interest in the regulation of political parties to protect the freedom of association of its citizens in the electoral process. It suggested that primary endorsements are more misleading than educational and claimed that state regulations ensured voters affiliated with a particular party the right to make a "free, unfettered and intelligent choice as to the nominee" of their party.[75] Regarding the internal governance of parties, the state claimed a compelling interest in party structure to discourage any faction from taking control of a party organization for its own purposes and denying party members an effective voice in party affairs.

The district court declined to rule on the question of party endorsements in nonpartisan elections because the matter was simultaneously at issue before the California Supreme Court.[76] On the other questions, however, it held substantially in favor of the plaintiffs. The court found state restrictions on party endorsements in primaries to be a "clear limitation on political expression," which took the form of a "total bar." "There is no greater burden on the freedom of speech," the court noted, "than the outright government prohibition of any kind of expression."[77] The court found too that the ban on endorsements presented a substantial burden to the freedom of association but delivered a divided opinion on the issue of internal party governance, yet one clearly more favorable to the plaintiffs.[78] California appealed the district court decision, but the federal circuit court and the Supreme Court sustained the lower court's judgment, holding the state statutes unconstitutional intrusions upon the associational rights of parties.[79]

The California suit thus freed the state's political parties from some of the more odious state regulations that infringed their basic rights of self-governance. But it also opened wider the door of opportunity for party self-determination in matters of internal governance. Substantively, the California case, like those in Massachusetts and Connecticut, gives political parties more room to explore, as the APSA Committee on Political Parties urged, just what parties can be in the American setting. Tactically, it differs from the Massachusetts and Connecticut cases, being more narrowly judicial in character while the others were more political, but this suggests that American parties have a range of viable strategies in their quest for a more effective role in our constitutional system.

Conclusion

The historian Richard Hofstadter observes that America has a Constitution against parties, and surely this is true of the separated and divided structure of government it provides.[80] In the last three decades, however, political parties have found that part of the Constitution, the First and Fourteenth amendments, is friendly to them. These amendments, from which the right of association derives, are not pro-party per se, but pro-voluntary association, of which parties are but one example. The right-of-association cases liberate parties from the entanglements of excessively restrictive state regulation of their organization and conduct, but they neither confer greater powers on the parties nor secure their place as privileged institutions in American politics. Indeed, some, like Leon Epstein, conclude that the most striking thing about these decisions is "their failure *so far* to do more than modify the twentieth century status of parties under state law."[81] Others, like Daniel Lowenthal, go further to argue that these cases are "unlikely to have any but the blueprint, but it remains the point of departure for those who would draft most marginal consequences either for the basic party structure or the overall future of American politics."[82]

In itself, the right of association is no solution to the problem of party government with which the Committee on Political Parties grappled. It does not even point in the direction of a solution. It is at most a tool the parties can use to create greater space, constitutionally and politically, within which to search for a larger and more effective role in American politics. Indeed the committee urges the parties to do just this—to explore opportunities for strengthening themselves within the framework of the Constitution, and the right of association can help in this endeavor. But the parties must be willing to launch the exploration; they must be willing to take on the political and intellectual challenges that party building entails. For forty years, the report of the committee has stood as a guide for party builders, analyzing problems and exploring ideas. It is not a workable blueprint, but it remains the point of departure for those who would draft one. In the absence of a blueprint, Epstein and Lowenthal are surely correct in their assessment of what the right of association means for the condition of America's parties.

Notes

1. Austin Ranney, "Toward a More Responsible Two-Party System: A Commentary," *American Political Science Review*, 45 (June 1951): 492–99.

2. Committee on Political Parties, "Toward a More Responsible Two-Party System," *American Political Science Review*, 44 (September 1950): vi (hereinafter, CPP).

3. Richard Hofstadter, *The Idea of a Party System* (Berkeley, Calif.: University of California Press, 1972), p. 204.

4. CPP, pp. 26–27.

5. This reflects the position of E. E. Schattschneider, chairman of the APSA Committee on Political Parties. In his textbook *Party Government* (New York: Farrar and Rinehart, 1942), Schattschneider observes that the Constitution is "proparty in one sense and antiparty in another" (p. 7), that it secures the liberties that make parties possible but that its design of government makes parties ineffective. "The Constitution made the rise of parties inevitable," he writes, "yet was incompatible with party government;" parties and the Constitution are simply the "unhappy marriage" of an irresistible force and an immovable object (p. 8). But as the Constitution has shaped the parties, so the parties have changed the Constitution, popularizing the presidency and democratizing the government (pp. 124–26).

6. For a summary list of the ways in which state legislation affects party

organization, see Samuel J. Eldersveld, *Political Parties in American Society* (New York: Basic Books, 1982), p. 96.

7. F. Morstein Marx, "Party Responsibility and Legislative Program," *Columbia Law Review*, (March 1950): 281, 197.

8. Wallace Sayre and Judith Parris, *Voting for President* (Washington, D.C.: Brookings Institution, 1970), pp. 26ff.

9. Joseph Harris, *Registration of Voters in the United States* (Washington, D.C.: Brookings Institution, 1929), pp. 65ff.

10. William Crotty, *Political Reform & the American Experiment* (New York: Crowell, 1977), p. 169ff.

11. In 1870, during the period of Reconstruction after the Civil War, Congress enacted comprehensive legislation governing the conduct of House elections in the South. This was repealed in 1894. See United States v. Gradwell, 243 U.S. 476 (1917), 482.

12. Eldon C. Evans, *A History of the Australian Ballot System in the United States* (Chicago: University of Chicago Press, 1917), Ch. 6; L. E. Freedman, *The Australian Ballot: The Story of an American Reform* (Lansing, Mich.: Michigan State University Press).

13. Charles Merriam and Louise Overacker, *Primary Elections* (Chicago: University of Chicago Press, 1928), pp. 24ff.

14. New York also enacted a primary law in 1866 that was mandatory in character but far less comprehensive than the California statute. The New York law made certain practices, like bribery, illegal and punishable by fine or imprisonment, but it made no provision for a party primary process per se. A number of early state primary laws followed the New York example. The first mandatory state primary laws governing procedures applied only to particular cities or other limited jurisdictions. Merriam and Overacker, *Primary*, Chs. 1–4.

15. Wisconsin was the first state to adopt a comprehensive mandatory statewide primary law in 1903 and, within 20 years, all but four states followed suit with some kind of mandatory statewide primary legislation. Ibid., Ch. 3.

16. Austin Ranney, *Curing the Mischiefs of Faction* (Berkeley, Calif.: University of California Press, 1975), p. 18. Similarly, Robert Brooks describes the direct primary as "perhaps the most sweeping change that has occurred in our party history. Taken in connection with the Australian ballot," he continues, "it has brought a large part of our extra constitutional governmental machinery under legal control, while at the same time it has given parties a legal standing which formerly they did not possess." Brooks, *Political Parties and Electoral Problems* (New York: Harper and Brothers, 1923), p. 242.

17. Merriam and Overacker, *Primary*, p. 118. They cite a 1901 Oregon case, Ladd v. Holmes, 66 P. 714 (1901), in which the court said, "Party management is of such vital importance to the public and the state that its operation, in so far as it respects the naming of candidates for public office, is an object of special legislative concern, to see that the purposes of the Constitution are not perverted, and the people shorn of a free choice." Ibid., p. 116.

18. Ibid., p. 120.

19. Ibid., p. 140. On this, see Stephen Gottlieb, "Rebuilding the Right of Association: The Right to Hold a Convention as a Test Case," *Hofstra Law Review*, 11 (Fall 1982): 196ff.

20. Joseph R. Starr, "The Legal Status of American Political Parties," *American Political Science Review*, 34 (June 1940): 443–44.

21. Ibid., p. 445.

22. Ibid., p. 448.

23. Nixon v. Herndon, 273 U.S. 536 (1924).

24. Nixon v. Condon, 286 U.S. 73 (1932).

25. Grovey v. Townsend, 295 U.S. 45 (1935).

26. Smith v. Allwright, 321 U.S 649 (1944).

27. *United States v. Classic*, 313 U.S. 299, 314, 318 (1941). In the *Townsend* decision, the Court's view of primaries relied on Newberry v. U.S., 256 US. 232 (1921), which held that "primaries . . . are in no sense elections for an office, but merely methods by which party adherents agree upon candidates whom they intend to offer and support for ultimate choice by all qualified electors. General provisions touching elections in constitutions or statutes are not necessarily applicable to primaries—the two things are radically different" (250). *Newberry* was reversed by *Classic*, which in turn became the basis for the Court's decision in *Allwright*.

28. Avery Leiserson, *Parties and Politics* (New York: Alfred A. Knopf, 1958), p. 89.

29. Austin Ranney and Willmoore Kendall, *Democracy and the American Party System* (New York: Harcourt, Brace and World, 1956), pp. 218ff.

30. Walter Dean Burnham, *Critical Elections and the Mainsprings of American Politics* (New York: W. W. Norton, 1970).

31. NAACP v. Alabama, 357 U.S. 449 (1958), 460.

32. Like many states, Alabama required out-of-state corporations to register with the state. The NAACP was incorporated in New York and, though active in Alabama for 40 years, had never registered there—nor had it been asked to do so. As civil rights activism increased across the South in the 1950s, Alabama charged the NAACP with failure to register and ordered it to produce certain records including membership lists. The NAACP complied in all respects, except that it refused to disclose its members. A state court held the organization in contempt; the U.S. Supreme Court reversed this decision.

33. NAACP, p. 459.

34. Ibid., p. 462.

35. Ibid., p. 466.

36. Bates v. Little Rock, 361 U.S. 516 (1960). NAACP v. Button. 371 U.S. 415 (1963). In *Button*, the Court said, "There is no longer any doubt that the First and Fourteenth Amendments protect certain forms of orderly group activity for the advancement of beliefs and ideas," adding that "only a compelling state interest in the regulation of a subject within the State's constitutional power to regulate can justify limiting First Amendment freedoms."

37. Sweezy v. New Hampshire, 354 U.S. 234, 250, (1957). See Communist Party v. Control Board, 367 U.S. 1 (1961).

38. United States v. Robel, 389 U.S. 258 (1967). On the question of scrutiny, see Gerald Funther, *Constitutional Law*, 10th ed. (Mineola, N.Y.: Foundation Press, 1980), pp. 71ff., and Laurence Tribe, *American Constitutional Law* (Mineola, N.Y.: Foundation Press, 1978), pp. 703ff.

39. See Rosario v. Rockefeller, 410 U.S. 752 (1973) and Kusper v. Pontikes, 414 U.S. 51 (1973).

40. See Williams v. Rhodes, 393 U.S. 23 (1968), Anderson v. Celebreeze, 460 U.S. 780 (1983), and Storer v. Brown, 415 U.S. 724 (1974).

41. See Buckley v. Valeo, 424 U.S. 1 (1976).

42. William J. Crotty, *Decision for the Democrats* (Baltimore: Johns Hopkins University Press, 1978) and David E. Price, *Bringing Back the Parties* (Washington, D.C.: Congressional Quarterly, 1984).

43. Cousins v. Wigoda, 419 U.S. 477 (1974). In a related case, O'Brien v. Brown, 409 U.S. 1 (1972), the Court was asked to rule on the legality of the California delegation to the 1972 Democratic national convention. The Court noted that associational rights were involved but based its decision on the political question doctrine. The case came to the Court only a few days before the start of the convention, and it ruled that the dispute was best resolved by the convention because, historically, parties had been seen as the proper forum for the resolution of intraparty disputes.

44. Cousins, p. 489.

45. Ibid., p. 490.

46. Bruce A. Harris, "National Political Party Conventions: State's Interest Subordinate to Party's in Delegate Selection Process," *University of Miami Law Review*, 29 (Summer 1975): 810.

47. Democratic Party of U.S. v. Wisconsin, ex. rel. LaFollette, 450 U.S. 107.

48. Ibid., 122. The quotation within the quotation is from Ray v. Blair, 343 U.S. 214, 221 (1952).

49. Ibid., p. 123.

50. In a related case, Ferenc v. Austin, 666 F.2d 1023 (1981), the Michigan Democratic Party adopted a delegate selection plan that was at odds with state law but in conformity with national party rules. The court upheld the state party rules.

51. Christopher J. Martin, "Democratic Party v. Wisconsin ex. rel. LaFollette: May States Impose Open Primary Results Upon National Party Conventions?" *Denver Law Review*, 59 (1982): 624–25.

52. See the dissenting opinion of Justice Lewis Powell in LaFollette, p. 134.

53. See Laurence Tribe, *American Constitutional Law* (Mineola, N.Y.: Foundation Press, 1978), p. 786.

54. In Ripon Society v. National Republican Party, 525 F. 2d 548 (1975), the U.S. Court of Appeals in Washington, D.C. held a national Republican Party plan for the allocation of delegates to its 1976 convention unconstitutional as a denial of fair representation and a violation of one-person, one-vote decisions as constituting a compelling *national* interest—the right to vote—which, the court said "is itself rooted in the First Amendment." It is also noteworthy that the party plan invalidated by the court had not been approved by a party convention.

55. Charles Gardner Geyh, "It's My Party and I'll Cry If I Want To: State Intrusions Upon the Associational Freedoms of Political Parties," *Wisconsin Law Review*, (1983): 220ff.

56. The charter provision reads: "Endorsements for statewide office of enrolled Democrats nominated at the Convention shall be by majority vote of the delegates present and voting, with the proviso that any nominee who receives at least 15 percent of the Convention vote on any ballot for a particular office may challenge the Convention endorsement in a State Primary Election." *Charter of the Democratic Party of the Commonwealth of Massachusetts*, Article VI, Section 3 (Boston: Democratic State Committee).

57. A description of the process of charter adoption may be found in Jerome M. Mileur, "Massachusetts: The Democratic Party Charter Movement," in *Party Renewal in America*, ed. Gerald M. Pomper (New York: Praeger, 1980), pp. 159–75.

58. The amendment to state election law approved by the legislature read: "Notwithstanding the charter, rule or by-law of a political party, a candidate, who is enrolled in such political party, submitting nomination papers subject to the provisions of state law shall be a candidate for nomination at the state primary."

59. 385 Mass. 1201, at p. 1204.

60. Ibid., p. 1205.

61. Ibid., p. 1207.

62. Ibid., p. 1208.

63. 388 Mass. 1850.

64. Ibid., p. 1930; emphasis in Tribe quotation added by the Court.

65. Bellotti v. Connolly, 460 U.S. 1057 (1983).

66. Several aspects of the Massachusetts case are noteworthy. First, adoption of the state party charter and the 15 percent rule was achieved through an extensive grass roots, participatory process which left little doubt that it reflected the will of the party's rank-and-file membership. Moreover, ratification by the state convention required super majorities, which added to its authority. Second, the charter provisions are moderate and consistent with the intent of protecting the interests of significant minorities within the party.

67. U.S. Senator Lowell Weicker proposed this rule following the 1982 state elections. Weicker had been challenged for renomination by Prescott Bush, Jr., who won enough support at the party convention to enter the primary. Bush chose not to do so. The events, however, pointed up the problem confronting a liberal Republican like Weicker whose appeal to independents and Democrats made him a strong candidate in the general election, but whose liberalism left him vulnerable to a conservative challenge within his own party. Weicker's proposal was referred to a party commission, which recommended its adoption.

68. The Republicans argued that the closed primary law interfered with a number of their rights: the freedom to select candidates according to party rules and to encourage participation in the political process, the freedom to organize and govern their party in a manner those associated with it believe will make it more efficient and effective, and the freedom to advance the party's political beliefs and to

pursue its goal of winning elections. They also argued that the party had been prevented from implementing its rule through the legislative process by a Democratic majority that controlled both branches of the legislature and the governorship.

69. The state also argued that the Republican Party rule was itself unconstitutional because Article I, Section 2, of the Constitution and the Seventeenth Amendment require that the eligibility to vote in congressional elections must be "absolutely symmetrical" to requirements for voting in state legislative elections and that, by permitting independents to vote in the primary for Congress but not the state legislature, the party rule was in conflict with the Constitution.

70. Republican Party v. Tashjian, 599 F. Supp 1228, 1238 (1983).

71. Tashjian v, Republican Party.

72. *Congressional Quarterly Weekly Report*, 18 January 1986, p. 127.

73. Kay Lawson, "California: The Uncertainties of Reform," in *Party Renewal in America*, ed. Gerald M. Pomper (New York: Praeger, 1980), pp. 116–38; Lawson, "Challenging Regulation of Political Parties: The California Case," *Journal of Law and Politics*, 2 (Fall 1985): 263–85.

74. San Francisco County Democratic Committee v. March Fong Eu, No. C-83-5599-MHP (May 1984), typed "order" of the district court, p. 14. The plaintiffs included several Democratic county committees, the San Francisco Republican county committee, the state's Libertarian Party, some individual Democratic and Republican party members, and the northern and southern California and national Committees for Party Renewal.

75. Quoted in Lawson, *Law and Politics*, p. 270.

76. The California Supreme Court subsequently ruled that political parties did have the right to make endorsements in non-partisan races, reversing an earlier decision, Unger II, 37 Cal. 3d.

77. Democratic Committee v. Eu, p. 14.

78. Ibid., p. 15.

79. Eu v. San Francisco County Democratic Central Committee.

80. Richard Hofstadter, *The Idea of a Party System* (Berkeley: University of California Press, 1972), Ch. 2.

81. Leon D. Epstein, *Political Parties in the American Mold* (Madison: University of Wisconsin Press, 1986), p. 198.

82. Daniel Hays Lowenthal, "Constitutional Rights of Majority Political Parties: A Skeptical Inquiry," (paper prepared for the annual meeting of the American Political Science Association, Washington, D.C., 1–4 September 1988), p. 5.

9

Tocqueville and Responsible Parties

Individualism, Partisanship, and Citizenship in America

WILSON CAREY MCWILLIAMS

Like Pyrrhus, democracy has often been troubled by the price of victory. The bill for success in the cold war is still being totaled. Europeans face the burden of rebuilding the East: Americans worry that their military dominance may have been ruinous for their economy, and the United States is pressed to create a "new world order" and to address neglected problems at home without the negative commonality and directing purpose so long afforded by anticommunism.[1] Back in 1950, however, even the conflict with the Soviet Union could still be seen as only part of the reckoning of the Allied victory in World War II, hence an item in the broader modern "age of reconstruction."[2]

Yet our problems, like those of the Committee on Political Parties four decades ago, are incidents in a grander story. A century and a half ago, Alexis de Tocqueville warned that the providential triumph of democracy raised the danger of a political society fragmented into so many individuals, each engrossed with private interest and dominated by the psychological force of "tyranny of the majority," incapable of either high purpose or freedom. Democracy required a "new science of politics," Tocqueville argued, to help "lessen its vices and render its natural advantages more prominent."[3] In that science, party plays a vital role, and Tocqueville's teaching deserves to rank as a cornerstone of our own.

In *Democracy in America*, political parties are introduced as a part of a descent, the first institution discussed when Tocqueville turns from the Constitution to the "sovereign power" of the people. Treating the Constitution and the laws calls for a discussion of the principles of public philosophy, republicanism in words and in theory. Even under the Constitution, however, all public authority derives from the people; America's fundamental law recognizes no other title to rule—not birth or property, education or virtue, religion or natural right.[4] Except in the very short term, representative government must follow opinion, and no institution or right can resist a majority sufficiently large and sufficiently durable. In democratic practice, principles depend on how the people "acts"—on the ways it is organized and makes itself felt in politics—and speech is less important than the public's "propensities and passions" or those "secret springs" that "retard, accelerate or direct" the "irresistible course" of popular power.[5]

Given this descent, it is not surprising that Tocqueville's first comments on parties are sharply negative, following traditional republican theory.[6] In chapter 9, he introduces what is to be his discussion of parties a chapter later with the observation that Americans, "by inclination or by interest," desire the general welfare but are subject to the "incessant agitation" of parties seeking their support.[7] This argument suggests that parties create political divisions and turbulences that at most would be implicit without them: party is the serpent in the Eden of republican virtue and can claim to be no more than a "necessary evil," an inescapable consequence of political freedom.[8]

Yet at the same time, Tocqueville's ordering places parties closer than any other institution to the Constitution and the laws. By doing so, he indicates that parties are more inclusive and more genuinely public than the press or political associations, which, however general their principles, speak to narrower constituencies. Party appeals to prejudice and to interest, but it requires a broad extension of allegiance, a perception of self in relation to the country as a whole, and the structure of Tocqueville's argument hints that that partisan spirit is a near, and sometimes legitimate, relative of patriotism and civic virtue. This theme, the partisan ascent, becomes increasingly prominent in Tocqueville's discussion.

He begins with the "great distinction," basic to his classification, between parties in the strict sense and their communalistic counterfeits. In certain large states, Tocqueville observes, regional or ethnic populations may have lives and interests so fundamentally opposed as to constitute "distinct nations." In such cases, nominally partisan groupings are at bottom the organizations of "rival peoples," and their logic is separation or civil war.[9] Tocqueville gives no specific examples, and readers today probably think of multiethnic states like the Soviet Union; similar instances doubtless occurred to Tocqueville's contemporaries.[10] It seems likely, however, that Tocqueville was pointing to what he regarded as the great danger in the United States: later in the chapter, he refers to the North and South as virtually "rival nations rather than parties," an observation soon to be confirmed in blood.[11]

By contrast, parties properly so called arise from differing opinions regarding the "principles upon which the government is to be conducted."[12] Parties, then, accept and presume the continued existence of the political society and a common government, recognizing the larger political whole and hence, to some degree, their own partiality. In this sense, parties are the great rivals of political communalism and separatism, just as the strength of party was able for a time to slow or deflect the development of "rival peoples" in the United States.[13]

Within this more restricted definition, Tocqueville distinguishes between "great parties," inspired and governed by general principles, and "minor parties," more concerned with interests and particular cases. Great parties have an undeniable grandeur; they make high moral claims on their members and encourage generous political feelings, prompting the disguising of self-interest if not its suppression. Ordinarily, Tocqueville observes, great parties are the result of political crisis, of conflict and felt injustice so intense as to aspire ideas of political or social transformation. Small parties are tied to periods of apparent calm, to the "normal times" in which continuing long-term change is so incremental as to become invisible, leading a people to accept the existing "horizon" as a given and to content itself with bargains and intrigue. Lacking "lofty purpose," minor parties, although they may use "vehement" rhetoric, are timid and irresolute in action, using means as "wretched" as their self-interested ends. On the other hand, while minor parties "agitate" and "degrade" a polity, they do not tear it apart as great parties may do. When heroic measures are called for, a great party may save a political society, but it is perilous, something to be avoided except in cases of political necessity. Minor parties, however, are incapable of addressing—and often recognizing—political problems, especially the long-term fault lines in a regime.[14]

Tocqueville's formulation points toward a desirable synthesis, a party both lion and fox that acknowledges self-interest but relates it to broader political principles. Such a party, in other words, follows the "self-interest rightly understood," which Tocqueville regards as the theory "best suited . . . to the wants of the men of our time."[15] Even in prosaic times, such middling parties preserve a certain appreciation for political poetry.

In any case, times and social circumstances set limits to the forms of party and party systems.[16] In the heroic age of its founding, America had great parties, but even at that time the United States was spared most of the violence associated with such a party system. The parties had only a moderate grandeur, agreeing on "the most essential points"—political precepts, but also the basics of moral life and social order—so that the high passion of the clash between Federalists and Jeffersonians was confined largely to words.[17] Moreover, the quasi-aristocratic doctrine of the Federalists was doomed because it was at odds with the fundamentally democratic character of American society, so that federalism collapsed as soon as the party lost power.[18]

The ordinary bases of great parties, Tocqueville asserts, were lacking in America. There was no "religious animosity," no "jealousy of rank," and no "public misery" (or, to modify Tocqueville's hyperbole, not enough to constitute a system of great parties).[19] But of course the Damoclean issue of slavery—not mentioned by Tocqueville in this context but very much on his mind—hung over the American system threatening to transform sectional conflict, heretofore fought on the limited terms of interest, into a war of principles. "At the present time," Tocqueville said carefully, there were no great parties in the United States; all parties accepted the form of government and the course of society, so that there was no danger of mortal combat in the contestation of parties.[20]

In fact, the mere formation of national parties demanded great political art. In James Madison's extended republic, opinion, then as now, is divided into "a thousand minute shades of difference," and it takes "inconceivable" pains to assemble a viable coalition. "Ambitious men," especially those out of power, discern those interests that may be aggregated with their own, and they then "discover" some "doctrine or principle" adapted to this party's use as a rallying cry.[21]

This is a fairly cynical picture, and Tocqueville acknowledges that in a "stranger" it might inspire contempt. This judgment, however, would be a superficial one since except at the margins, national parties must follow the main lines of division in a political society. Fundamentally, Tocqueville argues, American parties will be found to rest on great principles, support for or opposition to "popular authority." This implicit conflict of aristocracy and democracy is not ostensible; it is not even a conscious, though secret, aim of parties. Rather, it is rooted in passions or yearnings, below the surface but still the "main point and the very soul" of American partisan conflict.[22]

In other words, Tocqueville, anticipating Karl Mannheim, held that something like an ideology or utopia underlies any partisan coalition, ordinarily fuzzy or distorted but ready to be articulated should time and circumstance so intensify conflict as to make comfortable ambiguities untenable.[23] Tocqueville implies, however, that democracy cannot be content with parties whose greatness is *simply* latent or potential. If citizens feel no relation between their high yearnings and the practice of politics, they will, like the "remains of the aristocratic party" in

Tocqueville's America, retreat into private life, secretly despising the government and setting in motion the individualistic logic that ultimately threatens society itself.[24] In ordinary times American parties need leaders who can connect great principles with small parties, revealing some of the high stakes in low politics, the momentous aspects of the momentary.[25]

But parties are more than leaders and doctrines, and Tocqueville's discussion integrates the press and political associations, the "chief weapons" of party in striving for success but also the building stones that shape and constitute parties themselves.[26]

As he did when speaking of parties, Tocqueville begins with the negative virtues of the press. Despite its excesses, it cannot be regulated without worse evils, and as an "axiom of political science" holds in America, the multiplicity and variety of journals fragments the press's power.[27] Radically decentralized, the press speaks in "a thousand different ways" and for that reason cannot form "great currents of opinion."[28]

Still, taken as a whole, the press is undeniably vulgar, shaped by the tastes and passions of the mass audience, so that journalists habitually abandon the "principles of political science," reporting events in terms of individuals, dissecting their characters and pursuing them into private life.[29] This familiar tendency of the media obviously lessens the possibility of great parties, and it encourages public discussion that is seamy at best. Nevertheless, this gossipy local press, Tocqueville argues, is close to Americans, and it plays a decisive role in organizing the community for political life. It watches for the "secret springs of political designs" and especially when regarded collectively, sets the public agenda and shapes the alternatives for political debate.[30] This aspect of the press is central in the second volume of *Democracy in America* where Tocqueville emphasizes the role of newspapers as civic educators, essential in leading citizens to see and act on the connection between private interest and public policy. In this sense, the press is not merely a necessary evil but a bulwark of civilization.[31]

It is worth emphasizing that the force and effectiveness of the press in civic education depends on the extent to which it is seen as composed of gatekeepers, representatives who share the interests and feelings of their readers.[32] The civilizing role of the press, in other words, is better performed by media that are close to and dependent on groups and communities.[33]

Since the influence of newspapers grows in proportion to the weakness of individual readers, a mass press wields obvious power. At the same time, Tocqueville notices, increasing size attenuates the implicit association between a newspaper and its readership. The gain in power is purchased at the price of authority, so that mass media, like their audience, "more easily give way to the current of the multitude," becoming no more than echoes of the tyranny of the majority.[34] National mass media, in this sense, are weak teachers and no friends to strength or greatness in political parties.[35]

This implication is reinforced by Tocqueville's comments on the place of political associations in civic life.[36] Such associations, he argues, generally have more authority than the press in shaping the lives and opinions of their members because they have the "power of meeting" and are strengthened by acquaintance. Membership is something seen and experienced, part of the world of the senses and passions and able to enlist them, creating a specifically political sort of friendship. Numbers strengthen zeal, but the authority of associations is rooted in face-to-face relationships.[37]

American national parties, Tocqueville observed, were essentially local electoral bodies united by the representative system.[38] In fact, political parties were (and in a lessened way still are) a second, auxiliary system of representation. In the ratification debate, Anti-Federalists had worried that formal representation based on relatively large districts would result in too weak a bond of acquaintance and feeling between representatives and their constituents and would be too likely to exclude the "poor and middling classes" from office. The triumph of the large republic, accentuating these fears, led many Anti-Federalists to think better of party as a partial corrective.[39] In the same way, traditional party organization reflected Thomas Jefferson's desire for a "graduation of authorities" in which ward republics would delegate power "by a synthetical process to higher and higher orders of functionaries."[40] By the time the Committee on Political Parties was assembled, this had to seem axiomatic. In a modern democracy, Herman Finer wrote, "Representative government is party government."[41]

As Tocqueville notes, however, there is always the danger that party will become a rival of, rather than a support to, the formal system of representation. Parties are political societies that make high claims, and a party can constitute a "separate nation within a nation, a government within a government."[42] Despite the risk, relatively tolerable in the United States, Tocqueville thought the liberty of association, including the freedom of party organization, a "necessary guarantee against tyranny of the majority," strengthening the minority with a combination of friendship and shared conviction. Party, a "dangerous expedient," is needed to "obviate a still more formidable danger."[43]

We have already mentioned Tocqueville's warning that democracy tends to eliminate rank, only to leave individuals alone, without obligations to others but also without claims on them (a tendency strengthened by liberalism's individualistic premises). Isolated individuals are not free, Tocqueville observes, least of all in large states and mass societies; they are constantly aware of their relative weakness and insignificance and haunted by the anticipation of being forgotten, tending to surrender public life to the tyranny of the majority and retreating into the vulnerable fortress of the self. Only free institutions, Tocqueville maintains, stand any chance in combat with individualism. Democratic *politics* is the only possible cure for the fragmentations of democratic *society*.[44]

Public life, he notes, forces individuals to acknowledge their dependence and to cooperate with others, if only to defend themselves. Even such self-interested association has its liberative side since it reduces feelings of impotence and despair and encourages citizens to reach still farther beyond themselves. Tocqueville concedes the obvious: Elections are often mean contests between mean candidates, and political conflicts may divide friends and kindred. But partisan politics "brings a multitude of citizens permanently together, who would always have remained unknown to each other."[45] The enemy of indifference, partisanship is the ally of political freedom.

But in the school of citizenship parties are like institutions of higher education. They depend on prior preparation, habits of discipline, and quality of commitment. At bottom, partisanship is a matter of affect. E. E. Schattschneider once likened partisans to fans to argue that party identifiers, like fans, have no claim to participate in party decision making and should be seen as consumers in a political marketplace.[46] The Committee on Political Parties rejected this analogy to private enterprise, seeing parties as public bodies in which members have the right to a share in rule.[47] But the resemblance between partisans and fans is instructive. Fans have no serious bond of interest or material advantage linking them with their team, nor is their loyalty dependent on victory. A winning team increases the eagerness to buy tickets, and it may make fans insufferable, but allegiance often survives even repeated defeats.[48] And while a team symbolically represents its city, not all fans root for the home team. What defines a fan is the affective identification that makes fans feel a team's fortunes as their own. Similarly, political partisanship is rooted in a feeling of being *with* certain people more than being *for* certain programs or policies.[49]

After all, the word *affiliation*, which we use to describe the relation between members and their party, refers to entering a family. Like families, parties appeal to memory and hope against the allure of the present and of self-interest, narrowly defined. All of this indicates, as

Tocqueville did, that party and partisanship depend on the capacity to extend oneself, identifying with other persons and across time.[50]

In democratic regimes, Tocqueville wrote, the "laws that rule human societies" require the "art of associating together," the theoretical science of association applied as a rule of practice and a discipline of the soul.[51] The American excellence in that art, he observed, rested on the pervasive training in and for association that he saw in infancy, in the schools and social life.[52] And local politics was the indispensable palestra of citizenship.

In locality I can see or experience the connection between my interest and that of the community rather than having to reason it out more or less abstractly. Locality does not always make citizens generous: most of us are more apt to support housing for the homeless if it is to be located in someone else's backyard. For Tocqueville's purposes, however, what matters is that a housing project next door is likely to make me care about politics and to move me to form or join a political association. Wrestling with the problem, moreover, is likely to make me recognize, if dimly, that so long as there are homeless people, no home is secure.

In localities too, citizens are more apt to know one another and hence to see one another as relatively predictable if not benign. If the community is stable, that interpersonal knowledge goes deeper, and society seems even more reliable, holding the landmarks of life. "Love and respect," Tocqueville comments, are less likely to result from brilliant strokes and great achievements than from "a long succession of little services rendered and of obscure good deeds."[53]

In the little theater of local politics, a larger fraction of the citizenry can find roles on stage, and many people in the audience rank as personages in their own right. Entering the public sphere often brings greater dignity, reversing the ordinary rule in large states, so that in Tocqueville's America, "if an American were condemned to confine his activity to his own affairs, he would be robbed of one half of his existence."[54] Political participation and membership in associations can enlist the feelings and enlarge the heart, Tocqueville claims, so that subordinating one's effort to the "common impulse," even when it originates in calculations of interest, eventually becomes a habit and a taste.[55]

Learned in "small affairs," knowledge of public life and the "love and practice of association" are carried into "great undertakings." In that larger sphere, the discipline of association creates a disposition to partisanship, which is especially valuable in overcoming "whatever natural repugnance may retrain men from acting in concert."[56] Party and partisanship can overcome what might otherwise be unbridgeable gaps between individuals and between social groups. In the best case,

Tocqueville suggests, party mediates between pluralism and a public, aggregating groups and producing citizens.[57]

To sum up: (1) At least in normal times, Tocqueville implies a preference for middle-range parties, originating in interest but articulating implicit principles, and he calls attention to the special danger of communalism in the United States. (2) He argues that political parties and party systems are limited by, though they are not simply functions of, the times and the political culture in which they are situated. (3) Political parties are also integrally related to the character of the press and of political association, and decentralization in both is favorable to party strength and to civic education. (4) For similar reasons, parties should ideally be built from local bodies on the basis of representation, especially because local communities and political life strengthen political affects and the capacity for affiliation. It is theorizing that rings true, for all its echoes of another time.

Our near contemporaries, the Committee on Political Parties, shared much of Tocqueville's predilection for middling parties. The committee aspired, after all, only to a "more responsible" party system, not the genuine article. For the committee, however, "normal times" were no more than a memory, and American democracy faced an "explosive era" and "problems of unprecedented magnitude."[58] Foreign policy—a sphere, Tocqueville had argued, in which democracy is naturally deficient—had become a constant and urgent priority, and in economic and social life government's "far-flung" interventions also demanded the ability to act with speed and flexibility.[59] The committee's premise is the need for forceful, "effective" government, directed by policy and able to integrate power, the state envisioned as a powerhouse.[60]

The committee looks to political parties primarily to provide authorization, the "widest possible consent," sufficient public support for state policy to permit striking action. It hopes for majorities willing to alter habits and, probably, to make more material sacrifices.[61] At the same time, the committee recognizes the need for democratic regulation of the new American state, and it speaks of parties as a check on presidentialism and bureaucratic autonomy.[62] This is, however, very much a secondary concern in the committee's report. It expects that its recommendations will be supported by the president and by administrators, a sure sign that it expects responsible parties to empower the executive, while it anticipates similar backing only from "influential" members of Congress and "forward-looking" political leaders.[63] The committee's overriding concern is the need to "consolidate public attitudes toward the work plans of government."[64]

The committee emphasized that economics, technology, and political events had created an essentially national politics and opinion. Sectionalism was a declining force, and locality was increasingly regarded as small potatoes. The State House and Main Street were losing their audience to the White House and Wall Street. Consequently, parties could no longer be merely "loose associations" of local parties. Existing parties were the "most archaic institution in the United States," reflecting a kind of cultural lag, and no quality could have seemed more damning to the Progressive sensibility that dominated the committee.[65] Practical-minded, the committee had no desire to abandon federalism, but it did hope for a decisively heavier national weight in the balance.

In fact, the committee saw a special danger in failing to move in a national direction. The new state and the new politics had created something like a new public, tending to "broaden the base" of political parties, presumably by drawing into politics new voters oriented—pro or con—to the policies and goals of the New Deal.[66] It was evidently these voters the committee had in mind when it spoke of the risk that postelection coalitions—the alliance of Republicans and Dixiecrats in Congress—would promote political cynicism by making electoral choice something less than a "meaningful alternative."[67]

A great many southern white Democrats, however, appear to have *wanted* the alternative of voting for their party's presidential nominee while moderating his policies, especially regarding race, in a coalition-dominated Congress. The committee seems to have regarded that sort of choice as not "meaningful," for at least two reasons: (1) it denied the executive the authority necessary for effective government; (2) the intrusion of sectionalism muddled the national economic issues that were the main lines of division in modern government, the conflicts that really mattered. For the committee, the New Deal and the voters it brought to politics were the wave of the partisan future.[68]

The committee hoped, in other words, to sharpen and institutionalize what it took to be the existing and evolving distinction between the parties. In that spirit, the report asserted that its aim was parties as vehicles for coherent government, so that it urged greater discipline within parties, not greater differences between them.[69]

But whatever its members' thoughts, the committee was content to leave the definition of party very largely to the membership. Then as now, party membership was not defined by any clear rules or understandings, but the committee argued that the very idea of party implied "broadly like-minded voters" who had at least "something in common."[70]

And while parties had a "right and duty" to set terms for "participation in the common enterprise," the committee, as noted, rejected the view that party is an association of professionals in favor of the idea that the broad membership should control the party democratically, through "primaries, caucuses and conventions."[71] The committee favored a "representative political organization" in which ideas and programs "bubble up" from below, hoping to articulate the party's fundamental commonalities through structured deliberation, a position somewhat more democratic than Tocqueville's similar doctrine.[72]

Yet despite its regard for membership, the committee distrusted old-style partisan allegiance. "Yeller dog" straight-ticket voters might have seemed attractive to the committee since such voters, willing to support almost any policy or candidate endorsed by the party, give leaders broad discretion to act for the public good.

The loyalty of party regulars, however, provided no impetus for change and seemed to the committee part of the "inertia of the body politic." The committee expected only that "many" partisans would favor greater party responsibility and that the "rank and file" would support party government based on majority rule. For the achievement of its aims, the committee relied on the less than fully committed swing voter. "It is this group that is willing to make an electoral choice and wants a choice to make; that wants to vote for a program and resents not having carried it out." Since this group was "assiduously courted" by both parties, its disproportional strength gave the committee special hope for success.[73]

As an empirical matter, the committee's image of "swing" voters is very dubious, perhaps especially as a description of voters at that time.[74] Independent voters who feel pulled in conflicting directions are almost axiomatically eager to avoid sharp choices. Similarly, weakly committed voters must always be addressed in the short term since there are no reserves of loyalty to get leaders through the rough times.

The committee turned to such unlikely supporters because it was convinced that although traditional partisans gave their leaders authorization of impressive range and durability, they did so on a basis that was wrong, or at least unacceptably inarticulate. Allegiance on the basis of "personalities, patronage and local matters" had to give way to devotion to a national program.[75] To the committee, dominantly Progressive in persuasion, the rational issue-oriented voter was doubtless a more attractive partisan. Yet even if theoretically members of the committee had regarded local and personal attachments as a solider affective foundation for party identification, they would have pointed out that in practice, local community was declining and local allegiance with it. The committee was too optimistic to recognize the desperate quality in its conviction that it had no alternative but to attempt to base party loyalty on words and arguments rather than habits and feelings, relying on participation to an extent that went far beyond Tocqueville's already considerable confidence.

A "share in framing the party's objectives," the committee asserts, will encourage in members a "self-discipline" flowing from " free identification."[76] In that belief, it recommends frequent local meetings featuring discussions of policy and other "constructive alternatives," offering the assurance that this new direction will make "association with a party" more "interesting and attractive."[77]

Yet while the "opportunity to contribute" to forming a party's program probably does strengthen the willingness to support it, as the committee claimed, it does so in a way that is at least partly proportional to the sense of having contributed *effectively*.[78] Having a voice will not matter so much if one is heard only as crowd noise.

Even allowing for "two-way communication" with the national party council, any one of the committee's proposed local forums would have only the most limited impact on national policy, and to make matters worse, the committee envisages separating these policy leagues from local election committees.[79] Tocqueville spoke of a local politics that citizens entered from necessity or interest, going on to learn the importance of public principles. The committee relies on a prior concern for policy to bring people to party life in the absence of either clear material interests or significant power over policy. And the committee's seminars would have had to compete with entertainments and activities that did not exist for Tocqueville's Americans. It seems implausible that such policy leagues would have attracted more than a committed minority of activists and ideologues.[80]

This is especially true since in the committee's design so many of the party's decisions are to be made in primaries. The report leaves room for caucuses and conventions, especially in discussing policy, and it notes "recognized imperfections" in the primary, but it concludes that "no workable substitute" has been found for primaries as a basis for intraparty democracy.[81] It even looks with favor on a direct national presidential primary, although it also speaks well of preprimary screenings.[82] But even the closed primary, which the committee supported, leaves decisions to a mass electorate, not local associations.[83] The report speaks vaguely of "opportunities" offered by primaries "for the creation of a broad base on which to build the party structure"—presumably by drawing new voters into party life—but it admits that these chances "have rarely been fully utilized."[84] That considerable understatement implies that the committee envisioned primaries largely conducted by and through local membership committees, with a strong screening role played by the party council.[85] The evidence suggests that this was a forlorn hope, but even if we accept it on its own terms, the committee's reliance on primaries would have made its local gatherings seem less potent and less attractive.

Subtly but consistently, the committee was willing to trade accessibility and immediacy for parties centralized enough to be effective in mass politics.[86] Individualism and social fragmentation, nemeses for Tocqueville, scarcely counted as worries. For the committee, what mattered was organized power.

Like Tocqueville, the committee included political associations in its discussion of party, but where Tocqueville spoke of associations as weapons to be used by party, the committee worried that the reverse might become the rule. Part of the eclipse of the local witnessed by the committee was the rise of national interest groups, power accumulated on a grand scale to make private interests effective in public councils. Organized locally and in states, parties were at an increasing disadvantage, ill coordinated and lacking in resources. National responsible parties were needed to assert public principles against private interest and to avoid "government by pressure groups," the reduction of public policy to a parallelogram of forces.[87]

Shrewdly, the committee distinguishes between mass membership organizations—primarily the labor movement, although agricultural groups are also mentioned—and associations with little or no "direct voting power" that derive their strength from money, position, and the like. The latter, the report argues, prefer to deal with officials as isolated individuals, relatively vulnerable and out of the public eye; such groups, accordingly, can be expected to oppose stronger and more responsible parties. Mass membership organizations, by contrast, "find the public looking over their shoulders," and trading on electoral strength, are accustomed to thinking and speaking in more or less public terms. Such organizations, the committee notes, are more and more apt to act as virtual auxiliaries of political parties and despite a friction here and there, can be expected to support party reform.[88]

The committee did not anticipate the slow decline of organized labor or the other mass membership groups on which it relied. And it did not discern that the economic and social changes that were one of its premises would unsettle the social and moral foundations of American life. New mass movements and organizations have increasingly been responses to that disorder, articulating demands that are cultural and communal—the voices of race, ethnicity, gender, and televangelized religion—and far less easily subordinated to public norms.[89]

It is of a piece that unlike Tocqueville, the committee did not include the media in its treatment of party. Of course, by the time of the report, the party press of Tocqueville's day was long extinct. Yet this alone should have been worthy of comment. Advertising, the outgrowth of a national economy, had encouraged the growth of a mass circulation press and eventually the mass electronic media, free from dependence on party patronage. The media, consequently, have ceased to be the instruments of party and more often are its transformers.

Written before television's unequaled force made itself felt in American politics, the report did not seem to notice that the media were displacing local gatekeepers and in time would virtually eliminate them, shattering traditional party organization but also the reformed structures the committee favored.[90] Moreover, the electronic media, enormously increasing the importance of money in politics, have also increased the clout of the elite, less visible interest groups at the expense of the membership associations the committee favored. And the need for money, combined with communications technology, has brought about broad financial "participation" in response to direct solicitation.

The ability to engage in mass fund-raising has greatly added to the power of national party organizations, a result the committee would have approved.[91] Yet despite the Supreme Court's opinion in *Buckley v. Valeo*, the contribution of money, while undeniably "expression," is not speech; it does not give reasons or listen to arguments.[92] "Membership" through direct solicitation comes down to the relation of individuals with a central bureaucracy. It lacks the "power of meeting" so central to Tocqueville's hope of catching hearts or the committee's reliance on deliberation. A collection of private acts directed toward public ends, this version of association can aggregate individuals, but it cannot educate its citizens.

The media have created something close to a national culture, drawing us together in some ways but also creating new conflicts.[93] Among the democratic passions, Tocqueville argued, none is more fundamental than the people's resentment of any "great establishment" outside its authority. The majority rallied to Andrew Jackson, Tocqueville thought, out of "irritation" at the bank, not from settled ideas of policy.[94] When the committee wrote, *establishment* meant the economic elite, and the pattern of politics was shaped in the New Deal mold by one's identification with or against this "ruling class." The media, however, make symbol weigh more heavily on any balance with interest, and state regulation is now as ubiquitous as the impositions of economic power and more visible, an easy target for television reporting. As a political line of division, class is countered by resentment of the political and cultural establishment, the "new class" of neoconservative theory.[95]

The media themselves are the prototype of private government, an establishment on which we depend but practically beyond our control.[96] There is at least equal resentment of government, and especially of the law, which so often seems to thwart our ideas of justice. That distaste is amplified by hostility to legal entitlements, which appear to create specially advantaged groups. And intellectuals, with their tendency to combine democratic rhetoric with elitist sensibility, are at least a minor target. The "politically correct," after all, is unmistakably the creed of an establishment.

Clearly, Democrats have suffered most from these developments since as the party of the economic "outs" they have been cast as the champions of the cultural and governmental insiders. But the cause of responsible parties is also damaged: despite the increase in issue-oriented voting, the two cross-cutting lines of division define four persuasions or subparties, only uneasily and tentatively fitted into the two-party mold.[97]

Our evidence indicates, in fact, that voters are fearful of responsible party government and that they prefer divided authority, the new, partisan variation on checks and balances.[98] As the committee would have expected, this solution has problems of its own. There is plenty of rage against government's predictable inability to act decisively in domestic areas of concern, enough that in 1990 a large number of voters, however they voted in the end, were at least attracted by the appeal to turn incumbents out indiscriminately. The strong authorization the committee hoped for still ranks as an urgent need.

Barring a Depression-scale event, however, social and cultural issues will continue to add to political fragmentation. Assuming that Democrats are committed to economic equality—not as sure a thing as it once would have been—they have every reason to lessen the party's identification with social liberalism and the cultural establishment, just as Republicans have good cause to fudge the tension between traditional morals and the market.[99] Majority coalitions in Madison's extended republic have ordinarily been works of art, their contradictions softened by rhetoric, imagination, and charm, and the hope for party government today depends on leaders with the requisite craft and magic.[100]

Nevertheless, partisanship, as Tocqueville taught, is itself a partial antidote to communalism and fragmentation since it forces at least some effort to speak in terms of the good of the party and the public as a whole.[101] Patchwork, to use Jesse Jackson's 1988 metaphor, presumes the idea of a quilt, a design that orders the patches, just as diversity is defined and limited by the category of things to which it refers, whether menu items or citizens, so that implicitly the many is ruled by the one.[102] Still, working to discover and articulate a party's commonalities—and even more, subordinating our private nostrums to them—requires a commitment to the party's cause or at least the desire to defeat its enemies.[103]

Partisanship, like citizenship, is in need of policies to strengthen, or limit the damage to, those social and civil institutions, beginning with the family, that form the affective bases of affiliation and allegiance. Whatever their other satisfactions, civic participation and deliberation are time-consuming and invariably frustrating. In Albert Hirschman's terms, "voice" needs "loyalty" to countervail "exit," the disposition to seek private and individual solutions so powerfully positioned in America's culture and laws.[104]

The likelihood, though, is that party identification will grow weaker and that straight-ticket voters will become a rarer if not quite an endangered species.[105] Given increasing conditional commitment, what passes for a party's membership will resemble consumers with a certain degree of brand loyalty more than citizens of a community with a claim to share in its governance.[106] Under the circumstances, there is reason to reconsider Schattschneider's view that party government should be left to professionals, and at the margin where practice allows for it parties would be well advised to move in that direction.[107] As the committee recommended, for example, some sort of national party meetings should convene *before* the primaries to screen possible candidates, leaving the increasingly formal postprimary nominations to the traditional conventions.

In any event, the quality of deliberation in parties and the debate between them depends on the media that chair our national forum, recognizing speakers and setting the terms of discussion.[108] Responsible parties presuppose responsible media, especially media that fulfill some of their obligations in civic education.

The centralization of politics and political attention deprives almost all Americans of a public voice. All but a few of us must be listeners, yet that role, while an incomplete curriculum for civic virtue, can have its own excellence. As fans, Americans are engaged and often knowledgeable observers, and it would amount to an instauration if citizens approximated that level of commitment and skill. The emphasis on the visible in the electronic media, however, does nothing to develop an ear for politics, and politics ultimately comes down to speech, a quarrel about the just and unjust. In fact, driven by the competitive anxiety to please their audiences, the media tend to reduce coverage of politics and political speech to the lowest common denominator, promoting atrophy in the public's critical skills.[109]

Since the media seem incapable of restraining themselves, they need the support of law. The requirement that presidential candidates engage in four televised debates, recently approved by the Senate, is a step in the right direction.[110] There is also merit in Paul Taylor's suggestion that on alternating nights the candidates be given five minutes on every television and radio station on the condition that they appear in person.[111] Similarly, I think it would help to limit the percentage of federal funds that can be spent on television, directing money and attention to more traditional and local forms of campaigning. In any case, Americans need to do whatever they can to add to their powers of public speech and hearing.

With the ending of the cold war, America's political soul will be tried not against enemies but in the sounds of silence.[112] The media, vital as they are, only frame political debate. In American democracy it takes parties and partisanship to quicken and give substance to citizenship. Given their fading vitalities, reanimating the parties calls for help from all the sciences of politics, ancient and modern.

Notes

1. The economic worry is detailed in Paul Kennedy, *The Rise and Fall of Great Powers* (New York: Random House, 1987).

2. Karl Mannheim, *Man and Society in an Age of Reconstruction* (New York: Harcourt Brace, 1951).

3. Alexis de Tocqueville, *Democracy in America* (New York: Schoken, 1961), vol. 1, pp. lxxiii–lxxiv; see also vol. 1, pp. 304–18, and 2, pp. 118–20.

4. The exception, of course, is the requirement that the president be native-born.

5. *Democracy in America*, vol. 1, pp. 193–94.

6. Richard Hofstadter, *The Idea of a Party System* (Berkeley and Los Angeles: University of California Press, 1969), pp. 1–73.

7. *Democracy in America*, vol. 1, p. 194.

8. Ibid., vol. 1, p. 195. We need to remember the element of truth in this teaching. In 1980 Republican sorrow at the failure of Carter's rescue mission was at least tempered by its political advantages; and in 1991 most Democrats, sharing the elation of victory over Iraq, felt at least a twinge of partisan dismay.

9. *Democracy in America*, vol. 1, p. 195.

10. Tocqueville could easily have found small societies that fit this description, as we could (Sri Lanka, for example). His exclusion of such societies is thus indicative of his intent.

11. *Democracy in America*, vol. 1, p. 199.

12. Ibid., vol. 1, p. 195.

13. Robert V. Remini, *Martin Van Buren and the Making of the Democratic Party* (New York: Columbia University Press, 1959), p. 132; Joel Silbey, *The Partisan Imperative* (New York: Oxford University Press, 1985), pp. 33–49.

14. *Democracy in America*, vol. 1, pp. 195–97. A great party articulates and is devoted to a ruling principle, but such a principle taken on its own terms rejects the limits of partiality. A great party, consequently, tends to recognize its opponents only out of necessity or—as in Jefferson's analysis of Tories—a concession to temperamental "sickliness." *Life and Selected Writings of Thomas Jefferson*, Adrienne Koch and William Peden, eds. (New York: Modern Library, 1944), p. 715.

15. *Democracy in America*, vol. 2, pp. 145–49.

16.See Robert Harmel and Kenneth Janda, *Parties and Their Environments* (New York: Longmans, 1982).

17. *Democracy in America*, vol. 1, p. 197; see also vol. 1, p. 33.

18. Ibid., vol. 1, pp. 198–99.

19. Ibid., vol. 1, p. 200.

20. Ibid., vol. 1, p. 199; Harry V. Jaffa, *Crisis of the House Divided* (Chicago: University of Chicago Press, 1959).

21. *Democracy in America*, vol. 1, pp. 199–200.

22. Ibid., vol. 1, pp. 200–201. For a similar view, see E. E. Schattschneider, "The Functional Approach to Party Government," in Sigmund Neuman, ed., *Modern Political Parties* (Chicago: University of Chicago Press, 1956), pp. 194–215.

23. Karl Mannheim, *Ideology and Utopia* (New York: Harcourt Brace, 1936).

24. *Democracy in America*, vol. 1, pp. 201–3; vol. 2, 118–20.

25. It is always worth remembering that the nineteenth-century parties, less than great by our standards, seemed more significant to voters in that time than today's parties do to our contemporaries. Walter Dean Burnham, "The Changing Shape of the American Political Universe," *American Political Science Review*, 59 (1965): 12–13, 23.

26. He refers to the press and associations as "weapons" in vol. 1, where his argument descends from the inclusive to the particular; in vol. 2, this order is reversed, emphasizing the constituent role of associations. *Democracy in America*, vol. 1, p. 203; vol. 2, pp. 134–37.

27. Ibid., vol. 1, pp. 204–6, 209–10.

28. Ibid., vol. 1, pp. 210–11.

29. Ibid., vol. 1, p. 211.

30. Ibid., vol. 1, p. 212.

31. Ibid., vol. 2, p. 134.

32. Paul Lazarsfeld, Bernard Berelson, and Hazel Gaudet, *The People's Choice* (New York: Duell, Sloan and Pearce, 1944); Sally Foreman Griffith, *Home Town News* (New York: Oxford University Press, 1988).

33. *Democracy in America*, vol. 2, pp. 135–37.

34. Ibid., vol. 2, p. 137.

35. The national media would not have attempted to act like various radio talk shows as a catalyst in generating opposition to a pay raise for Congress. Nor, at a much higher level, could they have played anything like the role of the

National Review in unifying the American right. See E. J. Dionne, *Why Americans Hate Politics* (New York: Simon and Schuster, 1991), pp. 159–66.

36. Tocqueville's definition of association, "the public assent which a number of individuals give to certain doctrines," is a very broad one. Including political parties, it embraces "permanent associations . . . established by law" (primarily local governments) and groups "formed and maintained by . . . private individuals." Tocqueville, *Democracy in America*, vol. 1, pp. 216–17.

37. Ibid., vol. 1, pp. 217–18.

38. Ibid., vol. 1, p. 218.

39. See my "The Anti-Federalists, Representation and Party," *Northwestern Law Review*, 84 (1989): 26–37.

40. Koch and Peden, eds., *Life and Selected Writings of Thomas Jefferson*, pp. 661, 673; Richard K. Matthews, *The Radical Politics of Thomas Jefferson* (Lawrence: University Press of Kansas, 1984), pp. 81–89.

41. Herman Finer, *The Theory and Practice of Modern Government* (New York: Holt, 1949), p. 237.

42. *Democracy in America*, vol. 1, p. 218.

43. Ibid., vol. 1, pp. 220–21.

44. Ibid., vol. 2, pp. 118–20, 123–27; vol. 1, pp. 304–18.

45. Ibid., vol. 2, p. 124.

46. E. E. Schattschneider, *Party Government* (New York: Holt, Rinehart and Winston, 1942), p. 55.

47. Committee on Political Parties of the American Political Science Association, *Toward a More Responsible Two-Party System* (New York: Rinehart, 1950), p. 66; see also pp. 1, 10, 18, 70 (hereinafter, CPP).

48. Cubs fans are legendary longsufferers, for example, and my colleague Dennis Bathory is unshaken in his devotion to the Indians.

49. Ignazio Silone, "The Choice of Comrades," *Dissent*, 2 (1955): 7–19; John H. Schaar and Wilson C. McWilliams, "Uncle Sam Vanishes," *New University Thought*, 1 (1961) pp. 61–68; compare Angus Campbell, et al., *The American Voter* (New York: Wiley, 1960,) p. 121; Henry Valen and Daniel Katz, *Political Parties in Norway* (London: Tavistock, 1964).

50. *Democracy in America*, vol. 2, p. 131. This can be explained as a version of "interest rightly understood," but we should remember that Tocqueville was amused by the American tendency to explain all actions on the basis of self-interest. Americans, he noted, often acted from generous impulses, but were reluctant to admit yielding to such feelings: "They are more anxious to do honour to their philosophy than to themselves." Ibid., vol.2, pp. 146–47.

51. Ibid., vol. 2, p. 132. As the science of association is the "mother of science," the art of association is the "mother of action." Ibid.

52. Ibid., vol. 1, p. 216.

53. Ibid., vol. 1, p. 125.

54. Ibid., vol. 1, p. 293.

55. Ibid., vol. 2, pp. 140, 131, 127.

56. Ibid., vol. 2, pp. 139–140.

57. "This great and glorious country," Plunkitt asserted with considerable authority, "was built up by political parties." William Riordan, *Plunkitt of Tammany Hall* (New York: Dutton, 1963), p. 18. See also David Price, "Community, 'Mediating Structures' and Public Policy," *Soundings*, 62 (1970): 369–94.

58. CPP, pp. 92, 17.

59. Ibid., p. 1; see also pp. 4, 31–32; *Democracy in America*, vol. 1, pp. 269–75.

60. CPP, p. 16; the image of the state as a powerhouse is taken from Henry Adams, *The Education of Henry Adams* (Boston: Houghton Miffline, 1961), p. 421.

61. CPP, p. 18; see also pp. 4, 14, 31.

62. Ibid., p. 14.

63. Ibid., pp. 86–90.

64. Ibid., p. 16.

65. Ibid., pp. v, 3, 25, 33–34.

66. Ibid., p. 16.

67. Ibid., p. 19; see also p. 14.

68. The main lines of the committee's thinking seem to parallel Arthur N. Holcombe, *The New Party Politics* (New York: Norton, 1933).

69. CPP, p. 2.

70. Ibid., pp. 3, 27, 66–67.

71. Ibid., pp. 1, 2, 18, 21, 23.

72. Ibid., pp. 16, 66–67. Tocqueville, it will be remembered, relied on ambitious leaders to spell out the party's unifying themes.

73. Ibid., p. 91.

74. Phillip K. Hastings, "The Independent Voter in 1952: A Study of Pittsfield, Massachusetts," *American Political Science Review*, 47 (1953): 805ff.

75. CPP, pp. 11, 69.

76. Ibid., pp. 10, 70.

77. Ibid., pp. 6, 9, 10, 30, 67. It is worth noting that the committee preferred the term *association*, with its limited and contractual connotations, to the term *identification*.

78. Ibid., p. 69.

79. Ibid., p. 67.

80. For early evidence on the point, see Frank J. Sorauf, "Extra-Legal Parties in Wisconsin," *American Political Science Review*, 48 (1954): 692–704.

81. CPP, pp. 2, 23, 70–71.

82. Ibid., pp. 74, 72.

83. Ibid., p. 71.

84. Ibid., p. 30.

85. Ibid., pp. 71–73.

86. C. Wright Mills, *The Power Elite* (New York: Oxford University Press, 1956), pp. 306–10.

87. CPP, pp. 4, 19. In the succeeding decades political science often celebrated precisely the sort of brokerage the Committee feared. See, for example,

David Truman, *The Governmental Process* (New York: Norton, 1969), pp. 55–97.

88. CPP, pp. 4, 13, 20, 34-35, 85–86.

89. John K. White, *The New Politics of Old Values* (Hanover, N.H.: University Press of New England, 1988); Byron Shafer, "The New Cultural Politics," *PS* 18 (1985): 221–31; Christopher Lasch, *The True and Only Heaven* (New York: Norton, 1991), pp. 476–532. Of course, cultural conflict was a vital dimension in traditional party politics, but it was constrained within something much more like moral consensus. *Democracy in America*, vol. 1, p. 33; Paul Kleppner, *The Third Electoral System, 1853–1892* (Chapel Hill: University of North Carolina Press, 1979), p. 367.

90. Austin Ranney, *Channels of Power* (New York: Basic Books, 1983), p. 110.

91. CPP, p. 11.

92. Buckley v. Valeo, 424 U.S. 1 (1976); Wilson C. McWilliams, "The Discipline of Freedom," in *To Secure the Blessings of Liberty: First Principles of the Constitution*, ed. Sarah Baumgartner Thurow (Lanham, Md.: University Press of America, 1988) pp. 54–57.

93. Benjamin Barber, "The Tide in New Channels," *New York Times*, 21 April 1982.

94. *Democracy in America*, vol. 1, p. 201.

95. For example, Jeane Kirkpatrick, *The New Presidential Elite* (New York: Russell Sage, Twentieth Century Fund, 1976), pp. 246, 253, 360.

96. W. Russell Neuman, *The Paradox of Mass Politics* (Cambridge, Mass.: Harvard University Press, 1986). Kevin Phillips referred to a "knowledge elite"; *Mediacracy: American Parties and Politics in the Communications Age* (Garden City, N.Y.: Doubleday, 1975), p. 34.

97. William S. Maddox and Stuart A. Lilie, *Beyond Liberal and Conservative* (Washington, D.C.: Cato Institute, 1984); Dionne, *Why Americans Hate Politics*, pp. 276–80.

98. Joseph Schlesinger, "The New American Party System," *American Political Science Review*, 79 (1985): 1152–69; Walter Dean Burnham, "The Reagan Heritage," in Gerald M. Pomper, ed., *The Election of 1988* (Chatham, N.J.: Chatham House, 1989), pp. 16–25.

99. Christopher Lasch, "Traditional Values, Left, Right and Wrong," *Harpers*, 273 (September 1986): 13–16.

100. At crucial points the committee looked to party leaders, collected in the party council, to overcome the antinomies between local and national discipline, party leaders and elected officials, and party members and the mass electorate. CPP, pp. 23, 40–44, 52–53, 71–73.

101. Otto Kirchheimer, "The Party in Mass Society," *World Politics*, 10 (1958): 289–94.

102. See my "What Will Jackson Do?" *Commonweal*, 23 September 1988, p. 488; Aristotle, *Politics*, pp. 1281a39–1284a3.

103. David Carlin, "It's My Party," *Commonweal*, 7 October 1988, pp. 521–22.

104. Albert Hirschman, *Exit, Voice and Loyalty* (Cambridge, Mass.: Harvard University Press, 1970); Robert Reich, "The Secession of the Successful," *New York Times Magazine*, 20 January 1991, pp. 17ff.

105. Norman Nie, Sidney Verba and John Petrocik, *The Changing American Voter* (Cambridge, Mass.: Harvard University Press, 1979), pp. 62–64, 73, 363–65; Martin P. Wattenberg, *The Decline of American Political Parties* (Cambridge, Mass.: Harvard University Press, 1984), p. 89.

106. Leon Epstein likens parties to public utilities, but the moral is the same. *Political Parties in the American Mold* (Madison: University of Wisconsin Press, 1986). See also Gerald M. Pomper, "The Decline of Party in American Elections," *Political Science Quarterly*, 92 (1977): 23.

107. This is not a position I prefer, although it may be the best of a bad set of practical choices. See my "Political Parties as Civic Associations," in Gerald M. Pomper, ed., *Party Renewal in America* (New York: Praeger, 1980,) pp. 63–64.

108. Marc Landy and Dennis Hale, eds., *The Nature of Politics: Selected Essays of Bertrand de Jouvenel* (New York: Schocken, 1987), pp. 44–54.

109. Pomper, *Election of 1988*, pp. 180–83; on the problems and possibilities of the media, see Jeffrey Abramson, F. Christopher Arterton, and Gary Orren, *The Electronic Commonwealth* (New York: Basic Books, 1988).

110. *New York Times*, 18 May 1991, p. 10.

111. Paul Taylor, "The Five-Minute Fix," *Washington Post National Weekly*, 23–29 April 1990, p. 23. I am also attracted by Michael Woo's argument that parties and candidates should be required to purchase television time in longer blocks, in the hope of encouraging more serious discussion. *New York Times*, 13 November 1988, p. E-3.

112. Sidney Blumenthal, *Pledging Allegiance* (New York: HarperCollins, 1990).

Epilogue
Prospects for Party Government

JEROME M. MILEUR

What is to be made of America's political parties and the party system they embody? What is to be done about them? Are parties really the keystone of democracy, as E. E. Schattschneider argues, writing that modern democracy is "unthinkable save in terms of the parties"?[1] Or are they anachronisms—political dinosaurs, powerful in their time but ill-equipped for the modern political environment? Is the party over, as the journalist David Broder asks, or has it just begun, as the political scientist Larry Sabato contends?[2] Has electoral disaggregation so fragmented the American polity as to make the task of parties impossible, as Walter Dean Burnham suggests, or can they be brought back, as David Price argues?[3]

The essays that compose this volume offer no definitive answers to these questions. Their authors are all fans of America's parties, believe in them, want them to win out, and think it important they do. They are like baseball fans, rooting for *their team*, down four runs in the sixth inning on the road, hoping against hope that their favorites can prevail against the odds in a hostile environment. Outside academia, America's parties have few enthusiastic fans—here and there a journalist like Broder, now and again an elected official like Congressmen William Thomas and David Price in these pages. But far more often than not among press, politicians, and voters, parties are seen, in that withering sixties phrase, as part of the problem, not part of the solution. Yet the party goes on, and the contributors here are intent primarily upon charting the course of party evolution and assessing the character of America's parties today.[4]

The Committee on Political Parties of the American Political Science Association, whose 1950 report inspired this book, argues that changing America's parties, making them more suitable instruments of popular democracy in the nation's governance, is as simple as changing our collective minds. It is a wonderfully Progressive sentiment, a belief in civic education as the solvent of public problems. But the committee's faith in it wishes away the difficult realities that face political parties in America. It is hard to imagine a constitutional and legal terrain more forbidding to parties and the growth of party government. The Constitution disperses authority, dividing it between the levels and branches of government. Federalism and the separation of powers muddle notions of responsibility and accountability. Divided government in the states and nation, the antithesis of party government, is the by-product, but a symptom, not the disease. At the same time, the legal regulation of parties has stripped them of resources (patronage), powers (nominations), and roles (nonpartisan elections), the debilitating effects of which have been augmented by the changing nature of political campaigns (television, money).

The political culture in America—Jeffersonian to the core in its individualism, pluralism, and localism—reinforces the effects of the constitutional division of powers, making majorities yet harder to organize. The Puritan heritage adds to this, infecting public sentiments with a morality that is at once suspicious and certain. Haunted privately by sin and publicly by fraud, it is resolute in the belief that individuals are responsible for themselves and their condition—a sense of "responsibility" applicable to parties. The American party system, birthed by a Jacksonian democracy devoted in word to restoring Jeffersonian virtue but grounded in deed in a politics of patronage and favoritism, offends the values and beliefs of America's Jeffersonian and Puritan political culture. Indeed, as agencies of compromise alone, political parties are not institutions to be instinctively admired, much less revered, in such a milieu.

The history of party in America, moreover, gives little support to the friends of party government. As James Reichley details, the "golden age" of party government in America, the latter half of the nineteenth century, was a time of bosses who reigned supreme in cities, state legislatures, and Congress, largely indifferent to questions of responsibility and beyond the easy reach of accountability. The parties of these bosses may have expanded popular democracy in America, socializing waves of new Americans and empowering working- and lower-class voters, but their methods and those of their machines were an affront to the values of middle-class democracy. The Progressive reforms were aimed squarely at breaking the hold of bosses and party on government and voters alike, and in doing so, they made it more difficult intellectually and politically to make the case for party government in America.

The case for party government, however, has a long and honorable history in American political thought.[5] In its simple form, it is that popular democracy requires agencies of general interest to organize public opinion around competing programs of government, nominate candidates for office who embrace their respective programs, enact their program if they win control of the government, and answer to the electorate if they fail to do so. Voters at least vaguely understand the logic of party government. They know that their real political power lies in their ability to throw the rascals out, that as John Stuart Mill taught more than a century ago, they need the ballot not that they may govern but that they not be misgoverned. For the most part, however, the logic of party government has not been embraced by America's democrats in this century. They are wedded instead to the Progressive ideal of direct democracy and citizen empowerment; they want the ballot in order to govern. Parties may have done mischief to the ideal of political democracy in America, but Progressivism, in the name of reform, redefined it substantially, albeit subtly.

Progressivism and the Vocabulary of American Politics

Progressivism defines American democracy in the twentieth century. In its New Deal guise, it remade American constitutionalism and politics and along the way it changed the vocabulary of public discourse—not the words themselves, but their meanings. Political concepts like democracy, politics, and power are inherently fluid, not limitlessly so but importantly so. They are, to borrow William Connolly's useful term, "essentially contestable."[6] This is true on the vulgar plane of everyday politics where the definitional capture of a term like *reform*—or *progressive*—can be key to success. But it is also true on the intellectual plane of understanding and explanation. All of which is to say that words and their meanings are important for reasons both practical and analytical; they are the tools of intelligence. Progressivism crafted new tools for American politics, but not necessarily better tools.

In the Gettysburg Address, Abraham Lincoln defines political democracy as government *of* the people, *by* the people, and *for* the people. This prepositional trilogy is not mere rhetoric, nor is it redundant. It is, as Mortimer Adler and William Gorman note, "a compressed but accurate definition of the idea of democracy." It is an understanding of the term consonant with that of the Framers and of the Jacksonians.[7] Lincoln's trilogy recognizes three distinct dimensions of the term *democracy*. He understands that democratic government derives its authority and its continuing legitimacy from the people—that it is government *of* the people.[8] He understands too that democratic government, based on consent of the governed, requires the active participation of the people in their governance—that it is government *by* the people. And he understands that democratic government must serve the interests of justice, the public good—that it is government *for* the people.

Lincoln's simple trilogy defines a complex reality—the relation of the governed to their government and to the public good, and of the government to the governed and to the duties of citizenship. His formulation—democracy as free and representative government—is at home with the republicanism of the Founders. Progressivism, however, abandons Lincoln's formulation in favor of an understanding of democracy as direct citizen governance, modeled on their idea of the New England town meeting. In effect, it reduces Lincoln's trilogy to a single dimension: government *by* the people. Direct citizen participation in governance becomes the sole standard for political democracy. In this, Progressivism also remakes understandings of the public good and representation, of politics and political power.

Like the Framers, Lincoln understands the public good—justice as the goal of government—as an ideal, a measure above the clamor of ordinary politics beyond simple definition that encourages and guides deliberation in a representative system. Informed by the competition of interests, the democratic representative is to measure popular claims against this abstract standard and seek policies that are at once acceptable to the people and consistent with the ideal of justice. For Progressivism, however, the public good is defined by the people; it is less an abstract ideal and more a calculus of interests.[9] Public opinion becomes at once the expression of collective self-interest and the measure of justice. The voice of the people is to rule directly. Thus, rather than deliberation, the task of the democratic representative is to re-present—to mirror—the opinions of the people, to be a conduit linking the voters directly to their government.

The Progressive understanding of democracy changes other relationships. For Lincoln—and James Madison, for that matter—the public educates the representative as to its opinions on public matters and leaves the legislator to reflect upon and judge how to realize popular ends in ways consistent with ideals of justice and morality. For Progressivism, the representative is to educate the people, who in their wisdom direct him as to the preferred course of action. Not only does deliberation thus pass from the representative to the people, but the idea of a mandate, discussed by John White, changes from the Jacksonian standard of what the people oppose to the Progressive one of what the people have said. Where Madison sees breaking the effects of faction as essential to republican government, the Progressives see interest groups as organized expressions of popular sentiments, some good, others not.[10] There are "public" interests—for example, the National Civil Service Reform League—and there are "antipublic" interests—financial, industrial, and even political—which are the corrupting forces of private greed and power. Whatever else, this division of interests into good and bad confounds Madison's fear of factions.

Beyond the term *democracy*, Progressivism also embraces an idea of *politics* that departs from previous understandings. Classically, as Bernard Crick notes, politics is understood as the public activity by which free individuals through deliberation "conciliate competing interests in a given unit of rule by measuring them in proportion to their importance to the welfare and survival of the community."[11] In this view, politics is separated conceptually from the "political," from the claims made upon government and the interests behind them. In other words, politics is not democracy, ideology, or a program of reform like Progressivism and the New Deal. Progressivism, however, reduces politics to the political, from an activity for accommodating a plurality of claims to one for facilitating the realization of a single end. Progressives wanted to build the Good Society, and politics is to serve this objective. Where the American Founders took Aristotle for their teacher, the Progressives chose Plato.

In reducing politics to the political, Progressivism also equates politics with democracy because democracy is the political purpose politics is to serve. To say that democratic politics is the means to the end of democratic government is to say that democracy begets democracy. There is, then, no important difference between the Progressive idea of politics and the Progressive idea of democracy. This union of democracy with politics in no way enriches the one-dimensional democracy of Progressivism; it does, however, impoverish the idea and the activity of politics. Politics no longer mediates a plurality of interests; it serves one. It is no longer a creative enterprise, the invention of public order; it is the executor of democracy. This equation of democracy with politics is further confounded by Franklin Roosevelt's redefinition of rights, as described by Sidney Milkis, extending the idea of rights to include positive as well as negative claims upon the public. This move, as Milkis details, secures New Deal reforms against the debilitations of localism in American politics as represented in the Congress and the traditional party system, but it does so by narrowing further the ideas of democracy and politics.

In principle, rights are absolute claims upon both the government and its citizens, and while there may be practical limits at the extremes, the idea of rights is that they inhere in the nature of man and are not properly subject to the vicissitudes of politics and the whims of majorities. This is the genius of Roosevelt's capture of the term, for clothing the New Deal in the raiments of *rights* "liberates" his program from traditional politics. But this conception of rights protects New Deal programs at the expense of both democracy and politics. By transforming public questions from political issues into rights claims, the political legacy of FDR has been an increasingly strident politics in which voters questioning a range of rights-based policies from affirmative action to school busing have found their recourse to reason foreclosed by the absolutist character of rights-encased policies. This has enervated democracy by removing public questions from the easy reach of the citizenry, thus diminishing the role of reason in public decision and often dissolving discourse into a frenzy of claims and counterclaims with, as in the case of abortion, both sides asserting their interpretation of rights. The result, as E. J. Dionne explains, has been to freeze American politics into a combat between two relentless and unbending public philosophies, both of which are in important ways out of step with public opinion in the nation.[12]

The problems do not end here, for Roosevelt's conception of rights, defended as a simple extension of the traditional liberal idea, is in fact a sharp break with that tradition. In the older tradition, rights were understood as negative guarantees; rights such as speech, press, worship, and assembly are claims upon the government and its citizens that they not interfere with the free expression of individuals in those areas, that it is indeed the duty of government to protect minorities from majorities in the exercise of these inalienable rights. As negative guarantees, rights draw the line between the public and private spheres, between what government can and ought not to do—and they require of the citizenry only tolerance. They also define liberty, that realm of freedom citizens enjoy from their government and from other citizens.

Roosevelt's redefinition of rights changes all this. Rather than demands to be left alone, the positive conception of rights justifies claims upon the government for the provision of certain services to which citizens are entitled as a right. Of the general public this new notion of rights asks not just tolerance but also money to pay for the enlarged responsibilities of government.[13] As tolerance has weakened, owing to the diminished role of politics and deliberation in public decisions, the concern with money has provoked an antitax conservative, populist revolt that has remade American politics in the last quarter of the twentieth century. Moreover, this new idea of rights clouds understandings of liberty. It expands the realm of privacy and narrows that of the public, thus expanding liberty, but also enlarges the role of government as enforcer of rights and exposes more to its interventions, thus diminishing liberty. As a result, the line between the private and public spheres, which defines liberty, is made even more ambiguous. A restive public, concerned with its liberty, has been more and more receptive to political appeals to traditional values: freedom, privacy, less government, more family.[14]

The New Deal conception of rights also parallels a new understanding of *political power*, one consistent with the Progressive equation of democracy with politics. It understands power in personal and positive terms, as the ability of an individual to effect his will upon others. This reduces politics and democracy to power. Politics is understood as a process for determining who gets what, when, and how,[15] and in turn, democracy is measured by the distribution of power in society, by who can effect the outcomes of government. While consistent with FDR's idea of rights, this understanding of political power is at odds with that of the Framers. For them, political power, like rights, is an essentially negative concept; indeed the terms *power* and *rights* are commonly used interchangeably by them. They saw a political right as a check for individuals upon the public and its government, and a political power as a check of one division of government upon the others.

The idea of political power as a negative is central to the Founders' constitutionalism. They built it into the American system of government to protect and promote political liberty, whose security was their greatest goal. The idea of political power as a negative serves liberty because it evokes politics. Politics arises from constraints, from negatives, from a constitutional system of checks and balances, from a pluralistic political system awash in "veto groups," and from a political culture that sets value against value: majority rule versus minority rights, liberty versus equality, individualism versus community, and so on.[16] Moreover, by treating will power as political power, Progressivism and the New Deal personalize political power and thereby disconnect it from the institutions of government and politics and vest it wholly in the individual citizen. The individual, as Stuart Chase argues, becomes the measure of all things, a standard distant from that of the Framers.[17] In their reductionist disregard for distinctions between democracy, politics, and power, Progressivism and the New Deal alike were bent upon creating the Good Society, one in service to the national interest, organized politically by a direct link between the people and the national government, protected programmatically by a new concept of rights. This, they believed, would save American democracy from the corrupting clutches of a politics of local power and an economy of private greed. Their remedies may not have been worse than the disease they sought to cure, but they have, like much of modern medicine, given rise to new maladies. The report of the Committee on Political Parties, issued at midpassage from the liberalism of the Progressives to the conservatism of the Reagan ascendancy, may best be understood as at once a response to and a victim of these new maladies.

Democracy and Responsible Parties

Progressives in the tradition of Herbert Croly and Theodore Roosevelt wished to nationalize and democratize American government and politics. They wanted, as Milkis notes, an American state. They sought to defeat the localism that had dominated American politics and made a corrupt bed with powerful economic interests. Political parties were a prominent part of the system the Progressives sought to replace with a national scheme of government, and parties were of little importance in the Progressive reconstruction of American politics. The Progressives offered no institutional substitute for parties but pinned their hopes on the presidency and institutions of direct democracy like the primary. Indeed, the best friend of parties among the Progressives, Woodrow Wilson, conceived them as at best appendages of the presidency.

Franklin Roosevelt and the New Deal gave Progressivism its American state and vested it institutionally in a much-strengthened chief executive, embellished administratively by an array of experts in the White House and secured politically by a direct tie to the American people as their spokesman in national affairs. Seen at the time as a strong party leader, a model of presidential party government who transformed the Democrats from minority to majority party status, FDR is viewed by Milkis as having used his party to establish a national idea of the public good that would govern and thereby remove the need for party government.

The members of the Committee on Political Parties were for the most part children of Progressivism and in many instances were themselves New Dealers. Partisans of the new liberalism, as Everett Ladd observes, they were schooled in its understanding of American politics, frustrated that the idea of national reform was unfulfilled, and concerned that its completion and maintenance required more than a strong president, however enhanced the office and popular the incumbent.[18] The rise of the bipartisan conservative coalition in Congress to block Roosevelt's initiatives in the late 1930s had underscored the inability of the president alone to effect reform and pointed to the need for majorities in the Congress who shared his programmatic goals. Moreover, the committee had grown anxious that a greatly strengthened presidency, less restrained institutionally, could have grave consequences for the nation.

Like James Madison, they knew that great statesmen were unlikely always to be at the helm. Indeed, some of the most prescient passages in the committee report, especially in the aftermath of Vietnam and Watergate, are those that voice apprehension about a presidency grown too powerful and independent.

The committee locates the solution to these problems—how to advance national reform and also restrain a wanton presidency—in a reconstructed party system, national in focus, programmatic in content, and responsible in conduct. Where Progressivism and the New Deal had seen parties as agents of localism, the committee envisions a new kind of national party system, one of responsible parties, "agencies of the electorate," able to deal with the demands of modern government.[19] Unlike the old parties, these new parties would be organized around programs, not patronage, and would provide a permanent but still permeable *organized* institutional link between the public and its government. Structurally, this new party was to be at once representative and participatory—coherent in its national program, cohesive in its national elites, yet open and broadly activist at the grass roots. In this, the committee embraced the older and newer notions of democracy as one, evincing scant appreciation that they entail distinctive institutional forms and entail different styles of politics that are likely to collide if not carefully integrated.

In the forty years since the committee report, America's two major political parties have undergone significant change. In the 1960s and 1970s they pursued strikingly different paths to modernization, neither of them precisely what the committee recommends but both tests of many of the committee's proposals.[20] In its reforms, beginning in earnest after the 1968 convention, the Democratic Party adopted the Progressive idea of democracy, opening party processes for selecting delegates to their national convention to widespread participation at the grass roots through increased numbers of primaries and reformed caucuses, as well as affirmative action for underrepresented groups.[21] By contrast, with the presidential nomination of Barry Goldwater in 1964, the Republicans became increasingly dominated by a programmatically coherent, ideologically conservative elite who rebuilt the party nationally around its philosophy of government. Thus, where the Democrats sought to be responsible *to* all of the factions that compose their national party coalition, as enforced internally (by party members) in primaries and caucuses, the Republicans chose to be responsible *for* a philosophy and program of national government, as enforced externally (by the electorate) in general elections. The organizational strategies of the two parties thus represent, albeit crudely, the two ideas of democracy embodied in the committee report.

In its call for greater internal democracy, the committee argues that widespread participation at the grass roots in developing the party program will build consensus behind it and that this unity will in turn translate into broad public support for the party agenda and thus into victory at the polls. There is, however, little in the Democratic Party experience of the last two decades to support this view. Instead, the party's new openness has led to a kind of balkanization as numerous party factions—social, cultural, regional, categorical—have emerged to compete for standing and influence in the party. Moreover, many of the most prominent party factions have insisted upon their place in the party and its platform as a matter of right, understood in the New Deal sense of a positive claim. Framing claims as rights—whether to a clean environment, an education, or an abortion—has made party consensus less a matter of accommodation and conciliation than one of capitulation. Jesse Jackson's image of the party as a quilt may have been intended to portray its coalitional diversity, but it also pictures the party platform, which (1988 may be an exception) has been a patchwork of factional claims stitched together as if whole cloth.

Greater internal democracy has not produced greater unity among Democrats. Moderate and liberal wings of the party, factional fights aside, continue their decade-long struggle for preeminence in the party. Nor has internal democracy led the party to agreement on a clear and coherent program of government. Indeed, among the most common criticisms of the Democrats is that they lack a national vision.[22] Moreover, internal democracy has not led to expanded public support for the party. Not only has the reformed party lost four of five presidential elections since 1968, but it has lost its half-century lead in party identifiers among voters as well. Factors other than internal party democracy have undoubtedly shaped Democratic Party politics over the last five presidential elections, during which time the party has for the most part retained control of Congress, but the internal party dynamics released by reforms of the 1970s and early 1980s are not those anticipated by the Committee on Political Parties.

Unlike the Democrats, the Republican Party has not undergone internal procedural reform. Contests for the party's presidential nomination have been colored by the increased number of primaries that resulted from Democratic Party reform, but GOP rules governing the allocation and selection of delegates to their national convention, as well as those governing balloting at the convention, remain substantially unchanged. Yet the party has changed significantly. Since the Goldwater nomination, a conservative elite has come to power. Its public philosophy has given a unity to the Republicans, muting diversity within the party and enabling it to speak more clearly on national issues and to set government priorities. Control of the White House for twenty of the last twenty-four years has been key to the clarity of the party's voice, but the electoral success of the GOP in presidential races is clearly related to the party's philosophical consensus.

Over the past quarter century, the Republicans have concentrated on building a national party designed to serve the election needs of their candidates. Fueled by very successful direct-mail fund-raising, the GOP delivers not merely direct financial support but also a full array of campaign services to its candidates—training, polling, media, research, staffing, and more. In this, moreover, it has built an organizationally more unified and more professional national party, which has bridged operationally both the separation of powers and federalism, the national committee working more closely with House and Senate campaign committees on common strategies, as well as with state central committees. In this way, the Republicans have sought to maximize their resources and to target them as efficiently and effectively as possible in the hope of winning more offices but also in the belief that this will create a greater dependence of their candidates upon the party that will translate into their being more loyal to the party once in office.

The committee wanted national parties as well as democratic parties. It was the "ascendancy of national issues" and the need for a party system able to "set a general course of policy for the government as a whole" that led it to call for responsible party government.[23] There is much in the contemporary Republican party organization of which the committee would approve, but again the results have not been what it expected. The committee, for example, did not anticipate that divided government would become the norm rather than the exception in Washington, yet control of the national government has been split between the two parties for twenty-six of the forty-two years since the committee issued its report. Despite its resources, the GOP has been unable to win control of Congress. Though it has "owned" the presidency for most of the last twenty-five years, winning it several times by landslides of historic proportion, the Republican Party has made few inroads into Democratic majorities in the House of Representatives and has managed a majority in the Senate for only six years, from 1981 to 1986. The weakening of partisanship in the nation may be both cause and consequence of this.

Moreover, the committee seems clearly to assume that a national party will engage the problems of modern government and, in the fashion of Progressivism and the New Deal, seek public solutions to them. In short, it assumes that a national party will be liberal and activist. The Republicans are thus an anomaly: a conservative party opposed to big government using its national power to serve local and private interests as faithfully, if not as crudely, as the traditional party system so despised by Progressives like Croly and Robert LaFollette. Ironically, it is the Democrats in Congress, the bastion of localism to liberal reformers of this century, who seem now most concerned with national problems, at least those of a domestic nature, and who are most aggressive in seeking public responses to them.

The experiences of the two major parties suggest that the committee was correct to believe that strong national parties must be at once mass-based and elitist, that structurally they must incorporate both the participatory and representative dimensions of the democratic ideal. The question is *how*. For the most part, the committee seems to assume that wide participation at the base of the party combined with representative institutions at the top is sufficient, but the experience of the Democratic Party over the past two decades exposes problems with this answer. In truth, the answer to *how* is more complicated, for it requires an institutional design sensitive to the realities of power and politics as well as democracy. This can be seen more clearly by examining some of the committee's specific recommendations for institutional change within the parties.

Power, Politics, and Party Building

The Committee on Political Parties, wishing to redress the perceived imbalance of political forces within the federal system, offers a number of recommendations for change in America's parties, but two institutional reforms—a national party council and biennial national conventions—are seen as especially important in this redistribution of power. The council is to unify the party by bringing together national and state leaders, elected officials and leaders of constituency groups, and to have broad responsibilities for party affairs at the national level, especially as they involve interpretation and implementation of the party platform.[24] The biennial national convention is to augment the nominating convention, affording party members the opportunity to express and harmonize their views between presidential elections.[25]

The committee clearly expects the council and more frequent conventions to give national forces a more prominent role and a more audible voice in party affairs and thereby enhance their political power. In this it acts on the new understanding of political power as a gift of positive authority for the exercise of individual or institutional will, but it is one thing so to enhance the presidency in this way, for it is a constitutional office with significant veto powers over the other divisions of government. It is quite another to empower political parties in the same way, for they are without legal standing, constitutional or statutory, and have only electoral checks upon the institutions of national government, checks that were in decline at the time of the committee report and have declined further since. The committee can thus but hope that the reasonableness of party leaders, elected officials, and constituency groups will lead them to see the utility of these institutions and use them.[26]

In the forty years since the committee report, neither of America's major parties has adopted the idea of a party council, but the Democrats have created two national party agencies—the Democratic Advisory Council and the Compliance Review Commission—that had responsibilities akin to those suggested for the council. The Democrats, however, did adopt the idea of an off-year party conference as part of their 1970s reforms. If not perfect tests of the committee's proposals, these experiments offer insights into the problems that such institutions are likely to encounter in the American setting.

The Democratic Advisory Council, created in the late 1950s by Chairman Paul Butler, was intended to represent the national or presidential wing of the party. Having lost the presidency in 1952 and 1956, national Democrats, heirs to the New Deal and Fair Deal legacies, had no institutional forum from which their voices could be heard, no place to come together to shape the programmatic future of the party. The council filled that need. Featuring national figures like Adlai Stevenson and Eleanor Roosevelt, the council was designed as the party's national voice to speak on the range of public policy questions confronting the nation. Its statements drew national press attention as expressions of what the Democrats would do if restored to power and also found their way into the 1960 Democratic Party platform.

The incentives for the presidential wing of the party were clear. Lacking the White House as a platform from which to advance their program, they turned to the national party as the instrument of their advocacy, and they had figures who could command national attention. But the council was not welcomed by all Democrats in Washington. Both Speaker Sam Rayburn and Senate Majority Leader Lyndon Johnson declined invitations to join the council. As the party's highest-ranking elected officials in the national government, Rayburn and Johnson felt they were the spokesmen for the Democratic Party out of power, saw the council as a competitor, and saw no reason to join it as two voices among many. John Kennedy, the party's presidential nominee in 1960, was a latecomer to council membership, and upon his election as president, he abolished it. Kennedy too saw the council as a competitor with him as the voice of the party in national politics and apparently saw no other utility in it.

In the American system of separated powers, there is a void in national leadership of the party that does not occupy the White House. It is never entirely clear who speaks for it. The Democratic Advisory Council filled this void between the 1956 and 1960 elections. It was, however, a powerless institution with no capacity to unify the party's national leadership. There was no incentive for the party's congressional leaders to join the council, which for them meant joining a chorus instead of singing solos or duets. The national party council proposed by the committee is likewise a powerless institution with no independent base of authority and no effective checks or negatives upon any of its members.

Unlike the Democratic Advisory Council, the Democrats' Compliance Review Commission had nothing to do with developing a party platform. It was created in the early 1970s to enforce new national party rules governing delegate selection to the party's national convention. These rules, written and revised by a series of party commissions from the late 1960s and mid-1980s and approved quadrennially by the national committee, were an assertion of national party authority over state parties in the delegate selection process. Intended to encourage greater participation in party affairs, these rules set guidelines to open party procedures to grass-roots Democrats, require affirmative action for underrepresented groups, and generally reform internal operations in a way consonant with the Progressive idea of democracy. The Compliance Review Commission was empowered to interpret these guidelines, set standards, and judge whether state party plans for delegate selection conformed to national party rules. There were frequent conflicts between the commission and various state parties, some of which led to litigation in which the federal courts consistently upheld the national party's authority as an exercise of its constitutional right of association.

The Compliance Review Commission, as a creature of the national party, thus had a constitutionally protected power to veto state plans inconsistent with national party rules, which obliged state parties to deal politically with it in developing acceptable procedures. State laws and political practices had to be adapted to the national party rules on threat of state delegations not being seated at national conventions. A number of states felt aggrieved by this imposition of national party power, which led to a growing tension between the formal authority of the national party and the practical reality that the national party is heavily dependent upon its state parties for the conduct of national campaigns. Ultimately, this tension undercut the commission, and it was abolished as having become politically dysfunctional.

As institutions of the national party, the Democratic Advisory Council and Compliance Review Commission suggest the pitfalls of party building in national politics, derivative of the American Constitution and political culture. The council failed because it did not bridge the gaps created by the separation of powers in ways that were useful to the executive and legislative branches. The congressional leadership simply refused to associate with the council, and there were no penalties. In the end, the traditional independence of House, Senate, and White House prevailed over a mediating agency of the national party. The commission, on the other hand, fell victim to federalism, to the traditional independence of state parties and the diversity of state political practices and cultures. The commission's role provoked enough political objection from state parties that it became a political liability, and the national party, still insistent upon its rules, looked for a kinder and gentler method for their enforcement.

In the 1970s, the Democrats also experimented with a midterm national conference, similar in purpose to that proposed by the committee. The conference was to bring delegates together between national nominating conventions to conduct party business, review the party platform, and discuss questions of party and public policy. The first party conference in 1974, held with Republican Gerald Ford in the White House, adopted a charter for the national party and served too as a staging area for those considering a run for the party's presidential nomination two years later. The second party conference in 1978, held with Democrat Jimmy Carter in the Oval Office, became an arena of intraparty conflict as liberal and largely northern Democrats decried the moderate and lackluster leadership of their southern president. The conference gave Democrats unhappy with Carter's presidency a national forum from which to challenge his leadership and served as a launching pad for the 1980 challenge by Massachusetts Senator Edward Kennedy to Carter's renomination. In short, the conference became a second voice for the party in national affairs, much as John Kennedy seems to have feared the Democratic Advisory Council could become, and like the council, the midterm conference was soon dispatched to history.

These experiences suggest that party building in national politics will fail unless it entails institutional designs that create functional dependency upon the party among candidates, public officials, and voters alike. Institutionally, parties have to satisfy the needs and interests of candidates, officials, and voters as these individuals understand their needs and interests or can be persuaded to understand them. The party council proposed by the committee fails this test. The council is a microcosm of the party, an assemblage of government officials from the different branches and levels and of party officials and leaders from various levels and locations. It is intended as a representative body, a mirror of the party, but the committee never explains the incentives for anyone to participate in the council or the inducements it has to effect its decisions. In short, the committee offers an interesting idea but one not connected to the realities of political power. The Compliance Review Commission and the midterm conference failed less for lack of power than for its misplacement. Both had some value, at least short-term, but neither was consonant with the nature of American politics, nationally or otherwise.

The reconstruction of the national Republican Party, more than the experiments of the Democrats, affords a model of party building on the principle of functional dependency. By transforming itself into a candidate-service organization, the GOP has been able to assist its candidates in all aspects of modern campaigning. Its candidates have come to know they can depend upon the party for much of what they need in electioneering, and the party knows that it can use its resources to recruit candidates at all levels. This capacity, in a party unified by its public philosophy, has enabled the Republicans to bridge divisions both lateral and vertical in government with party officeholders defined by their beliefs and values backed by a party on which they can count for the delivery of critical election assistance, thus also affording them protection from the torments of narrow and passionate interests within and without the party.

Similarly, in describing the new spirit of party among Democrats in the House of Representatives, David Price ascribes it to the need members came to feel for more organized direction in a legislative process greatly decentralized by reforms of the 1970s. The party offices and agencies in the House filled this functional void, and members became increasingly dependent upon them as serving their needs and interests, not the least being that they formed a career ladder for advancement in the House. Likewise, in recommendations for campaign finance reform, William Thomas focuses on ways to strengthen parties by enlarging their role in the funding of campaigns to increase candidate dependence upon them as sources of money. In this way, he hopes, parties will become more effective institutions in American politics.

Underlying the idea of party building as the creation of functional dependency is an older understanding of political power as residing conceptually in institutions and not human will. Institutionally, power is defined by negatives, by the ability to block, check, veto, or otherwise obstruct action and thereby force consultation and deliberation. In this sense, power is not measured in the outcomes of decisions—not whether Jones prevails over Smith—but in who are the parties making the decisions. Positive grants of power to the people, as the Progressives intend, or to the parties, as the committee intends, are empty promises unless backed with an effective negative. Worse, they are prescriptions for cynicism, alienation, and a host of other modern societal diseases. To empower America's national parties requires an institutional design with enforceable negatives at critical junctures in the electoral and governmental processes that constrain and thereby oblige candidates and officials to deal with their party if they are to achieve the ends they desire. Such a design does not enable parties to *control* outcomes but builds real political relationships that necessitate taking parties seriously as independent institutions in the political process. In short, it gives parties leverage and thus makes them players in the game of politics, which is all that having *political* power can mean for anyone or any institution.

Toward National Political Parties

The Progressive dream of an American state national in its scope and power has for the most part been realized. Expanded domestically by the New Deal and Great Society and internationally by hot and cold wars, the national government's role has expanded dramatically in the twentieth century. The same, however, cannot be said of the nation's politics. More national today than in the past, the change is due in large part to a more national news media, especially television, and to the greatly increased number of political associations housed in Washington and concerned primarily with the activities of the national government. Responsibility for electoral politics remains with the states, and even campaigns for Congress and the presidency remain state-centered. Progressivism did not try to change this; it sought instead to circumvent it, and it succeeded impressively for a time. But its strategy, perhaps unwittingly has also succeeded in strengthening the centrifugal forces in American politics. Indeed, all of the direct democracy reforms of the Progressives—the initiative, referendum, and recall, as well as the primary—have been enacted into law by state governments, thus extending their dominion over the nation's electoral politics.

Moreover, Progressivism's understanding of democracy as participation requiring citizen politics linked directly to government has atomized the public. It has led to a politics corrosive to broad-based mediating institutions like political parties, replacing them with candidate-centered campaigns—self-promoting, increasingly negative, disconnected from governance—and with narrow special interest organizations, each promoting its cause, claiming its rights, and damning government for its failures.[27] "The process of politics today," according to a 1991 report of the Kettering Foundation, "is such that citizens no longer feel just discouraged, they believe that they are actually denied access to politics."[28] Rather than empowerment, the Kettering study describes a politics of citizen impotence. It is a milieu ripe for the antigovernment populism so widespread in America today and ironically the legacy, albeit unintended, of the Progressive disdain for politics.

The Committee on Political Parties, sympathetic in so many ways with the liberal democratic spirit of Progressivism and the New Deal, sought to nationalize politics in America through a kind of party system that would protect and advance the programs of "modern" government. The Kettering Foundation in its report of a year ago calls for a national discussion of the condition of American politics. Its second agenda item is "Find ways for citizens to form a public voice on policy issues—as an alternative to the clamor of special interests—and for public officials to hear that public voice."[29] This is precisely the objective of the Committee on Political Parties, and forty years ago it gave what remains the best answer: Renew America's political parties as genuinely national institutions linking voters to their government.

The committee, however, for all its appreciation of the need for truly national parties, seeks no changes in the existing electoral system. It makes clear that it has no wish that "the party system should be cut free from its federal basis" and dismisses any thought of constitutional amendment as "not a practical way of getting more effective parties."[30] It notes Woodrow Wilson's call for a national presidential primary and the "persistent agitation for change in the Electoral College system" but endorses neither.[31] It is an approach to party building rather like calling for a stronger presidency while denying the need to change power relations between the branches and levels of government.

The last quarter century has seen changes in America's two major parties that in different ways have resulted in stronger national party organizations. The increased strength of the national parties, however, has occurred in something of a political vacuum, for America's electoral system remains firmly rooted in state soil. Other than the Hatch Acts, restricting the political activities of federal employees, and the Federal Election Campaign Acts, regulating sources and uses of money in federal elections, there is no important national election law, and neither of these bodies of law is particularly encouraging to national parties. Insofar as the United States has a "national" electoral system, it is still a collection of the myriad state laws in all their dazzling variety, complemented by a similarly varied collection of state and national party rules.

Truly national parties require a national election system. The Progressive dream of a stable national government cannot be realized through a system of regressive politics. The committee points to two reforms in the structure of American politics that rightly designed would move the United States toward a more national politics and do so in a way that satisfies the committee's criteria of a more democratic, responsible, and effective system.

1. Adopt a national primary for presidential nominations, *and* change the timing of national party conventions from after to before the primary.[32] These preprimary conventions should be empowered, as they are in a number of American states, to reduce the field of candidates for the nomination by requiring them to obtain a minimum vote from delegates at the convention to qualify for the party's primary ballot.[33] This gives the party a significant negative at a critical juncture in the nominating process and will change the way candidates pursue the nomination, giving more importance to direct contact with party members and voters in all of the states and reducing the importance of money, media, and special interests in the nominating process. The national primary, coming after the conventions, will replace the present piecemeal process of state primaries that has been dominated in the past two decades by two small and hardly representative states. It will oblige candidates for the party nomination to appeal to party voters across the nation, focus them on national issues, simplify choices for the voters, and enable voters in all the states to cast ballots on the same day for the same field of candidates.

2. Abolish the Electoral College. Politically, the Electoral College turns the contest for the presidency, both nomination and election, into a series of state elections. This distorts national issues by forcing them through the prisms of state politics and increases the importance of small blocs of voters important in a particular state at the expense of large blocs of voters important to governing the nation. The presidency is the only office in American politics that is not filled by direct vote of the people, and the indirectness of that vote makes the office politically less national. In the interests of a more national and a more democratic politics, the president of the United States should be chosen by direct popular vote.

Neither of these reforms will suffice to produce a national politics in America, and indeed establishing a national primary without changing the timing and function of party conventions is likely to exacerbate the problems of money, media, and special interests in presidential nominations. But together they are a foundation upon which a national politics and a national party system can be built. The twentieth century has seen the construction of a national government in the United States. The challenge of the twenty-first century is to build a national politics to go with it.

Notes

1. E. E. Schattschneider, *Party Government* (New York: Farrar and Rinehart, 1942), p. 1.

2. David S. Broder, *The Party's Over* (New York: Harper and Row, 1971); Larry J. Sabato, *The Party's Just Begun* (Glenview, Ill.: Scott, Foresman, 1988).

3. Walter Dean Burnham, *Critical Elections and the Mainsprings of American Politics* (New York: Norton, 1970); David E. Price, *Bringing Back the Parties* (Washington: Congressional Quarterly, 1984).

4. Xandra Kayden and Eddie Mahe, Jr., *The Party Goes On* (New York: Basic Books, 1985).

5. Austin Ranney, *The Doctrine of Responsible Party Government* (Urbana: University of Illinois Press, 1962).

6. William E. Connolly, *The Terms of Political Discourse* (Lexington, Mass.: Heath, 1974).

7. Mortimer J. Adler and William Gorman, "Reflections on the Gettysburg Address," *The New Yorker*, 8 September 1975, pp. 42ff.

8. Adler and Gorman note Lincoln's use of the genitive, suggesting that, the "love of God" means both God's love of man and man's love of God, so too Lincoln's phrase "government of the people" means that the people are governed but by a government that is their's. Ibid.

9. Note that the Utilitarians and their calculus of felicity has often been treated by twentieth-century scholars as the "classical doctrine of democracy." See, for example, Joseph Schumpeter, *Capitalism, Socialism and Democracy* (New York: Harper and Row, 1942), Ch. 21.

10. See, for example, Arthur F. Bentley, *The Process of Government* (Chicago: University of Chicago Press, 1908). See Robert A. Dahl's interpretation of Madisonian democracy, *A Preface to Democracy* (Chicago: University of Chicago Press, 1956).

11. Bernard Crick, *In Defence of Politics* (Chicago: University of Chicago Press, 1962), Ch. 1.

12. E. J. Dionne, Jr., *Why Americans Hate Politics* (New York: Simon and Schuster, 1991).

13. Kevin Phillips distinguishes between the New Deal and Great Society, noting that the first taxes the few for the benefit of the many while the latter taxed the many on behalf of the few. Phillips, *The Emerging Republican Majority* (New Rochelle, N.Y.: Arlington House, 1969), p. 37.

14. John Kenneth White, *The New Politics of Old Values* (Hanover, N.H.: University Press of New England, 1988).

15. Harold Lasswell, *Politics: Who Gets What, When, How* (New York: McGraw-Hill, 1936).

16. On "veto groups," see David Riesman, *The Lonely Crowd* (Garden City, N.Y.: Doubleday, 1955). See Henry Steele Commager, *Majority Rule and Minority Rights* (New York: Oxford University Press, 1943).

17. Stuart Chase, *The Proper Study of Mankind* (New York: Harper and Row, 1948).

18. Paul T. David, "The APSA Committee on Political Parties: Some Reconsiderations of Its Work and Significance" (paper prepared for the annual meeting of the American Political Science Association, Chicago, Illinois, 1–4 September 1983).

19. Committee on Political Parties, *Toward a More Responsible Two-Party System*, (New York: Rinehart, 1950), p. 16 (hereinafter, CPP).

20. See Thomas Byrne Edsall, *The New Politics of Inequality* (New York: Norton, 1984), Chs. 1, 2.

21. William Crotty, *Party Reform* (New York: Longmans, 1983).

22. See forum on the Democratic Party, *Harper's Magazine*, January 1990.

23. CPP, p. 17.

24. Ibid., pp. 39ff.

25. Ibid., p. 38.

26. Ibid., pp. 85ff.

27. See Alan Ehrenhalt, *The United States of Ambition* (New York: Random House, 1991).

28. Kettering Foundation, "Citizens and Politics" (a report prepared by the Harwood Group, June 1991), p. 11.

29. Ibid., p. 8.

30. CPP, pp. 26, 35.

31. Ibid., pp. 37, 74.

32. See Thomas Cronin and Robert Loevy, "The Case for a National Preprimary Convention," *Public Opinion* (December–January 1983): 50–53; Martin P. Wattenberg, "When You Can't Beat Them, Join Them: Shaping the Presidential Nominating Process to the Television Age," *Polity* (Summer 1989): 587–97; and Jerome M. Mileur and John Kenneth White, "Where Angels Fear to Tread: Toward a Larger National Role in a Federal System of Presidential Nomination" (paper prepared for the annual meeting of the Midwest Political Science Association, Chicago, Illinois, 13–15 April 1989).

33. The percentage of delegates required should be large enough to enable the party to eliminate fringe and single-issue candidates, but small enough to enable significant minority blocs within the party to challenge the majority. The state of Connecticut uses 20 percent, a figure that seems to have worked well for them for over 30 years.

Appendix

Index

Appendix

Summary of Conclusions and Proposals

The Committee on Political Parties

Part I. The Need for Greater Party Responsibility

1. The Role of the Political Parties

1. *The Parties and Public Policy.* Popular government in a nation of more than 150 million people requires political parties which provide the electorate with a proper range of choice between alternatives of action. In order to keep the parties apart, one must consider the relations between each and public policy. The reasons for the growing emphasis on public policy in party politics are to be found, above all, in the very operations of modern government.

2. *The New Importance of Program.* The crux of public affairs lies in the necessity for more effective formulation of general policies and programs and for better integration of all of the far-flung activities of modern government. It is in terms of party programs that political leaders can attempt to consolidate public attitudes toward the work plans of government.

3. *The Potentialities of the Party System.* The potentialities of the two-party system are suggested, on the one hand, by the fact that for all practical purposes the major parties monopolize elections; and, on the other, by the fact that both parties have in the past managed to adapt themselves to the demands made upon them by external necessities. It is good practical politics to reconsider party organization in the light of the changing conditions of politics. Happily such an effort entails an application of ideas about the party system that are no longer unfamiliar.

22. What Kind of Party System Is Needed?

The party system that is needed must be democratic, responsible and effective.

Committee on Political Parties, "Toward a More Responsible Two-Party System," *American Political Science Review*, 44 (September 1950), pp. 1–14. Reprinted by permission of the American Political Science Association.

I. A Stronger Two-Party System

1. *The Need for an Effective Party System.* An effective party system requires, first, that the parties are able to bring forth programs to which they commit themselves and, second, that the parties possess sufficient internal cohesion to carry out these programs. Such a degree of unity within the parties cannot be brought about without party procedures that give a large body of people an opportunity to share in the development of the party program.

2. *The Need for an Effective Opposition Party.* The fundamental requirement of accountability is a two-party system in which the opposition party acts as the critic of the party in power, developing, defining and presenting the policy alternatives which are necessary for a true choice in reaching public decisions. The opposition most conducive to responsible government is an organized party opposition.

II. Better Integrated Parties

1. *The Need for a Party System with Greater Resistance to Pressure.* There is little to suggest that the phenomenal growth of interest organizations in recent decades has come to its end. The whole development makes necessary a reinforced party system that can cope with the multiplied organized pressures. Compromise among interests is compatible with the aims of a free society only when the terms of reference reflect an openly acknowledged concept of the public interest.

2. *The Need for a Party System with Sufficient Party Loyalty.* Needed clarification of party policy will not cause the parties to differ more fundamentally or more sharply than they have in the past. Nor is it to be assumed that increasing concern with their programs will cause the parties to erect between themselves an ideological wall. Parties have the right and the duty to announce the terms to govern participation in the common enterprise. The emphasis in all consideration of party discipline must be on positive measures to create a strong and general agreement on policies. A basis for party cohesion in Congress will be established as soon as the parties interest themselves sufficiently in their congressional candidates to set up strong and active campaign organizations in the constituencies.

III. More Responsible Parties

1. *The Need for Parties Responsible to the Public.* Party responsibility means the responsibility of both parties to the general public, as

enforced in elections. Party responsibility to the public, enforced in elections, implies that there be more than one party, for the public can hold a party responsible only if it has a choice. As a means of achieving responsibility, the clarification of party policy also tends to keep public debate on a more realistic level, restraining the inclination of party spokesmen to make unsubstantiated statements and charges.

2. *The Need for Parties Responsible to Their Members.* Party responsibility includes also the responsibility of party leaders to the party membership, as enforced in primaries, caucuses and conventions. The external and the internal kinds of party responsibility need not conflict. Intraparty conflict will be minimized if it is generally recognized that national, state and local party leaders have a common responsibility to the party membership. National party leaders have a legitimate interest in the nomination of congressional candidates.

3. The Inadequacy of the Existing Party System

I. Beginning Transition

1. *Change and Self-Examination.* Marked changes in the structure and processes of American society have necessarily affected the party system. The prevailing climate of self-examination as well as the current tendencies toward change in the party system give point to inquiries like that represented by our report.

2. *Burden of the Past.* Formal party organization in its main features is still substantially what it was before the Civil War. Under these circumstances the main trends of American politics have tended to out-flank the party system.

II. Some Basic Problems

1. *The Federal Basis.* The two parties are organized on a federal basis. The national and state party organizations are largely independent of one another, without appreciable common approach to problems of party policy and strategy. The real issue is not over the federal form of organization but over the right balance of forces within this type of organization. A corollary of the kind of federalism now expressed in the party system is an excessive measure of internal separatism.

2. *The Location of Leadership.* Party organization does not vest leadership of the party as a whole in either a single person or a committee.

There is at present no central figure or organ which could claim authority to take up party problems, policies, and strategy.

3. *The Ambiguity of Membership.* No understandings or rules or criteria exist with respect to membership in a party. Those who suggest that elections should deal with personalities but not with programs suggest at the same time that party membership should mean nothing at all.

III. Specific Deficiencies

1. *National Party Organs.* The National Convention, as at present constituted and operated, is an unwieldy, unrepresentative and less than responsible body. The National Committee is seldom a generally influential body and much less a working body. House and Senate campaign committees do not always have a good working relationship with the National Committee. Although interest in questions of party policy has grown, the national party organs are not so constituted nor so coordinated as to make it simple for them to pay enough attention to these questions.

2. *Party Platforms.* Alternatives between the parties are defined so badly that it is often difficult to determine what the election has decided even in broadest terms. The prevailing procedure for the writing and adoption of national party platforms is too hurried and too remote from the process by which actual decisions are made to command the respect of the whole party and the electorate. The platform should be the end product of a long search for a working agreement within the party.

3. *Intraparty Democracy.* Too little consideration has been given to ways and means of bringing about a constructive relationship between the party and its members. In making the most of popular participation, the performance of American parties is very unsatisfactory.

4. *Party Research.* A party stands as much in need of research as does business enterprise or the government itself.

4. New Demands upon Party Leadership

I. The Nature of Modern Public Policy

1. *Broad Range of Policy.* The expanding responsibilities of modern government have brought about so extensive an interlacing of governmental action with the country's economic and social life that the need

for coordinated and coherent programs, legislative as well as administrative, has become paramount. In a democracy no general program can be adopted and carried out without wide public support.

2. *Impact on the Public.* In a predominantly industrial society, public policy tends to be widely inclusive, involving in its objectives and effects very large segments of the public or even the whole country.

3. *Governmental Program Machinery.* On the side of government, in the administrative and the legislative spheres, the twin needs for program formulation and for program machinery have long been recognized. The governmental advance toward program formulation needs now to be paralleled in the political sphere proper—above all, in the party system.

II. Rise of Nation-wide Policy Issues

1. *An Historic Trend.* The changes in the nature and scope of public policy are the result of changes in the social structure and in the economy of the United States.

2. *Past and Present Factors.* There has been in recent decades a continuing decline of sectionalism. Party organization designed to deal with the increasing volume of national issues must give wide range to the national party leadership.

3. *New Interest Groups in Politics.* The economic and social factors that have reduced the weight of sectionalism have also resulted in the development of a new type of interest groups, built upon large membership. To a much greater extent than in the past, they operate as if they were auxiliary organizations of one or the other party.

5. The Question of Constitutional Amendment

1. *A Cabinet System?* A responsible cabinet system makes the leaders of the majority collectively accountable for the conduct of the government.

2. *Strong Parties as a Condition.* To amend the Constitution in order to create a responsible cabinet system is not a practicable way of getting more effective parties.

3. *Adaptation within the Constitution.* The parties can do much to adapt the usages under the Constitution to their purposes.

Part II. Proposals for Party Responsibility

6. National Party Organization

I. Principal Party Bodies

1. *The National Convention.* We assume its continuation as the principal representative and deliberative organ of the party. The convention should meet at least biennially, with easy provision for special meetings. It should also cease to be a delegate convention of unwieldy size.

2. *The National Committee.* It is highly desirable for the National Convention to reassert its authority over the National Committee through a more active participation in the final selection of the committee membership. It is also desirable that the members of the National Committee reflect the actual strength of the party within the areas they represent.

3. *The Party Council.* We propose a Party Council of fifty members. Such a Party Council should consider and settle the larger problems of party management, within limits prescribed by the National Convention; propose a preliminary draft of the party platform to the National Convention; interpret the platform in relation to current problems; choose for the National Convention the group of party leaders outside the party organizations; consider and make recommendations to appropriate party organs in respect to congressional candidates; and make recommendations to the National Convention, the National Committee or other appropriate party organs with respect to conspicuous departures from general party decisions by state or local party organizations. In presidential years, the council would naturally become a place for the discussion of presidential candidacies, and might well perform the useful function of screening these candidacies in a preliminary way. Within this Party Council there might well be a smaller group of party advisers to serve as a party cabinet.

II. Intraparty Relationships

1. *State and Local Party Organizations.* Organizational patterns of the parties are predicated on the assumption that a party committee is necessary for each electoral area. There is a growing dissatisfaction with the results of this system on the local level, especially the multiplicity of organizations. An increasing number of state legislators are noting the breakdown or lack of party responsibility and discipline and the growth of internal separatism in state government. It is necessary for both

parties to reexamine their purposes and functions in the light of the present-day environment, state and local, in which they operate.

2. *Relations between National, State and Local Organizations.* Establishment of a Party Council would do much to coordinate the different party organizations, and should be pressed with that objective in mind. Regional conferences held by both parties have clearly been fruitful. Regional party organizations should be encouraged. Local party organizations should be imbued with a stronger sense of loyalty to the entire party organization and feel their responsibility for promoting the broader policies of the party. This can be done by fostering local party meetings, regularly and frequently held, perhaps monthly. The national organization may deal with conspicuous or continued disloyalty on the part of any state organization. Consideration should be given to the development of additional means of dealing with rebellious and disloyal state organizations.

3. *Headquarters and Staff.* Both parties are now aware of the need to maintain permanent headquarters, with staff equipped for research and publicity. A beginning has been made, but much still remains to be done. Staff development at party headquarters provides the essential mechanism to enable each party to concern itself appropriately with its continuing responsibilities.

7. Party Platforms

I. Nature of the Platform

1. *Alternative Purposes.* Should the party platform be a statement of general principles representing the permanent or long-range philosophy of the party? Or should it state the party's position on immediate issues? Actually, the platform is usually made up of both the more permanent and the more fleeting elements.

2. *Interpretation of the Platform.* As a body representing the various parts of the party structure, the Party Council should be able to give authoritative and reasonably acceptable interpretations of the platform.

3. *National-state Platform Conflicts.* What is needed is better coordination in the declaration of party principles. The Party Council would be the appropriate party agency to interpret the respective platforms and determine the right position in case of conflict. There is very little likelihood indeed for the Party Council to be inconsiderate of arguable claims of state autonomy.

4. *Binding Character.* In spite of clear implications and express pledges,

there has been much difference of opinion as to the exact binding quality of a platform. All of this suggests the need for appropriate machinery, such as a Party Council, to interpret and apply the national program in respect to doubts or details. When that is done by way of authoritative and continuing statement, the party program should be considered generally binding.

II. Problems of Platform-making

1. *Method of Formulating Party Platforms.* Occasionally the state platforms are deliberately delayed until after the national platform has been adopted, in order to have a basis for conformity. Such practice is to be encouraged, and state legislation that prevents it ought to be changed. A method of platform-making that is closely related to the congressional as well as to the presidential campaign must be developed, and with more direct participation by the party members of Congress.

2. *Improvement of Platforms and Platform-making.* In both parties, the Platform Committee or a working part of it is now appointed some weeks in advance of the National Convention. The practice of holding public hearings on the policies to be incorporated into the platform has been fairly well established. This consultation is of importance, for it makes the parties aware of the interest in particular policies.

3. *Proposals.* Party platforms should be formulated at least every two years. National platforms should emphasize general party principles and national issues. State and local platforms should be expected to conform to the national platform on matters of general party principle or on national policies. To achieve better machinery for platform-making, the Party Council, when set up, should prepare a tentative draft well in advance of the National Convention for the consideration of the appropriate convention committee and the convention itself. Local party meetings should be held for the discussion and consideration of platform proposals.

8. Party Organization in Congress

I. Introduction

1. *External Factors.* A higher degree of party responsibility in Congress cannot be provided merely by actions taken within Congress. Nevertheless, action within Congress can be of decisive significance.

2. *Continuous Evolution.* The materials for responsible party operations in Congress are already on hand. The key to progress lies in making a full-scale effort to use them.

II. Tightening Up the Congressional Party Organization

1. *The Leaders.* For more than ten years now the press has carried news about regular meetings between the President and the Big Four of Congress—the Speaker of the House, the Majority Leader of the House, the Vice President and the Majority Leader of the Senate, when the four are of the President's party. It would be an error to attempt to supplant the relationship between the Big Four and the President by some new body. Whenever it becomes necessary for the President to meet with the leaders of both parties in Congress, it is a simple matter for the Big Four to be expanded to six or eight. In the public eye a party leader like these is a spokesman for his party as a whole. It is necessary that there be broad consultation throughout the national leadership of a party before a party leader is elected in either house.

2. *The Leadership Committees.* We submit these proposals: In both the Senate and the House, the various leadership groups should be consolidated into one truly effective and responsible leadership committee for each party. Each of these four committees should be responsible not only for submitting policy proposals to the party membership, but also for discharging certain functions with respect to the committee structure and the legislative schedule. Each of the four committees should be selected or come up for a vote of confidence no less often than every two years. Occasion must be found reasonably often for the leadership committees of each party in the two houses to meet together. Furthermore, the rival leadership committees in each house should meet together on a more regular basis. A case can also be made for the four leadership groups to meet on specific occasions.

3. *Caucuses or Conferences.* More frequent meetings of the party membership in each house should be held. A binding caucus decision on legislative policy should be used primarily to carry out the party's principles and program. When members of Congress disregard a caucus decision taken in furtherance of national party policy, they should expect disapproval. The party leadership committees should be responsible for calling more frequent caucuses or conferences and developing the agenda of points for discussion.

III. Party Responsibility for Committee Structure

1. *Selection of Committee Chairmen.* It is not playing the game fairly for party members who oppose the commitments in their party's platform to rely on seniority to carry them into committee chairmanships. Party

leaders have compelling reason to prevent such a member from becoming chairman—and they are entirely free so to exert their influence. The task of party leaders, when confronted with revolt on the part of committee chairmen, is not easy. Obviously problems of this sort must be handled in the electoral process itself as well as in the congressional arena.

2. *Assignment of Members to Committees.* The slates of committee assignments should be drawn up by the party leadership committees and presented to the appropriate party caucuses for approval or modification. There is nothing sound in having the party ratio on the committees always correspond closely to the party ratio in the House itself. Committee assignments should be subjected to regular reexamination by the party caucus or conference with reasonable frequency.

3. *Committee Staff.* Staff assistance should be available to minority as well as majority members of a committee whenever they want it. Where all committee staff is controlled by the majority, a change in power threatens continuity of service.

IV. Party Responsibility for the Legislative Schedule

1. *The Need for Scheduling.* Schedules should be openly explained on the floor in advance. No committee should be in charge of legislative scheduling except the party leadership committee.

2. *House Guidance of Legislative Traffic.* A democratic approach would be to substitute open party control for control by the Rules Committee or individual chairmen.

3. *The Right to Vote in the Senate.* The present cloture rule should be amended. The best rule is one that provides for majority cloture on all matters before the Senate.

9. Political Participation

Widespread political participation fosters responsibility as well as democratic control in the conduct of party affairs and the pursuit of party policies. A more responsible party system is intimately linked with the general level as well as the forms of political participation.

I. Intraparty Democracy

1. *Party Membership.* As stress is placed by the parties upon policy and the interrelationship of problems at various levels of government, asso-

ciation with a party should become more interesting and attractive to many who hold aloof today.

2. *Machinery of Intraparty Democracy.* If the National Convention is to serve as the grand assembly of the party, in which diverse viewpoints are compounded into a course of action, it must be nourished from below. To this end local party groups are needed that meet frequently to discuss and initiate policy.

3. *Toward a New Concept of Party Membership.* The existence of a national program, drafted at frequent intervals by a party convention both broadly representative and enjoying prestige, should make a great difference. It would prompt those who identify themselves as Republicans or Democrats to think in terms of support of that program, rather than in terms of personalities, patronage and local matters. Once machinery is established which gives the party member and his representative a share in framing the party's objectives, once there are safeguards against internal dictation by a few in positions of influence, members and representatives will feel readier to assume an obligation to support the program. Membership defined in these terms does not ask for mindless discipline enforced from above. It generates self-discipline which stems from free identification with aims one helps to define.

II. Nominating Procedures

1. *United States Senator and Representative.* Nominations for United States Senator and Representative are governed largely by state laws that vary radically in their provisions. National regulation would overcome the disadvantages of so much variety. But one must face the practical objections to national regulation. The direct primary probably can be adapted to the needs of parties unified in terms of national policy. The closed primary deserves preference because it is more readily compatible with the development of a responsible party system. The open primary tends to destroy the concept of membership as the basis of party organization. Cross filing is bound to obscure program differences between the parties, and to eliminate any sense of real membership on the part of the rank and file. The Washington blanket primary corrupts the meaning of party even further by permitting voters at the same primary to roam at will among the parties. The formal or informal proposal of candidates by preprimary meetings of responsible party committees or party councils is a healthy development. Quite appropriately the Party Council might become a testing ground for candidates for United States Senator or Representative.

2. *Presidential Nomination.* In the National Convention, delegates representative of the party membership should be chosen by direct vote of the rank and file. The Party Council naturally would concern itself with platform plans and the relative claims of those who might be considered for presidential and vice presidential nominations. In time it may be feasible and desirable to substitute a direct, national presidential primary for the indirect procedure of the convention.

III. Elections

1. *Election of the President.* The present method of electing the President and Vice President fosters the blight of one-party monopoly and results in concentration of campaign artillery in pivotal industrial states where minority groups hold the balance of power. In the persistent agitation for change in the Electoral College system, stress should be placed both upon giving all sections of the country a real voice in electing the President and the Vice President and upon developing a two-party system in present one-party areas.

2. *Term of Representative.* It appears desirable to lengthen the term of Representatives to four years.

3. *Campaign Funds.* Existing statutory limitations work toward a scattering of responsibility for the collecting of funds among a large number of independent party and nonparty committees. Repeal of these restrictions would make it possible for a national body to assume more responsibility in the field of party finance. The situation might be improved in still another way by giving a specified measure of government assistance to the parties. Everything that makes the party system more meaningful to all voters leads incidentally to a broadening of the base of financial support of the parties.

4. *Apportionment and Redistricting.* It is time to insist upon congressional districts approximately equal in population.

IV. Barriers to Voting

1. *Registration.* The system of permanent registration should be extended. Properly qualified newcomers to an area should be permitted to register and vote without undue delay.

2. *Access to the Polls.* Legislation establishing National Election Day would in all probability bring to the polls large numbers of people who would otherwise never come. Holding elections on Saturdays or Sundays

would probably also help to increase the size of the vote. Adequate voting time should be provided by opening the booths in the earlier morning hours and keeping them open into the late evening hours. There is room for much elaboration in laws governing absentee balloting.

3. *Undemocratic Limitations.* Intentionally limiting devices should be overcome by a combination of legal change and educational efforts. Action is indicated to extend the suffrage to the inhabitants of the District of Columbia.

4. *The Short Ballot.* Adoption of the short ballot would concentrate choice on contests with program implications and thus shift attention toward issues rather than personalities.

10. Research on Political Parties

I. Basic Facts and Figures

1. *Election Statistics.* We propose the publication of an election yearbook by the Bureau of the Census. The arrangement of the yearbook should probably be by states. In addition, a summary booklet for presidential and congressional elections should be issued.

2. *Party Activities.* Compilation and regular publication of information on party activities are no less urgently needed.

3. *Compilation of Party Regulations.* A third task is the collection of all major regulations relating to national parties and elections.

II. More Research by the Parties

1. *Party Research Staffs.* What is needed is a stronger full-time research organization adequately financed and working on a year-in, year-out basis.

2. *Areas of Work.* There are two fields of research that should always be of immediate interest to the national organization of every party. The first is the analysis of voting trends and voting behavior. A second research field is analysis of proposals dealing with changes in election methods.

III. More Studies of the Parties

1. *Types of Research Needed.* In a field in which much still remains to be done, specific priorities have little meaning. The basic need is for a combination of creative hypotheses and realistic investigations.

2. *Professors and Politics.* The character of political research cannot be dissociated from the general approach of academic institutions to politics as a whole. Increased faculty participation in political affairs would mean more practical, realistic and useful teaching as well as research in the field of political parties.

3. *Role of Research Foundations.* The private foundations should actively solicit new ideas and proposals for research on political parties.

4. *Role of American Political Science Association.* The presentation of this report is but one instance of the interest shown in the subject of political parties by the American Political Science Association. In making specific suggestions for the kinds of research projects that today appear most promising in this field, the Association could exert a further welcome influence.

Part III. The Prospect for Action

11. Sources of Support and Leadership

Readjustments in the structure and operation of the political parties call for a widespread appreciation, by influential parts of the public as well as by political leaders and party officials, of the kinds of change that are needed in order to bring about a more responsible operation of the two-party system.

1. *The Economic Pressure Groups.* Highly organized special interests with small or no direct voting power are best satisfied if the individual legislator and administrative official are kept defenseless in the face of their special pressure. Organizations with large membership are not in the same category. It is reasonable to expect that those large-membership organizations with wise leadership will generally support the turn toward more responsible parties.

2. *The Party Leaders.* Leaders who represent divergent sectional or other special interests within each party will look with disfavor upon any reforms that hit specifically at their personal vested interests. Most of the forward-looking leaders in each party are convinced that changes should be made.

3. *The Government Officialdom.* Greater program responsibility at the level of the political parties is likely to appeal to administrators and the career officialdom.

4. *Congress.* It cannot be expected that all congressional leaders will be sympathetic to the concept of party responsibility. As leaders of national opinion, influential members of each party in Congress can give strong support to the idea of party responsibility.

5. *The President.* The President can probably be more influential than any other single individual in attaining a better organized majority party, and thus also prompting the minority party to follow suit. With greater party responsibility, the President's position as party leader would correspond in strength to the greater strength of his party.

6. *The Electorate.* The electorate consists of three main groups: (1) those who seldom or never vote; (2) those who vote regularly for the party of their traditional affiliation; and (3) those who base their electoral choice upon the political performance of the two parties, as indicated by the programs they support and the candidates they succeed in putting forward. The rank and file in each party want their party so organized that the views of the party majority will be respected and carried out. It may well be the members of the third group who, in making their choices at election time, will decide the question of our country's progress in the direction of a more responsible party system. It is this group that occupies a place of critical importance in supporting a party system able to shoulder national responsibility.

12. The Dangers of Inaction

Four dangers warrant special emphasis. The first danger is that the inadequacy of the party system in sustaining well-considered programs and providing broad public support for them may lead to grave consequences in an explosive era. The second danger is that the American people may go too far for the safety of constitutional government in compensating for this inadequacy by shifting excessive responsibility to the President. The third danger is that with growing public cynicism and continuing proof of the ineffectiveness of the party system the nation may eventually witness the disintegration of the two major parties. The fourth danger is that the incapacity of the two parties for consistent action based on meaningful programs may rally support for extremist parties poles apart, each fanatically bent on imposing on the country its particular panacea.

1. *The Danger of an Explosive Era.* The political foundation of appropriate governmental programs is very unstable when it is not supplied by responsible party action.

2. *The Danger of Overextending the Presidency.* Dependable political support has to be built up for the governmental program. When there is no other place to get that done, when the political parties fail to do it, it is tempting to turn to the President. When the President's program actually is the sole program, either his party becomes a flock of sheep or the party falls apart. This concept of the presidency disposes of the party system by making the President reach directly for the support of a majority of the voters.

3. *The Danger of Disintegration of the Two Parties.* A chance that the electorate will turn its back upon the two parties is by no means academic. As a matter of fact, this development has already occurred in considerable part, and it is still going on. American political institutions are too firmly grounded upon the two-party system to make its collapse a small matter.

4. *The Danger of an Unbridgeable Political Cleavage.* If the two parties do not develop alternative programs that can be executed, the voter's frustration and the mounting ambiguities of national policy might set in motion more extreme tendencies to the political left and the political right. Once a deep political cleavage develops between opposing groups, each group naturally works to keep it deep. Orientation of the American two-party system along the lines of meaningful national programs is a significant step toward avoiding the development of such a cleavage.

Index